TEXT BOOK OF PHARMACEUTICS – I

[According to latest syllabus of B. Pharm – I semester of Pharmacy Council of India]

Dr. Ritesh Kumar
Professor
Department of Pharmaceutics
Sharda School of Pharmacy
Sharda University Agra, Uttar Pradesh

Dr. Jashanjit Singh
Associate Professor
Gurukul Institute of Pharmaceutical Sciences,
Badesh Kalan, Khamanon, Fatehgarh Sahib, Punjab

Dr. Rajkumari Thagele
Professor
Career Point School of Pharmacy
Career Point University
Kota, Rajasthan

Mr. Akash J. Nanaware
Pharmacy Officer
(Government of Maharashtra)
RH, Washi, District Dharashiv, Maharashtra

Prof. (Dr.) Jitendra Singh Chaudhary
Professor and Head of the Department of Pharmaceutics
Smt. Vidyawati College of Pharmacy
Jhansi, Uttar Pradesh

TEXT BOOK OF PHARMACEUTICS – I

First Edition 2024

Published by:

NOTION PRESS

Publisher and distributor

Head office: Notion press Media Pvt. Ltd.

7, Red cross Road,

Egmore, Chennai, Tamil Nadu 60008

TEXT BOOK OF PHARMACEUTICS – I

NOTION PRESS

PREFACE

The authors feel great pleasure in presenting the first edition of the book **"Text Book of Pharmaceutics – I"** for graduate and post graduate students. The present book on **Text Book of Pharmaceutics – I** has been written according to the syllabus of B. Pharm – I semester of Pharmacy Council of India and covers full course of the subject.

THE SALIENT FEATURES OF THE BOOK ARE: -

- *Easy to understand style of writing* which makes the book a self-study material.
- *Each new concept has been introduced through day-today problem of interest* to the students which makes the subject matter interesting.
- *The language of the book, on the whole, is lucid and easy to understand.*
- Wherever needed *neatly labeled figures have been drawn.*

The authors hope that the students, teachers and other readers will find the book interesting and to the point covering the course. We hope that the students will receive the book warmly.

I express a sincere thank you to the Management of Sharda School of Pharmacy, Gurukul Institute of Pharmaceutical Sciences, Sharda University, Career Point School of Pharmacy, Career Point University, RBMI Group of Institutions and Parmarth College of Pharmacy for their support during the writing of this book.

Every effort is made to keep the book error free. The author will gratefully acknowledge the suggestions to improve the book to make it more useful.

Wishing our readers success in examination and life ahead. The authors feel that their efforts will be fully rewarded if the book serves the purpose for which it is written.

TEXT BOOK OF PHARMACEUTICS – I

CONTENTS

CHAPTER – 1

HISTORICAL BACKGROUND AND DEVELOPMENT OF PROFESSION OF PHARMACY

INTRODUCTION:

1. Ancient Foundations

a. **Early Practices**: The roots of pharmacy trace back to ancient civilizations where herbs and natural substances were used for medicinal purposes. Ancient Egyptians, Greeks, Chinese, and Indians practiced early forms of pharmacy, with texts like the Ebers Papyrus and works by Hippocrates documenting medicinal practices.

b. **Ancient Greece and Rome**: Greek physicians like Hippocrates and Dioscorides contributed significantly to the understanding of medicinal plants. Dioscorides' work, *De Materia Medica*, became a foundational text in the study of medicinal substances.

2. Medieval Developments

a. **Islamic Golden Age**: During the medieval period, Islamic scholars preserved and expanded upon Greek and Roman knowledge. Figures like Avicenna (Ibn Sina) wrote influential texts like *The Canon of Medicine*, which integrated pharmacology with clinical practice.

b. **Monastic Pharmacy**: In Europe, monastic communities played a crucial role in preserving medicinal knowledge and practices. Monks often prepared medicines in their herb gardens and were among the earliest practitioners of pharmacy in Europe.

3. Renaissance and Early Modern Period

a. **Advancements in Chemistry**: The Renaissance saw a surge in scientific inquiry, including the study of chemistry and pharmacology. Paracelsus, a

Swiss physician, emphasized the use of chemical substances and mineral compounds in medicine.

b. **Pharmacy Guilds**: By the 16th and 17th centuries, pharmacy began to emerge as a distinct profession. Pharmacy guilds and organizations were established in various European cities, setting standards and regulating practice.

4. Emergence of Modern Pharmacy

a. **Pharmacy Schools**: The 19th century saw the establishment of formal pharmacy education and professional organizations. The Philadelphia College of Pharmacy, founded in 1821, was one of the first institutions dedicated to pharmaceutical education.

b. **Pharmacopoeias**: The creation of official pharmacopoeias, such as the United States Pharmacopeia (USP) in 1820, standardized drug formulations and quality, further professionalizing the field.

5. 20th Century and Beyond

a. **Scientific Advancements**: The 20th century brought significant advancements in drug development, including the discovery of antibiotics and the development of synthetic drugs. Pharmacy became increasingly focused on pharmaceutical sciences, including pharmacokinetics and pharmacodynamics.

b. **Regulatory Changes**: With the rise of pharmaceuticals as a major industry, regulatory agencies like the FDA were established to oversee drug safety and efficacy.

c. **Expansion of Roles**: The role of pharmacists expanded beyond dispensing medications to include clinical services, patient counseling, and involvement in healthcare teams.

6. Contemporary Pharmacy

a. **Clinical Pharmacy**: Today, pharmacy practice includes a broad range of services such as clinical pharmacy, which involves direct patient care and collaboration with other healthcare professionals.

b. **Pharmacy Informatics**: The integration of technology and informatics into pharmacy practice has improved medication management and patient safety.

c. **Pharmaceutical Research**: Ongoing research continues to drive innovation in drug development, personalized medicine, and therapeutic interventions.

HISTORY OF PROFESSION OF PHARMACY IN INDIA IN RELATION TO PHARMACY EDUCATION, INDUSTRY AND ORGANIZATION

1. Ancient and Medieval Period

a. **Ancient Practices**: Traditional Indian medicine, including Ayurveda and Unani, has a rich history of pharmaceutical practices. Texts such as the *Charaka Samhita* and *Sushruta Samhita* from ancient India document the preparation and use of medicinal herbs and compounds.

b. **Medieval Contributions**: During the medieval period, Indian scholars continued to advance pharmaceutical knowledge. The integration of Indian and Islamic medicinal practices further enriched the field.

2. Colonial Era (18th-19th Centuries)

a. **Early Developments**: The arrival of the British East India Company in the 18th century marked the beginning of a more formal approach to pharmacy in India. The British influence introduced Western medical practices and pharmaceuticals to India.

b. **First Pharmacy School**: The first formal institution for pharmacy education in India was established in 1845. The College of Pharmacy in Bombay (now Mumbai) was initially part of the Sir J.J. Group of

Hospitals and focused on training pharmacists in Western pharmaceutical practices.

3. **Early 20th Century**
    a. **Pharmacy Act of 1948**: Post-independence, the Indian government recognized the need for a structured approach to pharmacy education and practice. The Pharmacy Act of 1948 was enacted to regulate pharmacy education, practice, and professional standards. This act led to the establishment of the Pharmacy Council of India (PCI) to oversee pharmacy education and registration.
    b. **Growth of Pharmacy Education**: The 1950s and 1960s saw significant growth in pharmacy education with the establishment of several new pharmacy colleges across the country. Institutions such as the Jamia Hamdard in Delhi, and the Institute of Chemical Technology (formerly UDCT) in Mumbai, played pivotal roles in advancing pharmacy education and research.
4. **Development of Pharmacy Industry (Post-Independence)**
    a. **Expansion of the Industry**: The post-independence era saw the growth of the pharmaceutical industry in India. The 1960s and 1970s marked the beginning of domestic pharmaceutical manufacturing, with companies like Ranbaxy, Cipla, and Sun Pharma emerging as major players.
    b. **Regulation and Standards**: The Drug and Cosmetics Act of 1940, along with subsequent amendments, established regulatory standards for drug manufacturing and quality control. The National Pharmaceutical Pricing Authority (NPPA) was established in 1997 to regulate drug prices and ensure affordability.
5. **Modern Era**
    a. **Pharmacy Education Reforms**: In recent decades, pharmacy education in India has continued to evolve with the introduction of new curricula and programs. The rise of postgraduate and doctoral programs, along with

specialized fields like clinical pharmacy and pharmaceutical sciences, reflects the growing complexity of the profession.

b. **Pharmacy Organizations**: Various professional organizations, such as the Indian Pharmaceutical Association (IPA) and the Indian Pharmaceutical Congress (IPC), play crucial roles in advancing the profession, promoting research, and supporting pharmacists.

c. **Global Integration**: Indian pharmaceutical companies have gained international recognition for their production of generic drugs and active pharmaceutical ingredients (APIs). The country's pharmaceutical industry has become a global hub for drug manufacturing and exports.

6. Contemporary Trends

a. **Clinical Pharmacy and Patient Care**: The role of pharmacists in India has expanded to include clinical pharmacy practices, patient counseling, and participation in healthcare teams. This shift reflects a growing emphasis on patient-centered care.

b. **Pharmacy Informatics and Technology**: The integration of technology into pharmacy practice, including electronic health records and telemedicine, is shaping the future of the profession in India.

c. **Research and Innovation**: Indian pharmaceutical research continues to advance, with significant contributions to drug discovery, development, and biotechnology.

PHARMACY AS A CAREER

1. Early Developments

a. **Ancient Traditions**: The concept of pharmacy as a career can be traced back to ancient civilizations, where individuals who prepared and dispensed medicinal substances played a crucial role in healthcare. In ancient Egypt, Greece, China, and India, individuals engaged in medicinal practices often combined roles of healer, herbalist, and preparer of remedies.

b. **Medieval and Renaissance Periods**: In medieval Europe, the role of the apothecary emerged as a distinct career, with individuals responsible for preparing and selling medicines. The establishment of guilds and early pharmaceutical organizations helped formalize this role.

2. Formation of the Modern Profession

a. **18th and 19th Centuries**: The 18th and 19th centuries marked significant developments in pharmacy as a career. The professionalization of pharmacy began with the formation of pharmacy schools and the establishment of formal training programs. Early institutions like the Philadelphia College of Pharmacy (founded in 1821) in the United States played a pivotal role in shaping the career path for pharmacists.

b. **Pharmacy Act of 1948 (India)**: In India, the Pharmacy Act of 1948 was a milestone in the professionalization of pharmacy. It established regulatory standards, created the Pharmacy Council of India (PCI), and formalized the career structure for pharmacists, emphasizing education and ethical practice.

3. Evolution of Pharmacy Education and Training

a. **Formal Education**: Over time, the career of pharmacy has become increasingly specialized, with the introduction of formal education and training programs. Modern pharmacy education includes undergraduate, postgraduate, and doctoral programs, reflecting the evolving complexity of the profession.

b. **Licensing and Certification**: Licensing and certification processes have been developed to ensure that pharmacists meet professional standards. This includes passing examinations and meeting continuing education requirements to maintain competency and stay current with advancements in the field.

4. Expanding Roles and Specializations

a. **Clinical Pharmacy**: The role of pharmacists has expanded beyond traditional dispensing to include clinical practice. Clinical pharmacists work directly with patients and healthcare teams to manage medications, optimize therapy, and provide patient counseling.

b. **Pharmaceutical Industry**: Careers in the pharmaceutical industry have also become prominent. Pharmacists in this sector work in drug development, quality control, regulatory affairs, and marketing, contributing to the creation and distribution of medications.

c. **Academia and Research**: Pharmacy careers in academia and research involve teaching, conducting research, and advancing the science of pharmacology and pharmaceutical sciences. This area supports the development of new drugs and therapies and contributes to the overall growth of the profession.

5. Modern Trends and Future Directions

a. **Technology Integration**: The integration of technology into pharmacy practice, including electronic health records, telepharmacy, and data analytics, is shaping the future of the career. Pharmacists are increasingly involved in utilizing technology to improve patient care and streamline pharmacy operations.

b. **Patient-Centered Care**: There is a growing emphasis on patient-centered care, with pharmacists playing a critical role in managing chronic diseases, conducting health screenings, and providing personalized medication management.

c. **Global Opportunities**: The globalization of the pharmaceutical industry offers career opportunities for pharmacists around the world. International collaboration and the expansion of global health initiatives provide diverse career paths and professional growth.

PHARMACOPOEIAS

1. **Early Pharmacopoeias**

   a. **Ancient Texts**: The earliest known pharmacopoeias were compilations of medicinal substances and their uses found in ancient civilizations. For instance, the *Ebers Papyrus* from ancient Egypt (circa 1550 BCE) is one of the oldest surviving medical texts, detailing a variety of drugs and treatments.

   b. **Classical Greek and Roman Contributions**: Greek and Roman texts, such as Dioscorides' *De Materia Medica* (circa 50-70 CE), provided comprehensive lists of medicinal plants and substances, influencing later pharmacopoeias.

2. **Medieval and Renaissance Developments**

   a. **Islamic Contributions**: During the Islamic Golden Age (8th-14th centuries), scholars preserved and expanded upon Greek and Roman pharmacological knowledge. Works such as Avicenna's *Canon of Medicine* (11th century) were highly influential.

   b. **Medieval European Pharmacopoeias**: In medieval Europe, various local and regional pharmacopoeias emerged, often compiled by apothecaries and physicians. These texts provided guidelines for the preparation and use of medicines.

3. **Emergence of Modern Pharmacopoeias**

   a. **Pharmacopoeia Londinensis**: One of the earliest official pharmacopoeias, the *Pharmacopoeia Londinensis*, was published in 1618 by the Royal College of Physicians of London. It marked the beginning of standardized drug formulations in Britain.

   b. **Pharmacopoeia Galenica**: Published in the late 17th century, this pharmacopoeia in Italy was notable for its comprehensive approach to drug preparation and use.

4. Development in the 19th and 20th Centuries

a. **United States Pharmacopeia (USP)**: The USP was first published in 1820 in the United States and became a significant milestone in standardizing drug formulations. It aimed to ensure the quality, purity, and strength of drugs. The USP has undergone numerous revisions and updates to incorporate new scientific knowledge and practices.

b. **European Pharmacopoeia**: The European Pharmacopoeia was first published in 1964 and serves as a standard for drug quality across European countries. It has played a crucial role in harmonizing pharmaceutical standards across the continent.

5. Global Standardization and Harmonization

a. **International Pharmacopoeia**: Published by the World Health Organization (WHO), the International Pharmacopoeia provides a global standard for drug quality and manufacturing. It helps harmonize pharmaceutical practices and ensures the safety and efficacy of medicines worldwide.

b. **Pharmacopoeial Harmonization**: Efforts have been made to harmonize pharmacopoeias across different countries and regions. Organizations such as the International Council for Harmonisation of Technical Requirements for Pharmaceuticals for Human Use (ICH) work to align standards and practices internationally.

6. Contemporary Trends and Future Directions

a. **Technological Integration**: Modern pharmacopoeias increasingly incorporate advanced technologies, including digital platforms for real-time updates and access to drug information.

b. **Biotechnology and Novel Drugs**: The rise of biotechnology and the development of novel drugs require continuous updates to pharmacopoeias. New sections addressing biological products, biosimilars, and advanced therapeutics are being added.

c. **Regulatory Changes**: Ongoing changes in global regulations and standards influence the development and revision of pharmacopoeias. Continuous collaboration between regulatory agencies and pharmaceutical organizations helps maintain the relevance and accuracy of pharmacopoeial standards.

INTRODUCTION TO INDIAN PHARMACOPOEIA

1. **Early Developments and Historical Context**

   a. **Pre-Independence Era**: Before the establishment of an official Indian Pharmacopoeia, medicinal practices in India were guided by traditional systems like Ayurveda and Unani. During British rule, pharmaceutical practices began to adopt Western methods, but there was no standardized reference for drug quality and preparation in India.

2. **Establishment of the Indian Pharmacopoeia**

   a. **First Edition (1955)**: The Indian Pharmacopoeia (IP) was first published in 1955, shortly after India gained independence. This edition aimed to standardize drug formulations and ensure the quality and efficacy of medicines used in the country. The development of the IP was driven by the need for a comprehensive and official reference for pharmaceutical practices in India.

   b. **Pharmacy Act of 1948**: The foundation for the IP was laid by the Pharmacy Act of 1948, which established the Pharmacy Council of India (PCI). The act emphasized the need for a national pharmacopoeia to regulate drug standards and practices.

3. **Evolution and Revisions**

   a. **Subsequent Editions**: The Indian Pharmacopoeia has undergone several revisions since its first publication. Each edition has incorporated advancements in pharmaceutical science, changes in drug formulations, and new regulatory requirements.

i. **Second Edition (1966)**: The second edition reflected updates in drug standards and included new drugs and formulations.
ii. **Third Edition (1985)**: This edition included further revisions and expanded sections on drug quality and manufacturing processes.
iii. **Fourth Edition (1996)**: Introduced additional guidelines and updated monographs based on contemporary scientific knowledge.
iv. **Fifth Edition (2002)**: Focused on harmonizing with international standards and included updates on pharmacopoeial practices.
v. **Sixth Edition (2010)**: Added new sections on biological and biotechnological products, reflecting advances in these fields.

4. Role and Importance

a. **Standardization and Quality Control**: The Indian Pharmacopoeia plays a crucial role in ensuring the quality, purity, and strength of drugs manufactured and used in India. It provides official monographs for drugs, including their specifications, tests, and preparation methods.
b. **Regulatory Framework**: The IP serves as a regulatory tool for the Indian government and pharmaceutical industry. It helps enforce drug quality standards and supports the regulation of pharmaceutical practices.
c. **Guidance for Pharmacists and Manufacturers**: The IP provides valuable guidance for pharmacists, pharmaceutical manufacturers, and healthcare professionals, helping them adhere to established standards and practices.

5. Contemporary Trends and Updates

a. **Digital Access and Updates**: The Indian Pharmacopoeia is now available in digital formats, allowing for easier access and real-time updates. This shift helps in maintaining the relevance and accuracy of the pharmacopoeial standards.
b. **Integration with Global Standards**: Efforts have been made to align the Indian Pharmacopoeia with international standards, such as those set by

the United States Pharmacopeia (USP) and the European Pharmacopoeia. This alignment ensures consistency in drug quality and safety across global markets.

c. **Focus on New Therapies**: Recent editions of the IP have included guidelines for new therapies, including biopharmaceuticals, biosimilars, and advanced drug delivery systems. This focus reflects the evolving landscape of pharmaceutical science and technology.

INTRODUCTION TO BRITISH PHARMACOPOEIA

1. Historical Background

a. **Early Practices**: The concept of a standardized pharmacopoeia in Britain dates back to the early 17th century. Prior to this, medicinal practices were guided by various local and regional standards.

b. **Pharmacopoeia Londinensis**: The first official pharmacopoeia in Britain, *Pharmacopoeia Londinensis*, was published in 1618 by the Royal College of Physicians of London. This early pharmacopoeia aimed to standardize drug formulations and ensure consistency in medicinal preparations.

2. Establishment of the British Pharmacopoeia

a. **British Pharmacopoeia (1864)**: The British Pharmacopoeia as a national pharmacopoeia was first published in 1864. It was established to provide a comprehensive and standardized reference for the preparation and quality of medicines in Britain.

b. **Objectives**: The main objectives were to ensure the quality, safety, and efficacy of medicines, and to standardize pharmaceutical practices across the country.

3. Evolution and Revisions

a. **Regular Updates**: The British Pharmacopoeia has undergone regular updates and revisions to incorporate advancements in pharmaceutical science and changes in drug regulations.

   i. **Early Revisions**: The early 20th century saw several revisions to update drug standards and include new substances and formulations.

   ii. **Mid-20th Century**: The pharmacopoeia was revised to reflect new scientific knowledge and international harmonization efforts.

   iii. **Modern Editions**: Recent editions, such as the British Pharmacopoeia 2007, 2011, and 2016, have incorporated significant changes, including updates on biological products, advanced therapies, and harmonization with European and international standards.

4. Role and Importance

a. **Standardization**: The British Pharmacopoeia plays a crucial role in standardizing drug formulations and quality control in the UK. It provides official monographs for drugs, detailing their specifications, tests, and preparation methods.

b. **Regulatory Framework**: It serves as a key regulatory tool for the UK government and pharmaceutical industry, ensuring that medicines meet high standards of quality and safety.

c. **Guidance for Healthcare Professionals**: The pharmacopoeia provides valuable guidance for pharmacists, pharmaceutical manufacturers, and healthcare professionals, supporting consistent practices and adherence to established standards.

5. Contemporary Trends and Updates

a. **Harmonization with International Standards**: Efforts have been made to align the British Pharmacopoeia with international standards, such as those set by the European Pharmacopoeia and the United States

Pharmacopeia. This alignment promotes consistency in drug quality and regulatory practices across global markets.

b. **Digital Access**: The British Pharmacopoeia is available in digital formats, facilitating easier access and real-time updates. This shift helps maintain the relevance and accuracy of pharmacopoeial standards.

c. **Focus on Advanced Therapies**: Recent editions have included guidelines for new and advanced therapies, such as biologics, biosimilars, and complex drug formulations. This focus reflects the evolving landscape of pharmaceutical science and technology.

INTRODUCTION TO UNITED STATE PHARMACOPOEIA

1. **Historical Background**

a. **Early Pharmacopoeias**: Before the establishment of the United States Pharmacopeia (USP), the U.S. relied on British pharmacopoeias and various local and regional standards for medicinal practices.

b. **Founding of USP**: The USP was first published in 1820, marking a significant milestone in the formalization of pharmaceutical standards in the United States. It was initiated by the efforts of a group of physicians and pharmacists who sought to create a unified and authoritative reference for drug quality and preparation.

2. **Establishment and Development**

a. **First Edition (1820)**: The first edition of the USP was published in 1820 and included a list of drugs and their preparations. It aimed to standardize drug formulations and ensure the quality and efficacy of medicines used in the U.S.

b. **Early Revisions**: Subsequent editions of the USP were published periodically to incorporate new scientific knowledge, update drug standards, and address changes in pharmaceutical practices. The USP quickly became an essential reference for pharmacists and drug manufacturers.

3. **Evolution and Revisions**

   a. **19th Century Developments**: The USP continued to evolve throughout the 19th century, with revisions reflecting advancements in pharmaceutical science and changes in drug regulation.

   b. **20th Century Updates**: The 20th century saw significant updates to the USP, including the incorporation of new drug formulations, quality control measures, and regulatory changes. The USP expanded its scope to include guidelines for biologics, vaccines, and other advanced therapies.

   c. **Modern Editions**: Recent editions of the USP, such as the USP 37-NF 32 (2014) and later updates, have incorporated extensive revisions, including new monographs, updated testing methods, and harmonization with international standards.

4. **Role and Importance**

   a. **Standardization**: The USP plays a critical role in standardizing drug formulations and quality control in the United States. It provides official monographs for drugs, detailing their specifications, tests, and preparation methods.

   b. **Regulatory Framework**: The USP serves as a key regulatory tool for the U.S. Food and Drug Administration (FDA) and the pharmaceutical industry. It helps ensure that medicines meet high standards of quality, safety, and efficacy.

   c. **Guidance for Healthcare Professionals**: The USP provides valuable guidance for pharmacists, pharmaceutical manufacturers, and healthcare professionals, supporting consistent practices and adherence to established standards.

5. **Contemporary Trends and Updates**

a. **Harmonization with International Standards**: The USP has made efforts to align with international standards, such as those set by the European Pharmacopoeia and the International Pharmacopoeia. This alignment promotes consistency in drug quality and regulatory practices across global markets.

b. **Digital Access**: The USP is available in digital formats, allowing for easier access and real-time updates. This shift helps maintain the relevance and accuracy of pharmacopoeial standards.

c. **Focus on New Therapies**: Recent editions of the USP have included guidelines for new and advanced therapies, including biologics, biosimilars, and complex drug formulations. The USP continues to adapt to the evolving landscape of pharmaceutical science and technology.

INTRODUCTION TO EXTRA PHARMACOPOEIA

Historical Background

1. **Emergence of Supplementary Pharmacopoeias**

a. **Need for Comprehensive Information**: As the field of pharmacy advanced, it became apparent that national pharmacopoeias alone might not cover all the substances and methods required for pharmaceutical practice. There was a need for supplementary references that could provide additional information on substances and techniques not included in the primary pharmacopoeias.

2. Development of the British Extra Pharmacopoeia

a. **Early 20th Century Context**: By the mid-20th century, the British Pharmacopoeia was a comprehensive resource for drug standards in the UK. However, it did not cover all the chemicals, excipients, and less commonly used substances that pharmaceutical practitioners required. To address this, the concept of an "Extra Pharmacopoeia" was developed.

b. **Publication of British Extra Pharmacopoeia (1954)**: The *British Extra Pharmacopoeia* was first published in 1954. Its primary goal was to supplement the *British Pharmacopoeia* by providing detailed monographs on substances that were not included in the main pharmacopoeia. It aimed to fill gaps in the pharmacopoeial standards and offer additional guidance for pharmaceutical practitioners.

3. Content and Scope

a. **Supplementary Monographs**: The *British Extra Pharmacopoeia* included monographs on a wide range of substances, including drugs, chemicals, and excipients. It provided detailed specifications, testing methods, and preparation guidelines that were not covered in the main *British Pharmacopoeia*.

b. **Analytical Methods**: In addition to substance monographs, the *Extra Pharmacopoeia* also included analytical methods for testing the quality and purity of drugs and chemicals, offering valuable guidance for laboratory practices.

4. Integration and Evolution

a. **Integration into British Pharmacopoeia**: Over time, much of the content of the *British Extra Pharmacopoeia* was integrated into the main *British Pharmacopoeia*. This integration aimed to streamline pharmacopoeial standards and reduce redundancy, making it easier for practitioners to access comprehensive drug information in one reference.

b. **Regular Revisions**: The *British Extra Pharmacopoeia* underwent several revisions to incorporate new scientific knowledge and advancements. These updates ensured that the supplementary reference remained relevant and up-to-date with current pharmaceutical practices.

5. Decline and Legacy

a. **Transition to Digital Resources**: With the advent of digital technology and online resources, the need for separate supplementary pharmacopoeias like the *Extra Pharmacopoeia* diminished. Modern digital platforms now provide comprehensive and up-to-date drug information, integrating both standard and supplementary content.

b. **Harmonization Efforts**: Efforts to harmonize pharmacopoeial standards internationally have also contributed to the decline of separate supplementary pharmacopoeias. Global initiatives aim to provide unified standards and reduce the need for additional supplementary references.

Development of the British Extra Pharmacopoeia

1. **Context and Need**

   a. **Pre-1954 Era**: Prior to the introduction of the *British Extra Pharmacopoeia*, the *British Pharmacopoeia* served as the primary reference for drug standards in the UK. However, it did not cover all substances used in pharmaceutical practice, particularly less common drugs, chemicals, and excipients. This created a need for additional resources to address gaps and provide comprehensive guidance.

2. **Establishment**

   a. **Publication of the British Extra Pharmacopoeia (1954)**: The *British Extra Pharmacopoeia* was first published in 1954 to complement the *British Pharmacopoeia*. Its goal was to provide detailed monographs and specifications for substances not included in the main pharmacopoeia.

      i. **Purpose**: It aimed to address the increasing complexity of pharmaceutical formulations and provide additional information on various substances and methods.

      ii. **Scope**: The *Extra Pharmacopoeia* included a wide range of substances, including pharmaceuticals, chemicals, and excipients, as well as detailed analytical methods for their testing and quality control.

3. **Content and Features**

   a. **Supplementary Monographs**: The *British Extra Pharmacopoeia* provided monographs on substances and formulations that were not covered by the *British Pharmacopoeia*. These monographs included specifications, preparation methods, and quality control tests.

      i. **Detailed Specifications**: It offered comprehensive details on the physical and chemical properties of substances, including tests for purity and potency.

      ii. **Analytical Methods**: The *Extra Pharmacopoeia* included analytical methods for testing the quality of substances, which were essential for ensuring consistency and safety in pharmaceutical practice.

4. **Evolution and Revisions**

   a. **Regular Updates**: The *British Extra Pharmacopoeia* was regularly updated to incorporate new scientific knowledge and advancements in pharmaceutical science. These revisions aimed to keep the reference current and relevant.

      i. **Integration with British Pharmacopoeia**: Over time, much of the content from the *British Extra Pharmacopoeia* was integrated into the *British Pharmacopoeia*. This consolidation aimed to streamline pharmaceutical standards and reduce duplication.

      ii. **Revised Editions**: Subsequent editions of the *British Extra Pharmacopoeia* continued to expand and update its content, reflecting changes in drug formulations, analytical techniques, and regulatory requirements.

5. **Decline and Legacy**

   a. **Transition to Digital Resources**: With advancements in technology and the rise of digital platforms, the role of the *British Extra Pharmacopoeia* diminished. Modern digital resources now provide comprehensive and integrated drug information, reducing the need for separate supplementary pharmacopoeias.

i. **Harmonization and Integration**: Efforts to harmonize pharmacopoeial standards internationally have also contributed to the decline of separate supplementary references. Global harmonization aims to provide unified standards and reduce the need for additional resources.

ii. **Legacy**: Despite its decline, the *British Extra Pharmacopoeia* played a significant role in the development of pharmaceutical standards by providing valuable supplementary information and guidance for pharmaceutical practitioners.

Evolution and Revisions

1. **Initial Publication and Objectives**

a. **1954**: The *British Extra Pharmacopoeia* was first published with the intention of supplementing the *British Pharmacopoeia*. It aimed to provide additional information on substances and methods not included in the main pharmacopoeia, addressing gaps in drug standards and quality control.

2. Early Revisions and Updates

a. **1963 Edition**: The first major revision of the *British Extra Pharmacopoeia* occurred in 1963. This edition included updates to existing monographs and the addition of new substances, reflecting advances in pharmaceutical science and changes in drug formulations.

i. **Expansion of Content**: New monographs were added to cover a wider range of substances, and existing monographs were revised to include improved testing methods and updated specifications.

3. Integration with British Pharmacopoeia

a. **1973 Edition**: By the 1973 edition, there was a significant effort to integrate the *British Extra Pharmacopoeia* with the *British Pharmacopoeia*. This integration aimed to streamline the pharmacopoeial standards and reduce redundancy by consolidating information into a single, comprehensive reference.

    i. **Consolidation Efforts**: The integration involved merging relevant content from the *Extra Pharmacopoeia* into the main *British Pharmacopoeia*. This process helped in unifying standards and providing a more accessible resource for pharmaceutical practitioners.

4. Continued Revisions and Updates

a. **1980s to 1990s**: During the 1980s and 1990s, the *British Extra Pharmacopoeia* continued to be updated to reflect new scientific knowledge, advancements in pharmaceutical practices, and changes in regulatory requirements.

    i. **Inclusion of New Substances**: New substances, including emerging drugs and advanced therapeutic products, were added to the monographs.

    ii. **Refinement of Testing Methods**: Advances in analytical techniques led to the refinement of testing methods and quality control procedures.

5. Decline and Legacy

a. **Transition to Digital Resources**: In the late 20th and early 21st centuries, the role of the *British Extra Pharmacopoeia* began to diminish with the rise of digital resources and online platforms. Modern digital pharmacopoeias and databases now provide comprehensive and up-to-date information, reducing the need for separate supplementary pharmacopoeias.

i. **Integration into British Pharmacopoeia**: Much of the content from the *British Extra Pharmacopoeia* was fully integrated into the main *British Pharmacopoeia* to provide a consolidated reference. This integration aimed to streamline access to drug information and maintain consistency in pharmaceutical standards.

ii. **Harmonization with International Standards**: Efforts to harmonize pharmacopoeial standards globally have also contributed to the decline of separate supplementary pharmacopoeias. International harmonization aims to provide unified standards and reduce the need for additional supplementary references.

Role and Importance

1. **Supplementary Resource**

   a. **Filling Gaps in Existing Pharmacopoeias**: The *British Extra Pharmacopoeia* was created to address the limitations of the *British Pharmacopoeia* by providing detailed information on drugs, chemicals, and excipients that were not covered by the main pharmacopoeia. It filled important gaps in pharmaceutical standards.

2. **Standardization and Comprehensive Coverage**

   a. **Detailed Monographs**: It offered comprehensive monographs on a range of substances, including those not included in the primary pharmacopoeia. These monographs included specifications, preparation methods, and testing procedures.

   b. **Quality Control and Testing**: The *Extra Pharmacopoeia* provided standardized analytical methods for testing the purity, quality, and potency of substances. This helped ensure consistency in drug formulations and supported the reliability of pharmaceuticals.

3. **Practical Guidance for Professionals**

   a. **Support for Pharmaceutical Practice**: By providing additional guidelines and specifications, the *Extra Pharmacopoeia* served as a practical resource for pharmacists and drug manufacturers. It aided in the preparation, formulation, and quality control of medications.

   b. **Educational Tool**: It also functioned as an educational resource for students and professionals in the pharmaceutical field, offering detailed and authoritative information on various substances and methods.

4. **Regulatory and Compliance Support**

   a. **Regulatory Framework**: The *Extra Pharmacopoeia* played a role in the regulatory framework by providing detailed standards that supported compliance with pharmaceutical regulations. It helped ensure that medicines met required quality and safety standards.

   b. **Innovation and Adaptation**: It supported the pharmaceutical industry by providing updated information on new substances and formulations, facilitating the introduction of innovative products and practices.

5. **Historical Significance**

   a. **Contribution to Drug Standards**: The *Extra Pharmacopoeia* was significant in the historical development of drug standards by offering additional information and updating existing guidelines. Its integration into the main pharmacopoeia marked an evolution in the standardization of pharmaceutical practices.

   b. **Legacy**: While the role of the *Extra Pharmacopoeia* has diminished with the advent of digital resources and the integration of its content into the main pharmacopoeia, its historical contribution to the development of comprehensive pharmaceutical standards is noteworthy.

6. **Modern Implications**

   a. **Transition to Digital Platforms**: The rise of digital resources has led to the decline of separate supplementary pharmacopoeias. Modern digital pharmacopoeias provide integrated and up-to-date information, incorporating the content previously covered by the *Extra Pharmacopoeia*.

b. **Global Harmonization**: Efforts towards global harmonization of pharmacopoeial standards have reduced the need for separate supplementary references. International collaboration aims to provide consistent and unified drug standards worldwide.

Contemporary Trends and Updates

1. **Digital Transformation**

   a. **Shift to Electronic Resources**: The rise of digital technology has transformed how pharmaceutical information is accessed and utilized. Traditional printed pharmacopoeias, including the *British Extra Pharmacopoeia*, have largely been replaced by electronic resources.

      i. **Digital Pharmacopoeias**: Modern digital pharmacopoeias offer comprehensive, searchable databases that integrate information from various sources, including content formerly covered by supplementary pharmacopoeias like the *Extra Pharmacopoeia*. This shift improves accessibility and updates drug information more efficiently.

2. **Integration with Main Pharmacopoeias**

   a. **Consolidation of Content**: Much of the content from the *British Extra Pharmacopoeia* has been integrated into the main *British Pharmacopoeia*. This integration aims to streamline pharmacopoeial standards and provide a unified reference for pharmaceutical professionals.

      i. **Unified Standards**: The consolidation process helps eliminate redundancy and offers a more coherent and accessible source of drug information.

3. Global Harmonization Efforts

a. **International Collaboration**: Efforts to harmonize pharmacopoeial standards across different countries and regions have gained momentum. Organizations such as the International Council for Harmonisation (ICH) and the Pharmacopeial Discussion Group (PDG) work towards establishing global standards.

i. **International Pharmacopoeias**: Initiatives like the International Pharmacopoeia (Ph. Int.) and the European Pharmacopoeia aim to provide consistent drug standards and reduce the need for supplementary pharmacopoeias. This harmonization supports global trade and ensures consistent drug quality across borders.

4. Enhanced Regulatory Frameworks

a. **Regulatory Updates**: Modern regulatory frameworks have evolved to incorporate updated scientific knowledge and technological advancements. Regulatory agencies now use integrated digital resources and international standards to ensure drug quality and safety.

i. **Adaptation to New Technologies**: The regulatory landscape has adapted to new technologies, such as advanced analytical techniques and novel drug delivery systems, further reducing the reliance on separate supplementary pharmacopoeias.

5. Focus on Evidence-Based Medicine

a. **Incorporation of Clinical Evidence**: Contemporary trends in pharmaceutical practice emphasize evidence-based medicine. Pharmacopoeial standards now consider clinical evidence and real-world data to support drug efficacy and safety.

i. **Data-Driven Updates**: Updates to pharmacopoeias are increasingly informed by clinical trials and observational studies, ensuring that drug standards reflect the latest evidence and best practices.

6. Emerging Trends and Future Directions

a. **Personalized Medicine**: Advances in genomics and biotechnology are driving the development of personalized medicine, which may influence future pharmacopoeial updates. Pharmacopoeias will need to address standards for personalized therapies and biopharmaceuticals.

   i. **Digital Health Tools**: The integration of digital health tools, such as mobile apps and wearables, may impact drug monitoring and management. Pharmacopoeias may evolve to include guidelines for these emerging technologies.

Multiple Choice Questions (MCQs)

1. The roots of pharmacy trace back to which ancient civilization?

   A) Romans

   B) Greeks

   C) Egyptians

   D) Chinese

2. Which ancient text is considered one of the oldest surviving medical texts?

   A) De Materia Medica

   B) The Canon of Medicine

   C) Ebers Papyrus

   D) Charaka Samhita

3. Who wrote "De Materia Medica," a foundational text in the study of medicinal substances?

   A) Hippocrates

   B) Dioscorides

   C) Avicenna

   D) Paracelsus

4. During the Islamic Golden Age, which scholar's work integrated pharmacology with clinical practice?

   A) Dioscorides

   B) Avicenna (Ibn Sina)

   C) Hippocrates

   D) Paracelsus

5. The establishment of pharmacy guilds in the 16th and 17th centuries marked the emergence of pharmacy as:

   A) A religious practice

   B) A distinct profession

   C) An informal trade

   D) A literary tradition

6. The first formal pharmacy school in the United States was established in which year?

   A) 1820

   B) 1821

   C) 1845

   D) 1864

7. The Pharmacy Act of 1948 in India led to the establishment of which regulatory body?

   A) Indian Medical Association

   B) Pharmacy Council of India (PCI)

   C) Indian Pharmaceutical Congress

   D) National Pharmaceutical Pricing Authority (NPPA)

8. Which institution is known as one of the first dedicated to pharmaceutical education?

   A) The Philadelphia College of Pharmacy

   B) The College of Pharmacy, Bombay

   C) Jamia Hamdard

D) Institute of Chemical Technology (ICT)

9. What was the primary objective of the first edition of the Indian Pharmacopoeia published in 1955?

A) To regulate the prices of drugs

B) To standardize drug formulations and ensure quality

C) To provide legal guidelines for pharmacists

D) To promote herbal medicine

10. The British Pharmacopoeia was first published in:

A) 1618

B) 1820

C) 1864

D) 1954

11. The United States Pharmacopeia (USP) was first published in which year?

A) 1820

B) 1845

C) 1864

D) 1955

12. The integration of technology and informatics into pharmacy practice primarily aims to:

A) Increase the number of prescriptions filled

B) Improve medication management and patient safety

C) Reduce the need for pharmacists

D) Expand the role of herbal medicines

13. Which period saw the rise of domestic pharmaceutical manufacturing in India?

A) Ancient Period

B) Colonial Era

C) Post-Independence Era

D) Modern Era

14. What was the purpose of the British Extra Pharmacopoeia, first published in 1954?

A) To provide guidelines for herbal medicine

B) To supplement the British Pharmacopoeia with additional monographs

C) To introduce new drugs in the British market

D) To harmonize international drug standards

15. Which organization publishes the International Pharmacopoeia?

A) World Health Organization (WHO)

B) European Union (EU)

C) United States Pharmacopeia (USP)

D) Indian Pharmacopoeia Commission (IPC)

16. The Pharmacy Act of 1948 in India was crucial for:

A) Establishing pharmacy guilds

B) Regulating pharmacy education and practice

C) Promoting Ayurvedic medicine

D) Expanding the pharmaceutical industry

17. What does the process of pharmacopoeial harmonization aim to achieve?

A) Increase the diversity of pharmacopoeias

B) Establish global standards for drug quality and safety

C) Promote the use of local herbs

D) Expand the pharmaceutical market in developing countries

18. What is a significant modern trend in the field of pharmacy?

A) Decrease in the use of technology

B) Focus on patient-centered care

C) Reduction in clinical pharmacy roles

D) Decline in pharmaceutical research

19. Which edition of the Indian Pharmacopoeia introduced sections on biological and biotechnological products?

A) 1955 Edition

B) 1966 Edition

C) 1996 Edition

D) 2010 Edition

20. The primary role of pharmacopoeias throughout history has been to:

A) Increase the cost of drugs

B) Provide entertainment

C) Standardize drug quality and preparation

D) Reduce the number of pharmacies

Short Answer Type Questions (Subjective)

1. Describe the significance of the Pharmacy Act of 1948 in India.
2. How did ancient civilizations contribute to the foundation of pharmacy?
3. What role did the Islamic Golden Age play in the development of pharmacy?
4. Explain the impact of the Renaissance on the evolution of pharmacy as a profession.
5. What were the primary objectives of the first edition of the Indian Pharmacopoeia?
6. Discuss the importance of the British Pharmacopoeia in the standardization of drug quality.
7. How has pharmacy education evolved in India since independence?
8. What is the role of the United States Pharmacopeia in global pharmaceutical standards?
9. Explain the concept of pharmacopoeial harmonization.
10. How did the British Extra Pharmacopoeia complement the British Pharmacopoeia?
11. What are the key components of modern pharmacy practice?
12. Describe the historical development of pharmacy in India during the colonial era.

13. How has the role of pharmacists expanded in contemporary healthcare?
14. What was the purpose of the establishment of pharmacy guilds in Europe?
15. How did the development of pharmacy schools contribute to the professionalization of pharmacy?
16. What impact did the discovery of antibiotics have on the field of pharmacy in the 20th century?
17. How has the role of pharmacopoeias changed with the advent of digital resources?
18. Explain the role of the World Health Organization in the development of the International Pharmacopoeia.
19. What are the primary challenges faced in the standardization of global pharmacopoeias?
20. Discuss the role of pharmacy organizations in advancing the profession in India.

Long Answer Type Questions (Subjective)

1. Trace the historical development of pharmacy from ancient civilizations to the modern era, highlighting key milestones.
2. Discuss the evolution of pharmacy education and practice in India, focusing on the impact of the Pharmacy Act of 1948.
3. Explain the significance of pharmacopoeias in the standardization of drug quality and safety, with a focus on the British Pharmacopoeia, United States Pharmacopeia, and Indian Pharmacopoeia.
4. Analyze the role of the Islamic Golden Age in preserving and advancing pharmaceutical knowledge, with reference to key figures and texts.
5. Discuss the challenges and opportunities in the global harmonization of pharmacopoeias and the role of international organizations in this process.

6. Describe the development and evolution of the Indian pharmaceutical industry post-independence, including key regulatory changes and industry growth.
7. Explain the contributions of the Renaissance to the scientific foundation of pharmacy, focusing on the work of Paracelsus and other key figures.
8. Discuss the role of technology and informatics in the evolution of pharmacy practice, particularly in clinical pharmacy and patient care.
9. Analyze the historical and contemporary significance of the British Extra Pharmacopoeia in the development of pharmaceutical standards.
10. Explore the future trends in pharmacy practice, including personalized medicine, biotechnology, and the integration of digital health tools.

Answer Key for MCQs

1. C) Egyptians
2. C) Ebers Papyrus
3. B) Dioscorides
4. B) Avicenna (Ibn Sina)
5. B) A distinct profession
6. B) 1821
7. B) Pharmacy Council of India (PCI)
8. A) The Philadelphia College of Pharmacy
9. B) To standardize drug formulations and ensure quality
10. C) 1864
11. A) 1820
12. B) Improve medication management and patient safety
13. C) Post-Independence Era
14. B) To supplement the British Pharmacopoeia with additional monographs
15. A) World Health Organization (WHO)
16. B) Regulating pharmacy education and practice

17.B) Establish global standards for drug quality and safety

18.B) Focus on patient-centered care

19.D) 2010 Edition

20.C) Standardize drug quality and preparation

CHAPTER – 2

DOSAGE FORMS

INTRODUCTION:

Dosage forms are the various forms in which medications are manufactured and administered. They play a crucial role in the delivery of drugs to achieve the desired therapeutic effect while minimizing side effects. Here's a detailed introduction to the different types of dosage forms:

1. Solid Dosage Forms

a. Tablets:

i. **Description:** Solid doses of medication that are usually round, oval, or square. They can be uncoated or coated.

ii. **Types:**

1. **Oral Tablets:** Designed to be swallowed.
2. **Chewable Tablets:** Designed to be chewed before swallowing.
3. **Effervescent Tablets:** Dissolve in water before ingestion.
4. **Extended-Release Tablets:** Release medication gradually over time.

b. Capsules:

i. **Description:** Gelatin shells containing medication in powder, liquid, or granule form.

ii. **Types:**

1. **Hard Gelatin Capsules:** Consist of two pieces that fit together.
2. **Soft Gelatin Capsules:** One-piece capsules with a soft shell that can contain liquid medication.

c. Powders:

i. **Description:** Finely ground drugs that can be mixed with liquids or taken directly.

ii. **Types:**

    1. **Oral Powders:** Mixed with water or other liquids.
    2. **Topical Powders:** Applied directly to the skin.

d. Granules:

i. **Description:** Small, irregularly shaped particles of medication.

ii. **Types:**

    1. **Effervescent Granules:** Dissolve in water to release medication.
    2. **Sustained-Release Granules:** Provide a controlled release of medication.

2. Liquid Dosage Forms

a. Solutions:

i. **Description:** Homogeneous mixtures of drugs dissolved in a solvent.

ii. **Types:**

    1. **Oral Solutions:** Taken by mouth.
    2. **Injectable Solutions:** Administered via injection.

b. Suspensions:

i. **Description:** Liquid preparations containing solid particles suspended in a liquid.

ii. **Types:**

    1. **Oral Suspensions:** Taken by mouth.
    2. **Injectable Suspensions:** Administered via injection.

c. Emulsions:

i. **Description:** Mixtures of two immiscible liquids, such as oil and water, with medication dispersed throughout.

ii. **Types:**

    1. **Oral Emulsions:** Taken by mouth.
    2. **Topical Emulsions:** Applied to the skin.

d. Syrups:

i. **Description:** Sweetened solutions of medication, often used for oral administration.

ii. **Types:**

   1. **Simple Syrups:** Contain medication dissolved in a sugar solution.
   2. **Medicated Syrups:** Contain additional therapeutic agents.

3. Semi-Solid Dosage Forms

a. Ointments:

i. **Description:** Thick, greasy preparations intended for external use.

ii. **Types:**

   1. **Hydrophilic Ointments:** Water-loving, non-greasy.
   2. **Oleaginous Ointments:** Greasy, oil-based.

b. Creams:

i. **Description:** Semi-solid emulsions that are less greasy than ointments.

ii. **Types:**

   1. **Oil-in-Water Creams:** Oil droplets dispersed in water.
   2. **Water-in-Oil Creams:** Water droplets dispersed in oil.

c. Gels:

i. **Description:** Semi-solid systems in which a liquid phase is trapped in a gel-like matrix.

ii. **Types:**

   1. **Hydrogel Gels:** Water-based.
   2. **Alcohol Gels:** Alcohol-based, often used for antiseptic purposes.

d. Pastes:

i. **Description:** Thick, adhesive preparations used for topical application.

ii. **Types:**

   1. **Adhesive Pastes:** Provide a protective layer on the skin.
   2. **Non-Adhesive Pastes:** Used for their therapeutic properties.

4. Transdermal Dosage Forms

a. Patches:

i. **Description:** Adhesive patches placed on the skin to deliver medication over a prolonged period.

ii. **Types:**

1. **Matrix Patches:** Contain medication in a matrix that releases it gradually.
2. **Reservoir Patches:** Contain medication in a reservoir with a controlled release mechanism.

5. Inhalation Dosage Forms

a. Aerosols:

i. **Description:** Medications delivered in fine particles or droplets via an inhaler.

ii. **Types:**

1. **Metered-Dose Inhalers (MDIs):** Deliver a specific dose of medication.
2. **Dry Powder Inhalers (DPIs):** Deliver medication in a dry powder form.

b. Nebulizers:

i. **Description:** Devices that convert liquid medication into a mist for inhalation.

6. Other Dosage Forms

a. Suppositories:

i. **Description:** Solid or semi-solid medications designed to be inserted into the body cavities (rectal, vaginal).

ii. **Types:**

1. **Rectal Suppositories:** Administered through the rectum.
2. **Vaginal Suppositories:** Administered through the vagina.

b. Implants:

i. **Description:** Solid dosage forms placed under the skin to release medication over time.

CLASSIFICATION OF DOSAGE FORMS

Dosage forms can be classified based on their physical state, route of administration, and release mechanism. Here's a detailed classification with examples for each type:

1. Solid Dosage Forms

a. Tablets:

i. **Oral Tablets:** Swallowed and absorbed in the digestive tract.
   1. **Example:** Paracetamol tablets.

ii. **Chewable Tablets:** Chewed before swallowing.
   1. **Example:** Children's aspirin tablets.

iii. **Effervescent Tablets:** Dissolve in water before ingestion.
   1. **Example:** Alka-Seltzer.

iv. **Extended-Release Tablets:** Release medication gradually.
   1. **Example:** Metformin extended-release tablets.

b. Capsules:

i. **Hard Gelatin Capsules:** Two-piece capsules with powdered or granular medication.
   1. **Example:** Amoxicillin capsules.

ii. **Soft Gelatin Capsules:** Single-piece capsules with liquid or semi-solid medication.
   1. **Example:** Fish oil capsules.

c. Powders:

i. **Oral Powders:** Mixed with liquids or taken directly.
   1. **Example:** Antibiotic powders for suspension (e.g., amoxicillin powder).

ii. **Topical Powders:** Applied directly to the skin.
   1. **Example:** Talcum powder.

d. Granules:

i. **Effervescent Granules:** Dissolve in water before ingestion.

1. **Example:** Vitamin C granules.

ii. **Sustained-Release Granules:** Provide controlled release of medication.

1. **Example:** Certain forms of antidepressants.

2. Liquid Dosage Forms

a. Solutions:

i. **Oral Solutions:** Taken by mouth.

1. **Example:** Cough syrups.

ii. **Injectable Solutions:** Administered via injection.

1. **Example:** Insulin solution.

b. Suspensions:

i. **Oral Suspensions:** Medications suspended in a liquid for oral use.

1. **Example:** Antibiotic suspensions (e.g., amoxicillin suspension).

ii. **Injectable Suspensions:** Administered via injection, with medication particles suspended in a liquid.

1. **Example:** Certain types of antibiotics and hormones.

c. Emulsions:

i. **Oral Emulsions:** Medications suspended in an oil-water mixture for oral use.

1. **Example:** Some nutritional supplements.

ii. **Topical Emulsions:** Applied to the skin.

1. **Example:** Hydrocortisone cream.

d. Syrups:

i. **Simple Syrups:** Sweetened solutions containing medication.

1. **Example:** Cough syrup.

ii. **Medicated Syrups:** Contain both sweeteners and active drugs.

1. **Example:** Antihistamine syrups.

3. Semi-Solid Dosage Forms

a. Ointments:

i. **Hydrophilic Ointments:** Water-loving, non-greasy.

1. **Example:** Zinc oxide ointment.

ii. **Oleaginous Ointments:** Greasy, oil-based.

1. **Example:** Petrolatum-based ointments.

b. Creams:

i. **Oil-in-Water Creams:** Oil droplets dispersed in water.

1. **Example:** Moisturizing creams.

ii. **Water-in-Oil Creams:** Water droplets dispersed in oil.

1. **Example:** Emollient creams.

c. Gels:

i. **Hydrogel Gels:** Water-based, often used for topical applications.

1. **Example:** Aloe vera gel.

ii. **Alcohol Gels:** Alcohol-based, often used as antiseptics.

1. **Example:** Hand sanitizers.

d. Pastes:

i. **Adhesive Pastes:** Provide a protective layer on the skin.

1. **Example:** Zinc paste for diaper rash.

ii. **Non-Adhesive Pastes:** Used for therapeutic purposes.

1. **Example:** Some topical medications for pain relief.

4. Transdermal Dosage Forms

a. Patches:

i. **Matrix Patches:** Medication in a matrix that provides a controlled release.

1. **Example:** Nicotine patches for smoking cessation.

ii. **Reservoir Patches:** Medication contained in a reservoir with controlled release.

1. **Example:** Hormonal contraceptive patches.

5. Inhalation Dosage Forms

a. Aerosols:

i. **Metered-Dose Inhalers (MDIs):** Deliver a specific dose of medication as an aerosol.

   1. **Example:** Albuterol inhalers for asthma.

ii. **Dry Powder Inhalers (DPIs):** Deliver medication in a dry powder form.

   1. **Example:** Advair Diskus.

b. Nebulizers:

i. **Description:** Devices that convert liquid medication into a mist for inhalation.

   1. **Example:** Nebulized form of albuterol for respiratory conditions.

6. Other Dosage Forms

a. Suppositories:

i. **Rectal Suppositories:** Inserted into the rectum for local or systemic effect.

   1. **Example:** Glycerin suppositories for constipation.

ii. **Vaginal Suppositories:** Inserted into the vagina.

   1. **Example:** Antifungal suppositories for yeast infections.

b. Implants:

i. **Description:** Solid dosage forms placed under the skin for prolonged drug release.

   1. **Example:** Hormonal contraceptive implants (e.g., Nexplanon).

DEFINITIONS OF DOSAGE FORMS

1.. Solid Dosage Forms

a. Tablets:

i. **Definition:** Solid, flat or cylindrical medications that are typically compressed into a specific shape and dosage. Tablets can be designed to dissolve quickly or release their medication slowly over time.

ii. **Characteristics:** Tablets are usually taken orally and can come in various forms, such as immediate-release, extended-release, or chewable.

b. Capsules:

i. **Definition:** Solid dosage forms where the drug is enclosed in a gelatin shell. Capsules can be made in two pieces (hard capsules) or as a single piece (soft capsules).

ii. **Characteristics:** Hard capsules typically contain powdered or granulated medication, while soft capsules are usually used for liquid or semi-solid medications.

c. Powders:

i. **Definition:** Finely ground drugs that are usually mixed with a liquid or taken directly. Powders can be used for internal or external use.

ii. **Characteristics:** Powders can be prepared in bulk or as single-dose packets and are often used when precise dosing is required or when the medication needs to be mixed with a liquid.

d. Granules:

i. **Definition:** Small particles of medication that are often used in oral or topical preparations. Granules are typically larger than powders and may be used to make suspensions or for sustained-release formulations.

ii. **Characteristics:** Granules can dissolve in water or other liquids and are used for both immediate and extended-release effects.

2. Liquid Dosage Forms

a. Solutions:

i. **Definition:** Homogeneous mixtures of a drug dissolved in a liquid solvent. Solutions can be used for oral or injectable administration.

ii. **Characteristics:** Solutions are clear and provide a uniform dosage of the medication in each dose.

b. Suspensions:

i. **Definition:** Liquid preparations where solid drug particles are dispersed in a liquid medium but are not completely dissolved. Suspensions require shaking before use to ensure uniform distribution of the drug.

ii. **Characteristics:** Suspensions are used when a drug is insoluble in a liquid or when a slow-release formulation is desired.

c. Emulsions:

i. **Definition:** Mixtures of two immiscible liquids (usually oil and water) stabilized by emulsifiers. Emulsions can be used for oral or topical administration.

ii. **Characteristics:** Emulsions are used to deliver medications that are not soluble in water, and can be formulated to provide a sustained release of the drug.

d. Syrups:

i. **Definition:** Sweetened, viscous solutions containing dissolved medication. Syrups are usually used for oral administration.

ii. **Characteristics:** Syrups often have a pleasant taste, making them suitable for pediatric use, and can also include therapeutic agents.

3. Semi-Solid Dosage Forms

a. Ointments:

i. **Definition:** Thick, greasy preparations intended for topical application. Ointments typically contain a high proportion of fat or oil.

ii. **Characteristics:** They form a protective barrier on the skin and are used for their emollient or therapeutic effects.

b. Creams:

i. **Definition:** Semi-solid emulsions that can be either oil-in-water or water-in-oil, intended for topical application.

ii. **Characteristics:** Creams are less greasy than ointments and are easily absorbed by the skin. They are often used for moisturizing or delivering medication.

c. Gels:

i. **Definition:** Semi-solid systems where a liquid phase is dispersed in a three-dimensional gel matrix. Gels are used for topical administration.

ii. **Characteristics:** Gels have a smooth texture and are often used to deliver medication with minimal greasiness.

d. Pastes:

i. **Definition:** Thick, sticky preparations used for topical application, containing a high percentage of solid substances.

ii. **Characteristics:** Pastes provide a protective layer on the skin and are used for their therapeutic or adhesive properties.

4. Transdermal Dosage Forms

a. Patches:

i. **Definition:** Adhesive patches placed on the skin to deliver medication over a prolonged period. They can contain a reservoir or matrix for controlled release.

ii. **Characteristics:** Patches provide a continuous, controlled release of medication and are used for conditions requiring long-term therapy.

5. Inhalation Dosage Forms

a. Aerosols:

i. **Definition:** Medications delivered in a fine mist or spray via inhalers or nebulizers. Aerosols are used for respiratory conditions.

ii. **Characteristics:** Aerosols can be in the form of metered-dose inhalers (MDIs) or dry powder inhalers (DPIs), delivering medication directly to the lungs.

b. Nebulizers:

i. **Definition:** Devices that convert liquid medication into a fine mist for inhalation. Nebulizers are used for treating respiratory conditions.

ii. **Characteristics:** Nebulizers are often used for patients who cannot use inhalers effectively, allowing for the direct delivery of medication to the respiratory tract.

6. Other Dosage Forms

a. Suppositories:

i. **Definition:** Solid or semi-solid dosage forms designed to be inserted into body cavities (rectal, vaginal) where they dissolve or melt.

ii. **Characteristics:** Suppositories are used for local or systemic effects and are beneficial for patients who cannot take oral medications.

b. Implants:

i. **Definition:** Solid dosage forms that are surgically inserted under the skin to provide a prolonged release of medication.

ii. **Characteristics:** Implants are used for continuous medication delivery over an extended period, such as hormonal implants for contraception.

A. Paracetamol Tablets:

1. **Introduction:**
   a. **Drug Name:** Paracetamol (also known as Acetaminophen)
   b. **Dosage Form:** Tablets
   c. **Common Brand Names:** Tylenol, Panadol

2. **Mechanism of Action:**
   a. **Analgesic Effect:** Paracetamol is believed to act centrally in the brain and spinal cord. It inhibits the enzyme cyclooxygenase (COX), specifically COX-3, in the central nervous system (CNS), which reduces the production of prostaglandins—chemicals involved in the sensation of pain.
   b. **Antipyretic Effect:** It reduces fever by acting on the hypothalamic heat-regulating center, leading to vasodilation and increased heat loss.

3. **Pharmacokinetics:**
   a. **Absorption:** Paracetamol is well-absorbed from the gastrointestinal tract. After oral administration, peak plasma concentrations are typically reached within 30 to 60 minutes.
   b. **Distribution:** It is widely distributed throughout the body and crosses the blood-brain barrier. It also crosses the placenta.

c. **Metabolism:** Paracetamol is primarily metabolized in the liver via conjugation with glucuronic acid and sulfuric acid. A small amount is metabolized via the cytochrome P450 system to a highly reactive metabolite that can be detoxified by glutathione.

d. **Excretion:** The majority of paracetamol is excreted in the urine as conjugates (mainly glucuronides and sulfates).

4. **Pharmacodynamics:**
   a. **Onset of Action:** Typically within 30 minutes after ingestion.
   b. **Duration of Action:** Approximately 4 to 6 hours.

5. **Therapeutic Uses:**
   a. **Analgesic:** For the relief of mild to moderate pain, such as headaches, muscle aches, backaches, and toothaches.
   b. **Antipyretic:** To reduce fever.

6. **Side Effects:**
   a. **Common:** Nausea, rash.
   b. **Serious:** Liver toxicity in cases of overdose or chronic excessive use, allergic reactions.

7. **Contraindications:**
   a. **Liver Disease:** Caution is needed in patients with liver impairment.
   b. **Alcohol Use:** Chronic alcohol users are at increased risk of hepatotoxicity.

8. **Interactions:**
   a. **Alcohol:** Increases the risk of liver damage.
   b. **Warfarin:** Chronic use can enhance the effects of warfarin.

B. Children's Aspirin Tablets:

1. **Introduction:**
   a. **Drug Name:** Aspirin (Acetylsalicylic Acid)
   b. **Dosage Form:** Tablets (often chewable for children)
   c. **Common Brand Names:** Bayer Aspirin, St. Joseph Aspirin

2. **Mechanism of Action:**
    a. **Analgesic and Antipyretic Effect:** Aspirin inhibits cyclooxygenase enzymes (COX-1 and COX-2), leading to decreased synthesis of prostaglandins involved in pain and fever.
    b. **Anti-inflammatory Effect:** By inhibiting COX-2, aspirin reduces inflammation.
3. **Pharmacokinetics:**
    a. **Absorption:** Aspirin is rapidly absorbed from the gastrointestinal tract. Chewable tablets dissolve faster, leading to quicker onset.
    b. **Distribution:** Aspirin is widely distributed in body tissues and fluids, including the CNS.
    c. **Metabolism:** Aspirin is metabolized in the liver to salicylic acid, its active form. Further metabolism occurs via conjugation.
    d. **Excretion:** Salicylic acid is excreted in the urine, mainly as conjugated metabolites.
4. **Pharmacodynamics:**
    a. **Onset of Action:** Generally within 30 to 60 minutes.
    b. **Duration of Action:** 4 to 6 hours, depending on the dose and individual metabolism.
5. **Therapeutic Uses:**
    a. **Analgesic:** For the relief of mild to moderate pain, such as headaches and muscle pain.
    b. **Antipyretic:** To reduce fever.
    c. **Anti-inflammatory:** Used in specific conditions like juvenile idiopathic arthritis, although not as commonly prescribed for this purpose in children due to potential risks.
6. **Side Effects:**
    a. **Common:** Stomach upset, nausea, heartburn.

b. **Serious:** Gastrointestinal bleeding, ulceration, Reye's syndrome (a rare but serious condition in children with viral infections).

7. **Contraindications:**

a. **Reye's Syndrome Risk:** Avoid use in children with viral infections (e.g., flu, chickenpox) due to the risk of Reye's syndrome.

b. **Gastrointestinal Issues:** Should be avoided in individuals with active peptic ulcer disease or certain gastrointestinal conditions.

8. **Interactions:**

a. **Anticoagulants:** Increased risk of bleeding when used with anticoagulants.

b. **Methotrexate:** May increase the risk of methotrexate toxicity.

C. Aloe Vera Gel:

1. **Introduction:**

a. **Product:** Aloe Vera Gel

b. **Common Uses:** Topical application for skin conditions, hydration, and wound healing.

2. **Mechanism of Action:**

a. **Anti-inflammatory:** Aloe vera contains compounds like acemannan that can reduce inflammation by inhibiting inflammatory mediators such as cytokines and prostaglandins.

b. **Antioxidant:** Aloe vera has antioxidant properties due to the presence of vitamins (e.g., vitamin C, vitamin E) and other bioactive compounds, which help in neutralizing free radicals and protecting skin cells from oxidative damage.

c. **Wound Healing:** The gel promotes wound healing by stimulating fibroblast proliferation and collagen synthesis. It enhances the skin's repair processes and may speed up the healing of minor burns and abrasions.

d. **Moisturizing:** Aloe vera gel acts as a natural moisturizer. It provides hydration by forming a protective layer on the skin, reducing transepidermal water loss.

3. Pharmacokinetics:

a. **Absorption:** When applied topically, aloe vera gel is not systemically absorbed. It works locally at the site of application.

b. **Distribution:** Aloe vera components remain in the local area of application, primarily affecting the skin and underlying tissues.

4. Pharmacodynamics:

a. **Onset of Action:** Immediate relief upon application, with noticeable effects on skin hydration and inflammation within a few hours to days.

b. **Duration of Action:** Effects can last as long as the gel remains on the skin and its components remain active.

5. Therapeutic Uses:

a. **Skin Moisturizer:** Used to hydrate and soothe dry or irritated skin.

b. **Burns and Wounds:** Applied to minor burns, cuts, and abrasions to promote healing and reduce discomfort.

c. **Sunburn Relief:** Provides cooling and soothing relief from sunburn.

d. **Anti-aging:** Sometimes included in skincare products for its potential to reduce the appearance of fine lines and wrinkles.

6. Side Effects:

a. **Common:** Mild irritation or allergic reactions (e.g., redness, itching) in sensitive individuals.

b. **Serious:** Rare cases of severe allergic reactions or dermatitis.

7. Contraindications:

a. **Allergy:** Should be avoided by individuals with known allergies to aloe vera or related plants.

b. **Open Wounds:** Caution is advised if applied to large open wounds or severe burns.

8. Interactions:

a. **Drug Interactions:** Generally minimal, but excessive use could theoretically affect the absorption of topical medications applied concurrently.

D. Hand Sanitizers:

1. Introduction:

a. **Product:** Hand Sanitizers

b. **Common Uses:** Antiseptic agents for hand hygiene to reduce or eliminate pathogens.

2. Mechanism of Action:

a. **Alcohol-based Sanitizers:**

i. **Ethanol (Ethyl Alcohol):** Disrupts the cell membrane of microorganisms, leading to cell lysis and death. Effective against a wide range of bacteria and some viruses.

ii. **Isopropanol (Isopropyl Alcohol):** Similar to ethanol, it denatures proteins and disrupts microbial cell membranes.

b. **Non-Alcohol-based Sanitizers:**

i. **Chlorhexidine:** Disrupts bacterial cell membranes and coagulates cellular contents, providing a broad spectrum of antimicrobial activity.

ii. **Triclosan:** Inhibits bacterial fatty acid synthesis, leading to bacterial cell death. However, it is less commonly used due to concerns about resistance and environmental impact.

3. Pharmacokinetics:

a. **Absorption:** Hand sanitizers are applied topically and generally do not enter systemic circulation. Alcohol-based sanitizers are rapidly absorbed by the skin but are not intended to be absorbed into the bloodstream

b. **Distribution:** The antimicrobial agents remain on the skin surface and do not distribute into internal tissues.

4. Pharmacodynamics:

a. **Onset of Action:** Immediate antimicrobial activity upon application.

b. **Duration of Action:** The antimicrobial effect persists for a short period after application, depending on the formulation and amount used. Reapplication is necessary for continued protection.

5. Therapeutic Uses:

a. **Hand Hygiene:** Used to reduce or eliminate pathogens on the hands when soap and water are not available.

b. **Infection Control:** Employed in healthcare settings to prevent the spread of infections.

6. Side Effects:

a. **Common:** Skin dryness, irritation, and redness.

b. **Serious:** Rarely, allergic reactions or dermatitis can occur, especially with frequent use.

7. Contraindications:

a. **Sensitive Skin:** Use with caution in individuals with sensitive skin or pre-existing skin conditions.

b. **Open Wounds:** Should not be used on open wounds or severely damaged skin due to potential irritation or delayed healing.

8. Interactions:

a. **Drug Interactions:** Minimal systemic interactions are expected since hand sanitizers are not intended for internal use. However, the use of sanitizers may interact with topical treatments if used simultaneously.

E. Moisturizing Creams:

1. Introduction:

a. **Product:** Moisturizing Creams

b. **Common Uses:** Hydration and protection of the skin.

2. Mechanism of Action:

a. **Hydration:** Moisturizing creams contain occlusive agents (e.g., petrolatum, dimethicone) and humectants (e.g., glycerin, hyaluronic acid). Occlusive agents form a barrier on the skin's surface to prevent water loss, while humectants attract water from the environment or deeper layers of the skin into the outer layer (stratum corneum).

b. **Emollience:** These creams often contain emollients that smooth and soften the skin by filling in gaps between skin cells and enhancing the skin's lipid barrier.

3. **Pharmacokinetics:**

a. **Absorption:** Moisturizing creams are primarily designed to act on the skin's surface. Minimal systemic absorption occurs, though some ingredients may penetrate the upper layers of the skin.

b. **Distribution:** The active ingredients remain localized in the stratum corneum and may influence deeper layers of the epidermis.

4. **Pharmacodynamics:**

a. **Onset of Action:** Immediate improvement in skin hydration and smoothness upon application.

b. **Duration of Action:** Effects can last as long as the cream remains on the skin, often requiring reapplication to maintain skin moisture levels.

5. **Therapeutic Uses:**

a. **Dry Skin Relief:** Used to hydrate and relieve symptoms of dry, flaky, or rough skin.

b. **Barrier Protection:** Provides a protective layer to prevent moisture loss and protect the skin from environmental factors.

c. **Skin Softening:** Enhances skin texture and reduces roughness.

6. **Side Effects:**

a. **Common:** Skin irritation, redness, or allergic reactions in sensitive individuals.

b. **Serious:** Rare cases of severe allergic reactions or dermatitis.

7. Contraindications:

a. **Allergy:** Should be avoided by individuals with known allergies to specific ingredients in the cream.

b. **Open Wounds:** Caution is advised when applying to large or severe open wounds.

8. Interactions:

a. **Drug Interactions:** Minimal, as these creams are applied topically. However, simultaneous use of other topical treatments may affect the efficacy or absorption of the cream.

F. Emollient Creams:

1. Introduction:

a. **Product:** Emollient Creams

b. **Common Uses:** Skin conditioning, moisturizing, and protection.

2. Mechanism of Action:

a. **Skin Barrier Repair:** Emollient creams contain lipids and fatty acids (e.g., ceramides, shea butter) that restore the skin's natural barrier function by replenishing lipids and enhancing the integrity of the skin barrier.

b. **Occlusion:** Like moisturizing creams, emollients form a barrier on the skin's surface to prevent moisture loss and protect against environmental irritants.

c. **Softening:** Emollients smooth and soften the skin by filling in gaps between skin cells and reducing roughness.

3. Pharmacokinetics:

a. **Absorption:** Emollient creams are primarily effective on the skin's surface. They are designed for minimal systemic absorption, focusing on local effects.

b. **Distribution:** Ingredients remain primarily in the stratum corneum and may have a localized effect on the skin's deeper layers.

4. **Pharmacodynamics:**
   a. **Onset of Action:** Immediate improvement in skin texture and softness upon application.
   b. **Duration of Action:** The effects can last as long as the cream remains on the skin. Regular application may be required for ongoing benefits.
5. **Therapeutic Uses:**
   a. **Dry and Rough Skin:** Used to treat and prevent dry, rough, or scaly skin conditions by restoring skin moisture and barrier function.
   b. **Eczema and Dermatitis:** Often used as part of the management of eczema or dermatitis to alleviate symptoms and improve skin condition.
   c. **Skin Protection:** Provides a protective layer against irritants and environmental factors.
6. **Side Effects:**
   a. **Common:** Possible irritation or allergic reactions in individuals with sensitive skin.
   b. **Serious:** Rare but potential for severe allergic reactions or dermatitis.
7. **Contraindications:**
   a. **Allergy:** Avoid use in individuals with known hypersensitivity to the ingredients.
   b. **Severe Skin Conditions:** Caution with use on severe open wounds or infections.

Multiple-Choice Questions (MCQs)

1. What is a common characteristic of tablets as a dosage form?
   a) They are always coated.
   b) They dissolve in water.
   c) They are typically solid and compressed into a specific shape.
   d) They are always chewable.

2. Which type of capsule contains liquid or semi-solid medication?
    a) Hard Gelatin Capsules
    b) Soft Gelatin Capsules
    c) Effervescent Capsules
    d) Chewable Capsules
3. What is a suspension in the context of liquid dosage forms?
    a) A homogeneous mixture of a drug dissolved in a solvent
    b) A mixture where solid particles are dispersed in a liquid
    c) A concentrated sugar solution
    d) A mixture of oil and water
4. Which of the following is a type of semi-solid dosage form?
    a) Tablet
    b) Ointment
    c) Solution
    d) Aerosol
5. What is the primary use of transdermal patches?
    a) To provide immediate release of medication
    b) To deliver medication over a prolonged period
    c) To be dissolved in water before use
    d) To be chewed before swallowing
6. Which of the following is a characteristic of effervescent tablets?
    a) They are chewed before swallowing.
    b) They dissolve in water before ingestion.
    c) They provide controlled release of medication.
    d) They are used for topical application.
7. What is the role of emulsifiers in emulsions?
    a) To increase the sweetness of the formulation
    b) To stabilize the mixture of two immiscible liquids
    c) To enhance the flavor of the medication

d) To thicken the solution

8. Which dosage form is typically used for medications that need to act quickly?
   a) Extended-release tablets
   b) Oral solutions
   c) Transdermal patches
   d) Suppositories
9. Which of the following is a potential disadvantage of using ointments as a dosage form?
   a) They are non-greasy.
   b) They provide a cooling effect.
   c) They are greasy and may be difficult to wash off.
   d) They dissolve quickly in water.
10. What type of dosage form is a metered-dose inhaler (MDI)?
   a) Solution
   b) Aerosol
   c) Gel
   d) Patch
11. Which of the following is an advantage of using tablets as a dosage form?
   a) They are always sweet-tasting.
   b) They provide precise dosing and are easy to handle.
   c) They are the best option for patients with difficulty swallowing.
   d) They require refrigeration.
12. What is the primary function of gels in semi-solid dosage forms?
   a) To be taken orally for systemic effects
   b) To provide a topical effect with minimal greasiness
   c) To be used as inhalation therapy
   d) To be inserted into body cavities

13. Which dosage form is most suitable for patients who cannot take oral medications?

  a) Oral solution
  b) Tablet
  c) Suppository
  d) Capsule

14. What is a major benefit of using paracetamol tablets for pain relief?

  a) They are only available in chewable form.
  b) They have a prolonged effect that lasts for 24 hours.
  c) They are widely available and effective for mild to moderate pain.
  d) They must be dissolved in water before use.

15. Which of the following is a common use of aloe vera gel?

  a) Oral administration for fever reduction
  b) Topical application for skin hydration and healing
  c) Inhalation therapy for respiratory conditions
  d) Injectable solution for pain management

16. What is the primary concern when using children's aspirin tablets in viral infections?

  a) Risk of excessive drowsiness
  b) Potential for Reye's syndrome
  c) Delayed onset of action
  d) Development of antibiotic resistance

17. What is the purpose of hand sanitizers?

  a) To cleanse the skin for hydration
  b) To moisturize dry skin
  c) To reduce or eliminate pathogens on the hands
  d) To provide long-lasting fragrance

18. Which of the following best describes the action of moisturizing creams?

  a) They provide systemic hydration through oral absorption.

b) They hydrate the skin by forming a barrier to prevent moisture loss.
c) They are primarily used for treating infections.
d) They are used to anesthetize the skin.

19. How do emollient creams differ from regular moisturizing creams?

a) Emollient creams are designed to hydrate without softening the skin.
b) Emollient creams repair the skin's barrier function by replenishing lipids.
c) Emollient creams are intended for internal use.
d) Emollient creams are used exclusively for wound care.

20. What is a contraindication for the use of aloe vera gel?

a) Use on large open wounds
b) Application on dry skin
c) Topical use for sunburn
d) Use as an oral analgesic

Short Answer Type Questions (Subjective)

1. Define solid dosage forms and give two examples.
2. What are the main advantages of using capsules as a dosage form?
3. Explain the difference between a suspension and an emulsion.
4. Describe the key characteristics of transdermal patches.
5. What are the common uses of semi-solid dosage forms like creams and ointments?
6. How do extended-release tablets differ from regular oral tablets?
7. What are the primary functions of solutions as liquid dosage forms?
8. Discuss the therapeutic uses of paracetamol tablets.
9. What are the potential risks associated with the use of children's aspirin tablets?
10. How do hand sanitizers work to reduce the spread of pathogens?

11. Describe the pharmacokinetics of paracetamol.
12. What is the significance of using aloe vera gel for skin care?
13. Explain the role of emulsifiers in liquid dosage forms.
14. What are the benefits of using metered-dose inhalers (MDIs) for respiratory conditions?
15. Discuss the contraindications for the use of aspirin in children.
16. What are the main differences between hydrophilic and oleaginous ointments?
17. Describe the mechanism of action of emollient creams in skin care.
18. How do gels differ from creams in their application and effect on the skin?
19. What factors should be considered when choosing a dosage form for a medication?
20. Explain how moisturizing creams protect and hydrate the skin.

Long Answer Type Questions (Subjective)

1. Discuss the various types of solid dosage forms, including their characteristics, advantages, and examples.
2. Explain the different types of liquid dosage forms, focusing on solutions, suspensions, and emulsions, and their therapeutic uses.
3. Describe the role and importance of semi-solid dosage forms in topical therapy, with a focus on ointments, creams, and gels.
4. Discuss the pharmacology of paracetamol, including its mechanism of action, pharmacokinetics, therapeutic uses, and potential side effects.
5. Explain the advantages and challenges associated with the use of transdermal patches for drug delivery.
6. Compare and contrast hand sanitizers and moisturizing creams in terms of their composition, mechanism of action, and therapeutic applications.
7. Describe the pharmacological considerations for the use of aspirin in children, including its benefits, risks, and contraindications.

8. Discuss the therapeutic uses and benefits of aloe vera gel, focusing on its mechanism of action and applications in skin care.
9. Explain the classification and uses of inhalation dosage forms, including aerosols, metered-dose inhalers, and nebulizers.
10. Discuss the significance of emollient creams in dermatological therapy, including their mechanism of action, uses, and potential side effects.

Answer Key for 20 MCQs

1. (c) They are typically solid and compressed into a specific shape.
2. (b) Soft Gelatin Capsules
3. (b) A mixture where solid particles are dispersed in a liquid
4. (b) Ointment
5. (b) To deliver medication over a prolonged period
6. (b) They dissolve in water before ingestion.
7. (b) To stabilize the mixture of two immiscible liquids
8. (b) Oral solutions
9. (c) They are greasy and may be difficult to wash off.
10. (b) Aerosol
11. (b) They provide precise dosing and are easy to handle.
12. (b) To provide a topical effect with minimal greasiness
13. (c) Suppository
14. (c) They are widely available and effective for mild to moderate pain.
15. (b) Topical application for skin hydration and healing
16. (b) Potential for Reye's syndrome
17. (c) To reduce or eliminate pathogens on the hands
18. (b) They hydrate the skin by forming a barrier to prevent moisture loss.
19. (b) Emollient creams repair the skin's barrier function by replenishing lipids
20. (a) Use on large open wounds

CHAPTER – 3

PRESCRIPTION

INTRODUCTION:

A prescription is a formal order written by a licensed healthcare provider that authorizes a patient to obtain a specific medication or treatment. It serves several key purposes:

1. **Legal Requirement:** Prescriptions are legally required for many medications, particularly controlled substances. They ensure that medications are dispensed safely and appropriately.
2. **Patient Safety:** Prescriptions help ensure that patients receive the correct medication at the correct dose and for the correct duration. This minimizes the risk of adverse effects and interactions.
3. **Standardization:** Prescriptions follow a standardized format, which helps in maintaining consistency and clarity in communication between healthcare providers and pharmacists.

Key Components of a Prescription

1. **Patient Information:** This includes the patient's full name, address, and sometimes date of birth. This ensures that the medication is intended for the correct individual.
2. **Date:** The date when the prescription was written is crucial for determining the validity and duration of the prescription.
3. **Medication Details:**
    a. **Drug Name:** The specific name of the medication (e.g., Sildenafil, Tadalafil).

b. **Dosage Form:** The form in which the medication is to be taken (e.g., tablet, capsule, liquid).
c. **Strength:** The amount of active ingredient in the medication (e.g., 50 mg, 100 mg).
d. **Quantity:** The total amount of medication to be dispensed.

4. **Directions for Use:** Instructions on how the patient should take the medication, including dosage, frequency, and any special instructions (e.g., "take one tablet twice daily with food").
5. **Refills:** Information about how many times the prescription can be refilled before a new prescription is needed.
6. **Provider Information:** The name, contact information, and credentials of the healthcare provider who wrote the prescription.
7. **Signature:** The provider's signature is required to validate the prescription.

Types of Prescriptions

1. **Written Prescription:** Physically written on paper and signed by the provider. This is the most traditional form.
2. **Electronic Prescription:** Sent electronically to a pharmacy through a secure system. This method is becoming increasingly common due to its convenience and reduced risk of errors.
3. **Verbal Prescription:** Given orally by the provider to a pharmacist. This is less common and typically used in emergencies.
4. **Renewal Prescription:** A request to continue a medication beyond the initial prescription period, often requiring provider approval.

Key Considerations

1. **Legal and Regulatory Aspects:** Prescriptions must comply with local laws and regulations regarding medication dispensing, especially for controlled substances.
2. **Patient Education:** Clear instructions and patient education are essential to ensure adherence to the prescribed regimen and to avoid misuse.
3. **Pharmacy Interaction:** The pharmacist plays a crucial role in reviewing the prescription, verifying its accuracy, and providing patient counseling.

DEFINITION OF PRESCRIPTION

A prescription is a formal written or electronic order from a licensed healthcare provider that authorizes a patient to obtain and use a specific medication or treatment. It specifies the exact medication or therapy, dosage, frequency, and duration, and is intended to guide the dispensing and administration of the prescribed substance. Prescriptions are an essential component of the healthcare system, ensuring that medications are used safely, effectively, and in accordance with medical standards.

Key Aspects of a Prescription

1. **Healthcare Provider Authorization:**
   a. A prescription must be written by a licensed healthcare provider, such as a physician, dentist, or nurse practitioner, who has the authority to prescribe medications within their scope of practice.
2. **Medication Specificity:**
   a. It details the exact medication or treatment to be used, including the drug name, dosage form, strength, and quantity.
3. **Patient Information:**
   a. The prescription includes the patient's personal information to ensure that the medication is dispensed to the correct individual.
4. **Dosage Instructions:**

   a. Clear instructions on how the medication should be taken or used, including the dose, frequency, and any special administration guidelines.

5. **Legal and Regulatory Compliance:**
   a. Prescriptions must comply with legal regulations, especially for controlled substances, to prevent misuse and ensure proper medical use.
6. **Pharmacy Dispensing:**
   a. The prescription is used by pharmacists to prepare and dispense the medication according to the specified instructions.
7. **Validation and Refill Information:**
   a. The prescription may include information about refills and expiration, indicating how long the prescription is valid and how many times it can be renewed.

Purpose and Importance

1. **Ensures Proper Medication Use**: Prescriptions provide a standardized way to communicate the appropriate use of medications, reducing the risk of errors and misuse.
2. **Facilitates Safe Dispensing**: By detailing medication specifics and instructions, prescriptions help pharmacists accurately prepare and dispense medications.
3. **Regulates Medication Access**: Prescriptions help control access to medications, particularly those that are potentially dangerous or habit-forming.
4. **Provides Legal Protection**: Prescriptions protect both patients and providers by documenting the medical need and authorized use of a medication.

PARTS OF PRESCRIPTION

1. **Patient Information**
   a. **Name**: Full name of the patient.
   b. **Date of Birth**: Helps to verify the patient's identity and ensure the appropriate dosage.
   c. **Address**: Sometimes included for additional identification, particularly in controlled substances.
2. **Date**
   a. The date when the prescription is written. This is important for tracking the validity of the prescription and determining if it's still active.
3. **Medication Information**
   a. **Drug Name**: The name of the medication prescribed. It can be either the generic name or the brand name.
   b. **Dosage**: The amount of medication to be taken at one time (e.g., 500 mg).
   c. **Strength**: Concentration of the medication (e.g., 100 mg/ml).
   d. **Form**: The form of the medication (e.g., tablet, capsule, liquid).
   e. **Route of Administration**: How the medication should be taken (e.g., orally, intravenously).
   f. **Frequency**: How often the medication should be taken (e.g., once daily, every 8 hours).
   g. **Duration**: The length of time the medication should be used (e.g., 7 days, 1 month).
4. **Instructions**
   a. Detailed guidance on how to use the medication, including any special instructions (e.g., take with food, avoid alcohol).
5. **Prescriber Information**
   a. **Name**: Full name of the prescribing healthcare provider.

b. **Credentials**: Professional title or designation (e.g., MD, DO, NP).

c. **Contact Information**: Address and phone number for follow-up or clarification.

d. **Signature**: The prescriber's signature, which authorizes the prescription. For electronic prescriptions, a digital signature or authentication is used.

6. **Pharmacy Information**

   a. **Pharmacy Name**: Name of the pharmacy where the prescription is filled.

   b. **Pharmacy Address**: Physical address of the pharmacy.

   c. **Pharmacy Contact Information**: Phone number or other contact details.

7. **Prescription Number**

   a. A unique identifier assigned to the prescription by the pharmacy. This number helps in tracking and refilling the prescription.

8. **Refills**

   a. **Number of Refills**: Indicates how many times the prescription can be refilled before needing a new prescription from the healthcare provider.

   b. **Refill Instructions**: Any specific instructions related to refilling the medication.

9. **Legal and Regulatory Information**

   a. **Controlled Substance Schedule**: For medications classified as controlled substances, the prescription must include the schedule classification (e.g., Schedule II, III) to comply with regulations.

10. **Additional Notes**

    a. Any special instructions or comments from the prescriber, such as warnings about drug interactions or specific patient considerations.

HANDLING OF PRESCRIPTION

1. Receiving the Prescription

a. **Verification**: Check that the prescription is complete and legible. Verify the patient's name, medication details, and prescriber information. Ensure that the prescription is signed or appropriately authenticated.

b. **Validation**: Confirm that the prescription is written by a licensed healthcare provider and is valid according to local regulations. For controlled substances, additional verification of the prescriber's credentials and prescription legality may be required.

2. Entering Prescription Information

a. **Data Entry**: Input the prescription details into the pharmacy's computer system, including patient information, medication name, dosage, and instructions. Ensure accuracy to prevent dispensing errors.

b. **Label Generation**: Generate a prescription label that includes essential information such as the medication name, dosage, instructions, and any warnings or special notes.

3. Preparing the Medication

a. **Medication Selection**: Retrieve the correct medication from inventory, ensuring it matches the prescription details (e.g., drug name, strength, and form).

b. **Dosage Preparation**: Measure or count the correct amount of medication based on the prescription. For liquid medications, use appropriate measuring devices to ensure accuracy.

c. **Label Application**: Attach the prescription label to the medication container. Ensure that the label is clear and includes all necessary information.

4. Reviewing and Finalizing

a. **Double-Check**: Review the prepared medication against the prescription for accuracy. Verify the medication name, dosage, and quantity.
b. **Patient Information**: Ensure that the prescription label includes the patient's name, dosage instructions, and any specific warnings or precautions.
c. **Pharmacist Review**: Have a licensed pharmacist or pharmacy technician conduct a final check to confirm the correctness of the medication and prescription details.

5. Providing Patient Information

a. **Counseling**: Offer the patient or caregiver information about the medication, including how to take it, potential side effects, interactions with other drugs, and any special instructions. Provide written information if available.
b. **Answer Questions**: Address any questions or concerns the patient may have regarding the medication or its use.

6. Documentation and Record-Keeping

a. **Prescription Records**: Maintain accurate records of the prescription, including the patient's information, medication details, and dispensing date. This documentation is crucial for legal compliance and future reference.
b. **Controlled Substances**: For controlled substances, follow additional documentation requirements and regulations, including maintaining logs of dispensing and refills.

7. Handling Refills and Renewals

a. **Refill Requests**: Process refill requests according to the original prescription's instructions and the pharmacy's policies. Verify the request with the patient and ensure that it complies with legal and medical guidelines.

b. **Renewal Requests**: Contact the prescriber if a prescription renewal is needed. Obtain authorization and update the prescription as necessary.

8. Disposal and Security

a. **Medication Disposal**: Dispose of any expired or unused medications according to local regulations and pharmacy policies. Ensure that disposal methods prevent environmental contamination and unauthorized access.

b. **Security**: Safeguard all prescription records and medications to protect patient confidentiality and prevent misuse or theft.

ERRORS IN PRESCRIPTION

Errors in prescriptions can lead to significant health risks and complications. Identifying and understanding these errors is crucial for ensuring patient safety and effective treatment. Here's a detailed look at common types of prescription errors:

Types of Prescription Errors

1. **Incorrect Drug Name**
   a. **Description**: Prescribing the wrong medication due to a spelling error, similar-sounding drug names, or misunderstanding.
   b. **Impact**: Can lead to ineffective treatment or adverse effects if the wrong drug is given.
2. **Dosage Errors**
   a. **Description**: Incorrect dosage of medication, either too high or too low, due to misinterpretation of the prescription or calculation mistakes.
   b. **Impact**: Overdosing can cause toxicity, while underdosing may result in inadequate treatment.
3. **Incorrect Strength**
   a. **Description**: Prescribing a medication in the wrong strength (e.g., 10 mg instead of 100 mg).

   b. **Impact**: Similar to dosage errors, this can lead to ineffective treatment or toxicity.

4. **Wrong Route of Administration**
   a. **Description**: Incorrectly specifying the route of administration (e.g., oral instead of intravenous).
   b. **Impact**: Can result in ineffective treatment or harm if the medication is administered improperly.
5. **Incorrect Frequency or Duration**
   a. **Description**: Mistakes in how often or how long the medication should be taken.
   b. **Impact**: May lead to suboptimal therapy or increased risk of side effects.
6. **Illegible Prescriptions**
   a. **Description**: Handwritten prescriptions that are difficult to read.
   b. **Impact**: Can result in misinterpretation of medication details and improper dispensing.
7. **Drug Interactions**
   a. **Description**: Failing to account for potential interactions between the prescribed medication and other drugs the patient is taking.
   b. **Impact**: Can cause adverse effects or reduce the effectiveness of treatment.
8. **Allergic Reactions**
   a. **Description**: Prescribing a medication to which the patient is known to be allergic.
   b. **Impact**: Can lead to severe allergic reactions, including anaphylaxis.
9. **Incorrect Patient Information**
   a. **Description**: Mistakes in the patient's name, age, or medical history.

b. **Impact**: Can result in dispensing errors or inappropriate medication use.

10. **Failure to Consider Patient-Specific Factors**
    a. **Description**: Not accounting for factors such as renal or hepatic impairment, age, weight, or pregnancy.
    b. **Impact**: Can lead to ineffective or harmful treatment.
11. **Incomplete Prescriptions**
    a. **Description**: Missing key information such as dosage, frequency, or duration.
    b. **Impact**: Can cause confusion and improper use of the medication.
12. **Expired Prescriptions**
    a. **Description**: Fulfilling prescriptions that are past their validity date.
    b. **Impact**: May result in treatment that is no longer appropriate or safe.

Preventing Prescription Errors

1. **Verification and Double-Checking**
    a. Always verify the prescription details with the patient or healthcare provider and double-check all information before dispensing.
2. **Use of Electronic Prescriptions**
    a. Electronic prescriptions can reduce errors due to legibility issues and improve accuracy with built-in safety checks.
3. **Clear Communication**
    a. Ensure clear communication between healthcare providers, pharmacists, and patients. Verify any unclear instructions or potential drug interactions.
4. **Patient Counseling**
    a. Provide thorough counseling to patients about their medications, including correct usage, potential side effects, and what to do if they miss a dose.

5. **Staff Training**
    a. Regularly train pharmacy staff on prescription handling procedures, error identification, and patient safety practices.
6. **Implement Safety Protocols**
    a. Establish and follow standard operating procedures for prescription handling, including checking and rechecking medication orders.

Classification:

The classification of prescriptions can be categorized based on various criteria, such as the type of medication, the nature of the prescription, and its legal status. Here's a detailed classification with examples:

1. Classification by Medication Type

a. Prescription Medications

These are drugs that require a prescription due to their potential for misuse or because they require professional oversight for safe use.

1. **Example**:
    i. **Antibiotics** (e.g., Amoxicillin) – Used to treat bacterial infections.
    ii. **Antidepressants** (e.g., Fluoxetine) – Used to treat depression and other mental health conditions.

b. Over-the-Counter (OTC) Medications

These are medications available without a prescription, typically for less severe conditions and with a lower risk of misuse.

1. **Example**:
    i. **Acetaminophen** – Used for pain relief and fever reduction.
    ii. **Antihistamines** (e.g., Diphenhydramine) – Used for allergy symptoms.

2. Classification by Prescription Nature

a. Written Prescription

A physical document, handwritten or printed, that includes all necessary information for medication dispensing.

1. **Example**:
    i. **Chronic Disease Management**: A prescription for insulin for a diabetic patient.

b. Electronic Prescription

Sent electronically from the prescriber to the pharmacy, which helps in reducing errors and streamlining the process.

1. **Example**:
    i. **Maintenance Therapy**: A prescription for statins for managing high cholesterol.

c. Verbal Prescription

Given orally by a healthcare provider, usually in urgent situations. It must be documented in writing later.

1. **Example**:
    i. **Emergency Medication**: A verbal prescription for a painkiller following a minor surgical procedure.

3. Classification by Legal Status

a. Prescription for Controlled Substances

Medications that are regulated due to their potential for abuse and addiction. These require special handling and documentation.

1. **Example**:
    i. **Opioids** (e.g., Oxycodone) – Used for pain management, classified as Schedule II controlled substances.

b. Non-Controlled Prescription

Medications that do not fall under controlled substance regulations and typically have a lower risk of misuse.

1. **Example**:
    i. **Antihypertensives** (e.g., Lisinopril) – Used for managing high blood pressure.

4. Classification by Prescription Duration

a. Acute Prescription

Intended for a short-term condition or illness, usually with a fixed duration.

1. **Example**:
    i. **Antibiotics** (e.g., Azithromycin) – Prescribed for a 5-day course to treat a bacterial infection.

b. Chronic Prescription

Prescribed for long-term or ongoing conditions, often with refills.

1. **Example**:
    i. **Thyroid Hormones** (e.g., Levothyroxine) – Prescribed indefinitely for hypothyroidism.

5. Classification by Drug Administration Route

a. Oral Prescription

Medications taken by mouth.

1. **Example**:
    i. **Pain Relievers** (e.g., Ibuprofen) – Taken orally for pain and inflammation.

b. Topical Prescription

Medications applied to the skin or mucous membranes.

1. **Example**:
    i. **Topical Steroids** (e.g., Hydrocortisone cream) – Used for skin conditions like eczema.

c. Injectable Prescription

Medications administered via injection.

1. **Example**:
    i. **Insulin** – Injected for diabetes management.

d. Inhaled Prescription

Medications inhaled into the lungs.

1. **Example**:

i. **Asthma Inhalers** (e.g., Albuterol) – Used for acute asthma attacks.

according to the patient's needs and the medication's properties.

A. **Amoxicillin:**

1. Classification

a. **Drug Class**: Antibiotic

b. **Subclass**: Penicillin

2. Mechanism of Action

a. **Mode of Action**: Amoxicillin inhibits bacterial cell wall synthesis. It does this by binding to specific proteins known as penicillin-binding proteins (PBPs) located on the bacterial cell wall. This binding disrupts the formation of cross-links in the peptidoglycan layer of the bacterial cell wall, which is crucial for maintaining the cell's structural integrity. The result is weakened cell walls, leading to bacterial lysis and death.

b. **Spectrum**: Effective against a range of Gram-positive bacteria (e.g., Streptococcus species) and some Gram-negative bacteria (e.g., Escherichia coli, Haemophilus influenzae).

3. Pharmacokinetics

a. **Absorption**: Amoxicillin is well-absorbed from the gastrointestinal tract when administered orally. Peak plasma concentrations are typically reached within 1-2 hours after ingestion.

b. **Distribution**: It is widely distributed throughout body tissues and fluids, including the lungs, kidneys, and middle ear. It can cross the placenta and is present in breast milk.

c. **Metabolism**: Amoxicillin is minimally metabolized in the liver; most of the drug remains unchanged.

d. **Elimination**: Primarily excreted by the kidneys through glomerular filtration and tubular secretion. The drug has a half-life of approximately 1-1.5 hours.

4. **Clinical Uses**

a. **Infections**: Amoxicillin is used to treat various infections, including:

   i. **Upper Respiratory Tract Infections**: Sinusitis, pharyngitis.

   ii. **Lower Respiratory Tract Infections**: Pneumonia, bronchitis.

   iii. **Urinary Tract Infections**: Cystitis, pyelonephritis.

   iv. **Skin Infections**: Cellulitis, impetigo.

   v. **Sexually Transmitted Infections**: Gonorrhea.

b. **Prophylaxis**: It may be used to prevent endocarditis in high-risk patients undergoing certain dental or surgical procedures.

5. **Side Effects**

a. **Common**: Gastrointestinal disturbances such as nausea, vomiting, diarrhea, and abdominal pain. Rash may also occur.

b. **Serious**: Allergic reactions (e.g., anaphylaxis), pseudomembranous colitis (due to Clostridium difficile overgrowth), liver enzyme abnormalities.

6. **Contraindications**

a. **Allergy**: Contraindicated in patients with a known allergy to penicillins or other β-lactam antibiotics.

B. Fluoxetine:

1. **Classification**

a. **Drug Class**: Antidepressant

b. **Subclass**: Selective Serotonin Reuptake Inhibitor (SSRI)

2. **Mechanism of Action**

a. **Mode of Action**: Fluoxetine works by selectively inhibiting the reuptake of serotonin (5-HT) in the brain. It achieves this by blocking the serotonin transporter (SERT), which is responsible for the reabsorption of serotonin from the synaptic cleft back into the presynaptic neuron. Increased levels of serotonin in the synaptic cleft enhance serotonergic neurotransmission, which is believed to contribute to its antidepressant and anxiolytic effects.

b. **Specificity**: Fluoxetine's action is highly selective for serotonin reuptake with minimal impact on norepinephrine or dopamine reuptake.

3. Pharmacokinetics

a. **Absorption**: Fluoxetine is well-absorbed from the gastrointestinal tract. Peak plasma concentrations are typically reached within 6-8 hours of oral administration.

b. **Distribution**: It is extensively bound to plasma proteins and is widely distributed throughout the body. It crosses the blood-brain barrier and is also found in breast milk.

c. **Metabolism**: Fluoxetine is extensively metabolized in the liver, primarily by cytochrome P450 enzymes, especially CYP2D6. It has an active metabolite, norfluoxetine, which contributes to its therapeutic effects.

d. **Elimination**: Excreted mainly as metabolites in the urine. Fluoxetine has a long half-life of approximately 4-6 days, and its active metabolite, norfluoxetine, has a half-life of 7-15 days.

4. Clinical Uses

a. **Depression**: Used to treat major depressive disorder (MDD).

b. **Anxiety Disorders**: Effective in managing generalized anxiety disorder (GAD) and panic disorder.

c. **Obsessive-Compulsive Disorder (OCD)**: Used to treat OCD.

d. **Bulimia Nervosa**: Prescribed for the management of bulimia nervosa.

5. Side Effects

a. **Common**: Nausea, insomnia, headache, sexual dysfunction, and weight changes.

b. **Serious**: Serotonin syndrome (a potentially life-threatening condition caused by excessive serotonergic activity), suicidal thoughts or behavior, severe allergic reactions.

6. Contraindications

a. **Monoamine Oxidase Inhibitors (MAOIs)**: Contraindicated if used concurrently with or within 14 days of MAOIs due to the risk of serotonin syndrome.

b. **Hypersensitivity**: Contraindicated in patients with known hypersensitivity to fluoxetine or its components.

C. **Diphenhydramine:**

1. Classification

a. **Drug Class**: Antihistamine

b. **Subclass**: First-generation H1-receptor antagonist

2. Mechanism of Action

a. **Mode of Action**: Diphenhydramine competes with histamine for binding at H1-receptors located on smooth muscle, endothelial cells, and central nervous system tissues. By blocking these receptors, it inhibits the effects of histamine, such as vasodilation, increased vascular permeability, and bronchoconstriction, which contribute to allergic symptoms. Diphenhydramine also has significant anticholinergic properties, which contribute to its sedative effects.

b. **Additional Effects**: Sedation, antiemetic (prevents nausea and vomiting), and antitussive (cough suppression) properties due to its central nervous system activity.

3. Pharmacokinetics

a. **Absorption**: Rapidly absorbed from the gastrointestinal tract following oral administration. Peak plasma concentrations are typically reached within 1-2 hours.

b. **Distribution**: Widely distributed throughout the body, including the central nervous system. It crosses the blood-brain barrier and is present in breast milk.

c. **Metabolism**: Metabolized in the liver, primarily by cytochrome P450 enzymes.

d. **Elimination**: Excreted mainly via the kidneys. The half-life is approximately 4-8 hours.

4. Clinical Uses

a. **Allergic Reactions**: Used to relieve symptoms of allergic reactions, such as rhinitis, urticaria (hives), and conjunctivitis.

b. **Insomnia**: Often used off-label as a short-term treatment for insomnia due to its sedative properties.

c. **Motion Sickness**: Effective in preventing and treating motion sickness and nausea.

d. **Cough**: Used to suppress cough due to its antitussive properties.

5. Side Effects

a. **Common**: Drowsiness, dry mouth, dizziness, and blurred vision.

b. **Serious**: Anticholinergic effects such as urinary retention, constipation, and confusion, especially in elderly patients.

D. Oxycodone:

1. Classification

a. **Drug Class**: Opioid analgesic

b. **Subclass**: Semi-synthetic opioid

2. Mechanism of Action

a. **Mode of Action**: Oxycodone is an opioid agonist that binds primarily to μ-opioid receptors in the central nervous system. This binding inhibits the release of neurotransmitters involved in pain transmission, resulting in analgesia (pain relief) and euphoria. Oxycodone also has affinity for κ-opioid receptors, contributing to its analgesic effects.

b. **Additional Effects**: Can cause sedation, respiratory depression, and reduced gastrointestinal motility.

3. Pharmacokinetics

a. **Absorption**: Well-absorbed from the gastrointestinal tract. Peak plasma concentrations occur within 1-2 hours after oral administration.

b. **Distribution**: Widely distributed throughout the body and crosses the blood-brain barrier. It is highly bound to plasma proteins.

c. **Metabolism**: Metabolized primarily in the liver by cytochrome P450 enzymes, particularly CYP3A4 and CYP2D6, to various metabolites, including some active forms.

d. **Elimination**: Excreted mainly via the kidneys, with a half-life of approximately 3-5 hours, depending on the formulation.

4. Clinical Uses

a. **Pain Management**: Prescribed for the management of moderate to severe pain, such as postoperative pain, cancer pain, or chronic pain conditions.

b. **Chronic Pain**: Used for long-term pain management in patients with conditions such as osteoarthritis or severe back pain.

5. Side Effects

a. **Common**: Constipation, nausea, vomiting, drowsiness, and dizziness.

b. **Serious**: Respiratory depression (which can be life-threatening), opioid dependence and addiction, severe hypotension, and allergic reactions.

6. Contraindications

a. **Respiratory Depression**: Contraindicated in patients with significant respiratory depression or acute asthma.

b. **Hypersensitivity**: Contraindicated in individuals with known hypersensitivity to oxycodone or other opioids.

c. **Severe Liver Impairment**: Use with caution in patients with severe liver dysfunction due to altered metabolism and increased risk of toxicity.

E. **Lisinopril:**

1. Classification

a. **Drug Class**: Antihypertensive

b. **Subclass**: Angiotensin-Converting Enzyme (ACE) Inhibitor

2. Mechanism of Action

a. **Mode of Action**: Lisinopril inhibits the enzyme angiotensin-converting enzyme (ACE), which is responsible for converting angiotensin I to angiotensin II. Angiotensin II is a potent vasoconstrictor and stimulates the release of aldosterone, which leads to sodium and water retention. By inhibiting ACE, Lisinopril reduces the formation of angiotensin II, leading to vasodilation, decreased blood pressure, and reduced workload on the heart.
b. **Additional Effects**: Reduces the secretion of aldosterone, leading to decreased sodium and water retention and reduced blood pressure.

3. Pharmacokinetics

a. **Absorption**: Lisinopril is well-absorbed from the gastrointestinal tract with a bioavailability of approximately 25%. Peak plasma concentrations are reached within 6-8 hours after oral administration.
b. **Distribution**: It is widely distributed throughout the body and is not highly protein-bound. It crosses the placenta and is present in breast milk.
c. **Metabolism**: Lisinopril is not metabolized in the liver; it is excreted unchanged in the urine.
d. **Elimination**: Excreted primarily by the kidneys, with a half-life of approximately 12 hours, allowing for once-daily dosing.

4. Clinical Uses

a. **Hypertension**: Used to treat high blood pressure, both as a monotherapy and in combination with other antihypertensive agents.
b. **Heart Failure**: Prescribed to improve symptoms and reduce mortality in patients with heart failure.
c. **Chronic Kidney Disease**: Beneficial in slowing the progression of chronic kidney disease, particularly in diabetic nephropathy.
d. **Post-Myocardial Infarction**: Used to improve survival and reduce the risk of heart failure following a myocardial infarction.

5. **Side Effects**

a. **Common**: Dizziness, headache, persistent cough, fatigue.

b. **Serious**: Angioedema (swelling of the deeper layers of the skin), hyperkalemia (elevated potassium levels), hypotension (low blood pressure), renal impairment.

6. **Contraindications**

a. **Pregnancy**: Contraindicated in pregnancy, especially in the second and third trimesters, due to potential fetal harm.

b. **Renal Impairment**: Use with caution in patients with significant renal impairment as it may exacerbate renal dysfunction.

c. **Angioedema**: Contraindicated in patients with a history of angioedema related to previous ACE inhibitor therapy.

F. Azithromycin:

1. **Classification**

a. **Drug Class**: Antibiotic

b. **Subclass**: Macrolide

2. **Mechanism of Action**

a. **Mode of Action**: Azithromycin inhibits bacterial protein synthesis by binding to the 50S ribosomal subunit. This binding interferes with the translocation of peptidyl tRNA during translation, thus preventing the synthesis of essential bacterial proteins. The result is bacteriostatic, meaning it inhibits bacterial growth and reproduction.

b. **Spectrum**: Effective against a broad range of Gram-positive bacteria (e.g., Streptococcus pneumoniae) and some Gram-negative bacteria (e.g., Haemophilus influenzae), as well as atypical pathogens like Mycoplasma pneumoniae and Chlamydia trachomatis.

3. **Pharmacokinetics**

a. **Absorption**: Azithromycin is well-absorbed from the gastrointestinal tract with a bioavailability of approximately 37%. Peak plasma concentrations are typically reached within 2-3 hours after oral administration.

b. **Distribution**: It is widely distributed throughout the body and has a high tissue penetration. It accumulates in tissues like the lungs, prostate, and tonsils. It crosses the placenta and is present in breast milk.

c. **Metabolism**: Metabolized in the liver via CYP3A4, but it has minimal interaction with other drugs metabolized by this enzyme.

d. **Elimination**: Excreted primarily in the bile, with a small amount excreted in the urine. The half-life is approximately 68 hours, allowing for once-daily dosing.

4. Clinical Uses

a. **Infections**: Used to treat various infections, including:

   i. **Respiratory Tract Infections**: Such as community-acquired pneumonia, bronchitis.

   ii. **Skin Infections**: Including impetigo and cellulitis.

   iii. **Sexually Transmitted Infections**: Such as Chlamydia and gonorrhea.

   iv. **Ear Infections**: Otitis media.

b. **Prophylaxis**: Sometimes used to prevent infections in patients with specific conditions (e.g., prevention of Mycobacterium avium complex in HIV patients).

5. Side Effects

a. **Common**: Gastrointestinal disturbances such as nausea, vomiting, diarrhea, and abdominal pain.

b. **Serious**: Hepatotoxicity (liver damage), prolonged QT interval (risk of arrhythmias), allergic reactions.

6. Contraindications

a. **Hypersensitivity**: Contraindicated in individuals with a known hypersensitivity to azithromycin or other macrolide antibiotics.

b. **Liver Disease**: Use with caution in patients with liver disease due to potential for hepatotoxicity.

G. Albuterol:

1. Classification

a. **Drug Class**: Bronchodilator

b. **Subclass**: Beta-2 Adrenergic Agonist

2. Mechanism of Action

a. **Mode of Action**: Albuterol is a selective β2-adrenergic agonist that acts on β2-adrenergic receptors in the smooth muscle of the airways. Activation of these receptors leads to relaxation of bronchial smooth muscle, resulting in bronchodilation and improved airflow. This mechanism helps to relieve bronchospasm associated with asthma and chronic obstructive pulmonary disease (COPD).

b. **Additional Effects**: It also reduces mucus secretion and has some mild anti-inflammatory effects, although it is not primarily used as an anti-inflammatory medication.

3. Pharmacokinetics

a. **Absorption**: Albuterol is administered via inhalation, which allows it to act directly on the airways. When inhaled, it reaches the systemic circulation quickly, with peak plasma concentrations occurring within 1-2 hours.

b. **Distribution**: It is widely distributed throughout the body, but its primary action is in the lungs. It crosses the placenta but is minimally present in breast milk.

c. **Metabolism**: Metabolized in the liver by sulfation and conjugation to inactive metabolites.

d. **Elimination**: Excreted primarily in the urine. The half-life of albuterol is approximately 2.7 to 5 hours, depending on the formulation and route of administration.

4. Clinical Uses

a. **Asthma**: Used as a rescue inhaler to provide quick relief from acute asthma symptoms and bronchospasm.

b. **Chronic Obstructive Pulmonary Disease (COPD)**: Used to manage symptoms of COPD, including chronic bronchitis and emphysema.

c. **Exercise-Induced Bronchospasm**: Often used prophylactically to prevent bronchospasm induced by exercise.

5. Side Effects

a. **Common**: Tremor, palpitations, headache, dizziness, and nervousness.

b. **Serious**: Tachycardia, significant hypertension, hypokalemia (low potassium levels), and paradoxical bronchospasm (rare).

6. Contraindications

a. **Hypersensitivity**: Contraindicated in individuals with known hypersensitivity to albuterol or any of its components.

b. **Caution**: Use with caution in patients with cardiovascular disorders, diabetes, or hyperthyroidism due to potential exacerbation of these conditions.

Multiple choice question:

1. What is the primary purpose of a prescription?
   a) To provide patient education
   b) To authorize the dispensing of medication
   c) To record patient visits
   d) To diagnose a condition
2. Which of the following is a key component of a prescription?
   a) Patient's insurance details

b) Medication side effects

c) Patient's name and date of birth

d) Pharmacy name and contact information

3. What type of prescription is commonly used in emergencies?

a) Written prescription

b) Electronic prescription

c) Verbal prescription

d) Renewal prescription

4. Which part of the prescription indicates how many times it can be refilled?

a) Dosage form

b) Quantity

c) Directions for use

d) Refills

5. What should be verified first when receiving a prescription?

a) The patient's address

b) The medication's side effects

c) The prescription's validity and completeness

d) The pharmacy's contact details

6. Which of the following is a common error in prescriptions?

a) Correct dosage

b) Incorrect drug name

c) Accurate patient information

d) Correct route of administration

7. What is the classification of Amoxicillin?

a) Antidepressant

b) Antibiotic

c) Bronchodilator

d) Antihistamine

8. Which medication is classified as a Selective Serotonin Reuptake Inhibitor (SSRI)?
   a) Diphenhydramine
   b) Fluoxetine
   c) Lisinopril
   d) Albuterol
9. What is the primary mechanism of action of Oxycodone?
   a) Inhibiting bacterial cell wall synthesis
   b) Blocking serotonin reuptake
   c) Binding to μ-opioid receptors
   d) Reducing prostaglandin production
10. Which prescription component is essential for ensuring the medication is dispensed to the correct individual?
   a) Prescriber's signature
   b) Patient's information
   c) Pharmacy's address
   d) Medication's strength
11. Which type of prescription is becoming increasingly common due to its convenience and reduced risk of errors?
   a) Written prescription
   b) Verbal prescription
   c) Electronic prescription
   d) Renewal prescription
12. What should be done if a prescription is illegible?
   a) Guess the medication
   b) Fill the prescription anyway
   c) Contact the prescriber for clarification
   d) Ignore the prescription
13. What is a common side effect of Ibuprofen?

a) Tachycardia
b) Gastrointestinal disturbances
c) Respiratory depression
d) Hyperkalemia

14. What is the mechanism of action of Lisinopril?
    a) Inhibiting bacterial protein synthesis
    b) Blocking histamine receptors
    c) Inhibiting the enzyme angiotensin-converting enzyme (ACE)
    d) Binding to β2-adrenergic receptors

15. What is the primary use of Albuterol?
    a) Treating bacterial infections
    b) Relieving bronchospasm in asthma
    c) Reducing inflammation in arthritis
    d) Managing depression

16. Which classification does Azithromycin fall under?
    a) Opioid analgesic
    b) Antihistamine
    c) Antibiotic
    d) Antihypertensive

17. What type of prescription is used to continue a medication beyond the initial prescription period?
    a) Written prescription
    b) Renewal prescription
    c) Electronic prescription
    d) Verbal prescription

18. Which error in prescription involves prescribing a medication to which the patient is allergic?
    a) Dosage error
    b) Incorrect strength

c) Wrong route of administration

d) Allergic reaction

19. Which medication is classified as a Nonsteroidal Anti-Inflammatory Drug (NSAID)?

a) Oxycodone

b) Diphenhydramine

c) Ibuprofen

d) Fluoxetine

20. What does the pharmacist do during the final check of a prescription?

a) Fills the prescription immediately

b) Reviews the prepared medication against the prescription

c) Calls the patient for a consultation

d) Submits the prescription to the insurance company

Short Answer Type Questions (Subjective)

1. Define a prescription and its purpose in healthcare.
2. List and describe the key components of a prescription.
3. Explain the difference between a written prescription and an electronic prescription.
4. What are the common types of prescription errors?
5. Describe the importance of patient information on a prescription.
6. How does a pharmacist verify the accuracy of a prescription?
7. Explain the mechanism of action of Amoxicillin.
8. What are the common side effects of Fluoxetine?
9. Describe the role of a prescriber's signature in a prescription.
10. Explain the pharmacokinetics of Diphenhydramine.
11. What are the legal requirements for dispensing controlled substances?
12. How is Oxycodone used in pain management?
13. Discuss the importance of dosage instructions on a prescription.

14. Describe the mechanism of action of Lisinopril.
15. What are the clinical uses of Azithromycin?
16. Explain the difference between acute and chronic prescriptions.
17. What steps should be taken if a patient presents with a prescription error?
18. Describe the classification and clinical uses of Ibuprofen.
19. Explain how Albuterol is used in the management of asthma.
20. What are the risks associated with incorrect prescription handling?

Long Answer Type Questions (Subjective)

1. Discuss the role of prescriptions in patient safety and legal compliance in healthcare.
2. Explain the key components of a prescription and the significance of each part in ensuring safe and effective medication use.
3. Describe the process of handling and verifying prescriptions in a pharmacy, including the steps taken to prevent errors.
4. Compare and contrast the mechanisms of action of Amoxicillin, Fluoxetine, and Oxycodone, and discuss their clinical uses.
5. Discuss the types of prescription errors and the strategies pharmacists can use to prevent these errors in practice.
6. Explain the classification and pharmacokinetics of Lisinopril, including its clinical applications in hypertension and heart failure.
7. Discuss the legal and regulatory considerations involved in prescribing and dispensing controlled substances, including opioids like Oxycodone.
8. Describe the role of Diphenhydramine in managing allergic reactions, and discuss its pharmacokinetics and side effects.
9. Explain the importance of accurate prescription handling in preventing drug interactions and adverse effects, using examples such as Fluoxetine and Ibuprofen.

10. Discuss the challenges and benefits of transitioning from traditional written prescriptions to electronic prescriptions in modern healthcare.

Answer Key for 20 MCQs

1. (b) To authorize the dispensing of medication
2. (c) Patient's name and date of birth
3. (c) Verbal prescription
4. (d) Refills
5. (c) The prescription's validity and completeness
6. (b) Incorrect drug name
7. (b) Antibiotic
8. (b) Fluoxetine
9. (c) Binding to μ-opioid receptors
10. (b) Patient's information
11. (c) Electronic prescription
12. (c) Contact the prescriber for clarification
13. (b) Gastrointestinal disturbances
14. (c) Inhibiting the enzyme angiotensin-converting enzyme (ACE)
15. (b) Relieving bronchospasm in asthma
16. (c) Antibiotic
17. (b) Renewal prescription
18. (d) Allergic reaction
19. (c) Ibuprofen
20. (b) Reviews the prepared medication against the prescription

CHAPTER – 4

POSOLOGY

INTRODUCTION:

Posology is the branch of pharmacology that deals with the study of the dosage of drugs. It encompasses the principles and practices involved in determining the correct dose of a medication for a patient. Proper posology is essential for achieving therapeutic efficacy while minimizing the risk of toxicity. Here's a detailed overview:

1. Definition and Scope

a. **Definition:** Posology is the science of determining the appropriate dosage of medications, including how much of a drug to administer, how often to administer it, and the duration of treatment.

b. **Scope:** It involves understanding factors that influence dosage, including the drug's pharmacokinetics, pharmacodynamics, patient characteristics, and the nature of the disease.

2. Factors Affecting Dosage

a. Pharmacokinetics

a. **Absorption:** The rate and extent to which a drug is absorbed into the bloodstream.

b. **Distribution:** How the drug is distributed throughout the body's tissues and organs.

c. **Metabolism:** The process by which the drug is chemically altered in the body.

d. **Excretion:** The elimination of the drug from the body, primarily through the kidneys or liver.

b. Pharmacodynamics

a. **Drug-Receptor Interaction:** How the drug interacts with its target receptors to produce its effects.

b. **Therapeutic Window:** The range of drug concentrations in the blood that are effective without being toxic.

c. Patient Characteristics

a. **Age:** Dosage adjustments may be needed for pediatric or geriatric patients due to differences in metabolism and drug handling.

b. **Body Weight:** Dosage often needs to be adjusted based on body weight or body surface area.

c. **Gender:** Hormonal differences and body composition can affect drug metabolism and response.

d. **Genetics:** Genetic variations can influence drug metabolism and efficacy.

e. **Health Status:** Liver and kidney function, as well as the presence of other diseases, can impact drug dosage.

d. Disease Characteristics

a. **Severity of Disease:** The dosage may need to be adjusted based on the severity of the condition being treated.

b. **Drug Interactions:** Other medications the patient is taking can influence the required dosage.

3. Dosage Regimens

a. Single Dose

i. **Definition:** Administration of a drug once to achieve a therapeutic effect.

ii. **Example:** A single dose of an analgesic for acute pain relief.

b. Multiple Doses

i. **Definition:** Administration of the drug at regular intervals over time.

ii. **Example:** Antibiotics are often given multiple times daily for a specific period.

c. Loading Dose

i. **Definition:** An initial higher dose of a drug to quickly achieve therapeutic levels.

ii. **Example:** The initial dose of digoxin to rapidly reach therapeutic levels in heart failure.

d. Maintenance Dose

i. **Definition:** The dose given after the loading dose to maintain therapeutic drug levels.

ii. **Example:** The regular dose of a drug given after the initial loading dose.

e. Titration

i. **Definition:** Adjusting the dose of a drug based on the patient's response and tolerance.

ii. **Example:** Gradually increasing the dose of antihypertensive medication to find the optimal dose.

4. Methods of Dosage Calculation

a. Weight-Based Dosing

i. **Description:** Dosage is calculated based on the patient's weight (e.g., mg/kg).

ii. **Example:** Pediatric doses are often calculated based on weight.

b. Body Surface Area (BSA) Dosing

i. **Description:** Dosage is calculated based on the patient's BSA, often used in oncology.

ii. **Example:** Chemotherapy dosing is often based on BSA.

c. Fixed Dosing

i. **Description:** Standard doses are used regardless of patient characteristics.

ii. **Example:** Many over-the-counter medications use fixed dosing.

5. Dosage Forms and Administration Routes

a. Oral

i. **Description:** Administered by mouth (e.g., tablets, capsules, liquids).

ii. **Considerations:** Absorption can vary based on food intake and gastrointestinal conditions.

b. Intravenous (IV)

i. **Description:** Administered directly into the bloodstream.

ii. **Considerations:** Provides rapid drug action and precise control over dosage.

c. Intramuscular (IM)

i. **Description:** Administered into a muscle.

ii. **Considerations:** Drug absorption can be influenced by blood flow and muscle mass.

d. Subcutaneous (SC)

i. **Description:** Administered under the skin.

ii. **Considerations:** Suitable for self-administration and slow drug release.

e. Topical

i. **Description:** Applied to the skin or mucous membranes.

ii. **Considerations:** Provides localized effect and minimizes systemic exposure.

f. Inhalational

i. **Description:** Administered via inhalation (e.g., inhalers).

ii. **Considerations:** Effective for respiratory conditions.

6. Adjustments and Monitoring

a. Dose Adjustment

i. **Definition:** Modifying the dosage based on patient response or side effects.
ii. **Example:** Reducing the dose of a medication if adverse effects occur.

b. Monitoring

i. **Definition:** Regular assessment of drug levels, therapeutic response, and side effects.
ii. **Example:** Monitoring blood levels of anticoagulants to ensure effectiveness and safety.

DEFINITION OF POSOLOGY

Posology is a specialized branch of pharmacology that focuses on the study of drug dosages. Its primary concern is determining the appropriate amount of medication needed to achieve a therapeutic effect while minimizing potential side effects or toxicity. Here's a detailed definition:

Definition of Posology

Posology refers to:

1. **The Science of Drug Dosage**: It is concerned with calculating and administering the correct dose of a drug, ensuring that the patient receives the optimal amount to achieve therapeutic benefits without causing harm.
2. **Dosage Calculation**: Involves determining the amount and frequency of medication required for different therapeutic goals. This includes the initial dose, maintenance dose, and any adjustments needed based on patient response.
3. **Factors Influencing Dosage**: Takes into account various factors that affect how a drug works in the body, such as:
    a. **Patient Characteristics**: Age, weight, sex, and overall health.
    b. **Disease State**: The impact of specific diseases or conditions on drug metabolism and efficacy.

   c. **Pharmacokinetics**: How the body absorbs, distributes, metabolizes, and excretes the drug.
   d. **Pharmacodynamics**: The drug's effects on the body and its mechanism of action.
4. **Therapeutic and Toxic Doses**: Establishes the minimum effective dose required for therapeutic effects and the maximum allowable dose to avoid toxicity, defining the therapeutic window.
5. **Dose-Response Relationships**: Studies how varying doses of a drug affect the intensity and duration of its therapeutic and adverse effects.
6. **Dosage Regimens**: Determines how often and at what intervals a medication should be administered to maintain effective drug levels in the body.
7. **Adjustments and Individualization**: Involves tailoring drug dosages based on individual patient needs, response to treatment, and any changes in their condition or health status.

Importance in Medicine

1. **Optimizes Therapeutic Outcomes**: Ensures that patients receive the correct dose to achieve the best possible therapeutic effects.
2. **Minimizes Adverse Effects**: Helps in avoiding overdosage and reducing the risk of side effects or drug toxicity.
3. **Enhances Drug Safety**: Contributes to safe and effective medication practices by considering individual patient factors.

FACTORS AFFECTING POSOLOGY

Several factors influence posology, the study of drug dosage. These factors affect how a drug should be dosed to ensure efficacy and minimize risks. Here's a detailed overview of the key factors:

1. Patient Characteristics

a. **Age**:

i. **Pediatrics**: Children often require different dosages than adults due to variations in metabolism, body size, and organ function. Pediatric dosing is usually calculated based on weight or body surface area.

ii. **Geriatrics**: Elderly patients may need adjusted dosages because of changes in drug metabolism and excretion, as well as the potential for multiple medications (polypharmacy).

b. **Body Weight and Surface Area**:

i. Dosages are frequently calculated based on body weight (mg/kg) or body surface area (mg/m^2) to account for differences in metabolism and drug distribution.

c. **Sex**:

i. Differences in body composition and hormonal levels between sexes can affect drug metabolism and efficacy, sometimes necessitating different dosing.

d. **Genetic Factors**:

i. Genetic variations can influence how individuals metabolize drugs, impacting both the efficacy and safety of treatment. Genetic testing may guide dosing for certain medications.

2. Disease State

a. **Renal Function**:

i. Impaired kidney function can affect drug excretion, requiring dose adjustments to prevent accumulation and toxicity.

b. **Hepatic Function**:

i. Liver diseases can alter drug metabolism. Adjustments may be needed for drugs that are metabolized by the liver to avoid toxicity.

c. **Underlying Diseases**:

i. Conditions such as heart disease, diabetes, or infections can impact drug absorption, distribution, metabolism, and excretion, influencing dosage requirements.

3. Pharmacokinetics

a. **Absorption**:

i. Variations in drug absorption can result from different administration routes, gastrointestinal conditions, or interactions with food and other drugs.

b. **Distribution**:

i. Factors like blood flow, protein binding, and tissue permeability affect how a drug is distributed in the body. Conditions affecting these factors can alter drug dosages.

c. **Metabolism**:

i. The liver metabolizes many drugs, and variations in liver enzyme activity can influence how a drug is processed. Genetic variations, drug interactions, and liver diseases can affect metabolism rates.

d. **Excretion**:

i. Renal excretion is crucial for many drugs. Kidney function affects the clearance of drugs, and impaired renal function requires dose adjustments.

4. Pharmacodynamics

a. **Drug Receptor Interactions**:

i. The relationship between a drug and its target receptors can impact dosing. Variability in receptor sensitivity or density can alter the effective dose.

b. **Dose-Response Relationship**:

i. The relationship between drug dose and response helps in determining the most effective and safest dose. The therapeutic window defines the range of doses that produce the desired effect without causing toxicity.

5. **Drug Interactions**

   a. **Additive Effects**:

      i. Concurrent use of drugs with similar effects can increase the risk of adverse effects or toxicity, necessitating dose adjustments.

   b. **Antagonistic Effects**:

      i. Some drugs can interfere with the effects of others, potentially reducing efficacy and requiring dosage changes.

   c. **Altered Metabolism**:

      i. Interactions with other drugs can affect metabolism, either increasing the risk of toxicity or reducing therapeutic efficacy.

6. **Administration Route**

   a. **Oral, Intravenous, Intramuscular, etc.**:

      i. The route of administration affects drug absorption and bioavailability. Dosages may need adjustment based on the chosen route to achieve the desired effect.

7. **Environmental and Lifestyle Factors**

   a. **Diet**:

      i. Food and beverages can affect drug absorption and metabolism. For example, grapefruit juice can inhibit certain liver enzymes, altering drug levels.

   b. **Alcohol and Tobacco Use**:

      i. These substances can interact with medications, affecting their metabolism and efficacy.

8. **Compliance and Adherence**

   a. **Patient Adherence**:

i. Ensuring that patients follow prescribed dosing regimens is crucial for effective treatment. Non-adherence can lead to underdosing or overdosing, impacting therapeutic outcomes.

PEDIATRIC DOSE CALCULATIONS BASED ON AGE, BODY WEIGHT AND BODY SURFACE AREA

Pediatric dose calculations are crucial for ensuring that children receive the correct amount of medication for their age, body weight, and body surface area. Children's physiological differences from adults mean that dosing must be carefully adjusted to achieve therapeutic efficacy and safety. Here's a detailed look at how dosages are calculated for pediatric patients:

1. Age-Based Dosage

Age-based dosing is used when specific pediatric dosage guidelines are available for different age groups. Dosages can be expressed in various ways:

a. **Age Categories**:
   i. **Neonates**: 0-28 days
   ii. **Infants**: 1-12 months
   iii. **Children**: 1-12 years
   iv. **Adolescents**: 13-18 years

b. **Dosing Guidelines**:
   i. Some medications have specific dosing recommendations based on age groups. These are often provided in clinical guidelines or drug formularies.

Example: For an antibiotic with a recommended dose of 10 mg/kg/day divided into two doses for children aged 1-5 years, a 4-year-old weighing 15 kg would receive 150 mg per day (10 mg × 15 kg), divided into two doses of 75 mg each.

2. Body Weight-Based Dosage

Body weight-based dosing is calculated using the patient's weight to determine the appropriate dose. This approach is common for many medications and ensures that the dose is proportional to the child's weight.

a. **Calculation**:

   i. Dosage is usually expressed as mg/kg (milligrams per kilogram of body weight).

Formula:

$$\text{Dose} = \text{Weight (kg)} \times \text{Dosage (mg/kg)}$$

Example: For a medication with a dose of 5 mg/kg, a child weighing 20 kg would receive:

$$\text{Dose} = 20\,\text{kg} \times 5\,\text{mg/kg} = 100\,\text{mg}$$

3. Body Surface Area-Based Dosage

Body surface area (BSA) is another method for calculating pediatric dosages, especially for drugs with narrow therapeutic windows or in oncology. BSA accounts for the overall body size and is considered a more accurate representation of drug metabolism.

a. **Calculation**:

   i. BSA is typically calculated using formulas such as the Mosteller formula:

$$\text{BSA}(\text{m}^2) = \sqrt{\frac{\text{Height (cm)} \times \text{Weight (kg)}}{3600}}$$

b. **Dosage Calculation**:

   i. Dosage is often expressed in mg/m² (milligrams per square meter of body surface area).

Formula:

$$\text{Dose} = \text{BSA}\ (\text{m}^2) \times \text{Dosage}\ (\text{mg/m}^2)$$

Example: For a drug with a dose of 50 mg/m², a child with a BSA of 1.2 m² would receive:

$$\text{Dose} = 1.2\,\text{m}^2 \times 50\,\text{mg/m}^2 = 60\,\text{mg}$$

Practical Considerations

1. **Weight Measurement**: Accurate weight measurement is essential for body weight-based dosing. It should be regularly updated as the child grows.
2. **Height Measurement**: Accurate height measurement is crucial for BSA-based dosing. Heights should be measured in a standardized manner.
3. **Adjustment for Special Conditions**: Adjustments may be necessary for certain conditions such as renal or hepatic impairment, which can affect drug metabolism and excretion.
4. **Drug Formulations**: Pediatric formulations may differ (e.g., liquid vs. tablet). Ensure the dosage form is appropriate for the child's age and ability to take the medication.
5. **Monitoring and Adjustment**: Regular monitoring of therapeutic response and side effects is essential to adjust dosages as needed.
6. **Safety and Efficacy**: Always refer to pediatric dosing guidelines or consult a healthcare professional to ensure that dosages are within safe and effective ranges.

CLASSIFICATION:

Posology, or the study of drug dosage, can be classified based on several criteria. These classifications help in understanding how dosages are determined and applied in clinical practice. Here's a detailed classification of posology with examples:

1. Classification Based on Dosage Calculation Methods

a. Age-Based Dosage

i. **Description**: Dosing guidelines are provided based on the age of the patient. These guidelines are often available for different age groups like neonates, infants, children, and adolescents.

ii. **Example**: Acetaminophen (Tylenol) dosage for children is often recommended as 10-15 mg/kg every 4-6 hours, based on the child's age.

b. Body Weight-Based Dosage

i. **Description**: Dosages are calculated based on the body weight of the patient, usually expressed in mg/kg.

ii. **Example**: A common dosage for antibiotics like amoxicillin might be 20-40 mg/kg/day, divided into multiple doses.

c. Body Surface Area-Based Dosage

i. **Description**: Doses are calculated based on the body surface area (BSA) of the patient, typically used in oncology and for medications with a narrow therapeutic range. BSA is usually expressed in mg/m^2.

ii. **Example**: Methotrexate dosing in cancer treatment is often based on BSA, such as 10-15 mg/m^2 administered weekly.

2. Classification Based on Therapeutic Context

a. Fixed Dosage

i. **Description**: A standard dose is prescribed regardless of individual patient characteristics, often used when the therapeutic window is wide.

ii. **Example**: The usual dose of a medication like ibuprofen might be a fixed amount, such as 200 mg every 6-8 hours for adults.

b. Adjusted Dosage

i. **Description**: Dosage is adjusted based on specific patient characteristics or conditions, such as weight, age, or organ function.

ii. **Example**: Warfarin dosage is adjusted based on regular INR (International Normalized Ratio) monitoring, tailored to individual patient responses.

c. Individualized Dosage

i. **Description**: Dosage is tailored specifically to each patient's unique characteristics, including genetic factors and concurrent medications.

ii. **Example**: Pharmacogenomic-guided dosing of clopidogrel based on genetic testing to predict patient response and adjust the dose accordingly.

3. Classification Based on Dosage Regimen

a. **Single Dose**

i. **Description**: A one-time dose is administered, often used for medications that require a single, high impact dose.

ii. **Example**: A single dose of the antibiotic azithromycin (e.g., 1 gram) may be used to treat chlamydia infection.

b. **Repeated Dosing**

i. **Description**: Medication is administered in multiple doses over a period, commonly used for chronic conditions.

ii. **Example**: Insulin is administered multiple times daily to manage diabetes.

c. **Continuous Infusion**

i. **Description**: A medication is given continuously over a period of time, often used for drugs with narrow therapeutic windows.

ii. **Example**: Heparin is administered as a continuous intravenous infusion to manage anticoagulation.

4. Classification Based on Dosage Form

a. **Oral Dosage**

i. **Description**: Medication is taken by mouth in forms such as tablets, capsules, or liquid.

ii. **Example**: A standard dose of losartan might be 50 mg once daily, administered in tablet form.

b. **Injectable Dosage**

i. **Description**: Medication is administered via injection, including intravenous, intramuscular, or subcutaneous routes.

ii. **Example**: EpiPen (epinephrine) is administered as an intramuscular injection for severe allergic reactions.

c. **Topical Dosage**

i. **Description**: Medication is applied directly to the skin or mucous membranes.

ii. **Example**: Hydrocortisone cream applied topically for inflammation or itching.

5. Classification Based on Therapeutic Goal

a. Loading Dose

i. **Description**: An initial higher dose is given to rapidly achieve therapeutic drug levels.

ii. **Example**: A loading dose of digoxin might be administered to quickly achieve the desired blood levels in heart failure treatment.

b. Maintenance Dose

i. **Description**: The dose given after the loading dose to maintain therapeutic drug levels.

ii. **Example**: After the initial loading dose, a maintenance dose of digoxin is adjusted based on therapeutic levels.

c. Rescue Dose

i. **Description**: An additional dose used to counteract an acute problem or breakthrough symptoms.

ii. **Example**: Additional doses of bronchodilators during an acute asthma attack.

These classifications help guide the appropriate use of medications, ensuring they are administered effectively and safely based on various patient-specific and therapeutic factors.

A. Acetaminophen (Tylenol):

1. **Mechanism of Action**:

a. **Central Analgesic**: Acetaminophen is believed to exert its analgesic (pain-relieving) effects primarily through its action in the central nervous system (CNS). It is thought to inhibit the synthesis of prostaglandins in the brain, which are chemicals involved in pain and inflammation.

   b. **Antipyretic Effect**: Acetaminophen reduces fever by acting on the hypothalamic heat-regulating center, promoting heat loss and lowering body temperature.

2. **Pharmacokinetics**:
   a. **Absorption**: Acetaminophen is rapidly absorbed from the gastrointestinal tract, with peak plasma concentrations typically reached within 30 to 60 minutes after oral administration.
   b. **Distribution**: It is distributed throughout the body, including the brain. It crosses the placenta and is present in breast milk in small amounts.
   c. **Metabolism**: Acetaminophen is primarily metabolized in the liver. It undergoes conjugation with sulfate and glucuronide to form non-toxic metabolites. A small fraction is metabolized by cytochrome P450 enzymes to a reactive metabolite, which is usually detoxified by conjugation with glutathione.
   d. **Excretion**: The majority of acetaminophen and its metabolites are excreted in the urine.

3. **Uses**:
   a. **Analgesia**: Used to relieve mild to moderate pain, such as headaches, muscle aches, and arthritis.
   b. **Antipyresis**: Commonly used to reduce fever in various conditions, including infections.

4. **Dosage**:
   a. **Adults**: Typical dosage is 325 to 650 mg every 4 to 6 hours, with a maximum daily dose of 4 grams to avoid toxicity.
   b. **Pediatrics**: Dosage is usually based on weight, such as 10 to 15 mg/kg every 4 to 6 hours, not to exceed 5 doses per day.

5. **Side Effects**:
   a. **Common**: Generally well-tolerated, but can cause nausea, rash, and, rarely, allergic reactions.

   b. **Severe**: Overdose can lead to severe liver damage, manifesting as jaundice, hepatomegaly, and liver failure.
6. **Toxicity and Overdose**:
   a. **Signs of Overdose**: Nausea, vomiting, loss of appetite, confusion, and jaundice.
   b. **Treatment**: Activated charcoal may be used if overdose is detected early. N-acetylcysteine (NAC) is the antidote, which replenishes glutathione and detoxifies the harmful metabolite.

B. Amoxicillin:

1. **Mechanism of Action**:
   a. **Beta-Lactam Antibiotic**: Amoxicillin is a broad-spectrum penicillin antibiotic. It works by inhibiting bacterial cell wall synthesis. Specifically, it binds to and inactivates penicillin-binding proteins (PBPs) involved in the final stages of peptidoglycan synthesis, leading to cell lysis and death.
2. **Pharmacokinetics**:
   a. **Absorption**: Amoxicillin is well-absorbed from the gastrointestinal tract. Food does not significantly affect its absorption.
   b. **Distribution**: It is widely distributed throughout the body, including to the lungs, skin, urinary tract, and middle ear. It crosses the placenta and is excreted in breast milk.
   c. **Metabolism**: It is minimally metabolized in the liver.
   d. **Excretion**: Amoxicillin is primarily excreted unchanged in the urine. Renal function significantly impacts its clearance.
3. **Uses**:
   a. **Infections**: Used to treat various bacterial infections, including respiratory tract infections (e.g., pneumonia, bronchitis), otitis media, sinusitis, urinary tract infections, and skin infections.

b. **Combination Therapy**: Often used in combination with clavulanic acid (as in Augmentin) to overcome bacterial resistance by inhibiting beta-lactamases.

4. **Dosage**:

a. **Adults**: Commonly prescribed as 250 to 500 mg every 8 hours, with a maximum of 3 grams per day depending on the infection.

b. **Pediatrics**: Dosage is based on weight, typically 20 to 40 mg/kg/day divided into 3 doses.

5. **Side Effects**:

a. **Common**: Gastrointestinal disturbances such as nausea, vomiting, and diarrhea. Rash and allergic reactions can also occur.

b. **Severe**: Rare but serious side effects include anaphylaxis, Stevens-Johnson syndrome, and Clostridium difficile-associated diarrhea.

6. **Resistance and Considerations**:

a. **Resistance**: Bacterial resistance can occur due to the production of beta-lactamases that inactivate amoxicillin. Combination with beta-lactamase inhibitors can help address this issue.

b. **Allergy**: Patients with a history of penicillin allergy should use amoxicillin with caution or avoid it.

C. **Methotrexate:**

1. Mechanism of Action:

a. **Antimetabolite**: Methotrexate is a folic acid antagonist that inhibits the enzyme dihydrofolate reductase (DHFR). This enzyme is crucial for converting dihydrofolate to tetrahydrofolate, a form of folate essential for DNA synthesis and cell replication.

b. **Inhibition of DNA Synthesis**: By blocking DHFR, methotrexate reduces the availability of nucleotides required for DNA synthesis, which impairs cell division. This action is particularly effective against rapidly dividing cells, such as cancer cells and cells in inflammatory processes.

2. Pharmacokinetics:

a. **Absorption**: Methotrexate can be administered orally, intramuscularly, or intravenously. It is absorbed well from the gastrointestinal tract when given orally.

b. **Distribution**: It is distributed widely throughout the body, including the liver, kidneys, and central nervous system. Methotrexate crosses the placenta and is present in breast milk.

c. **Metabolism**: Methotrexate is metabolized in the liver to various metabolites. It is also subject to enterohepatic recirculation.

d. **Excretion**: It is primarily excreted unchanged in the urine. Renal function affects the clearance of methotrexate; impaired renal function can lead to increased toxicity.

3. Uses:

a. **Cancer Treatment**: Used in the treatment of various malignancies, including leukemia, lymphoma, and solid tumors (e.g., breast cancer, lung cancer).

b. **Autoimmune Diseases**: Used in lower doses for chronic inflammatory conditions such as rheumatoid arthritis, psoriasis, and Crohn's disease.

4. Dosage:

a. **Cancer**: Dosages vary depending on the type and stage of cancer. For example, high-dose methotrexate may be used in leukemia treatment, often followed by leucovorin rescue to mitigate toxicity.

b. **Autoimmune Conditions**: Typically dosed at 7.5 to 25 mg once weekly for rheumatoid arthritis, adjusted based on response and tolerability.

5. Side Effects:

a. **Common**: Nausea, vomiting, mucositis, and liver enzyme elevation.

b. **Severe**: Bone marrow suppression, hepatotoxicity, nephrotoxicity, pulmonary toxicity, and risk of opportunistic infections.

6. Toxicity and Management:

a. **Signs of Toxicity**: Myelosuppression, liver damage (elevated liver enzymes, jaundice), gastrointestinal symptoms, and renal impairment.
b. **Management**: Leucovorin (folinic acid) is used as an antidote to reduce methotrexate toxicity. Hydration and urinary alkalinization can help prevent renal toxicity.

D. Ibuprofen:

1. Mechanism of Action:

a. **Nonsteroidal Anti-Inflammatory Drug (NSAID)**: Ibuprofen works by inhibiting the enzyme cyclooxygenase (COX), which is involved in the production of prostaglandins.
b. **COX Inhibition**: By blocking COX-1 and COX-2, ibuprofen reduces the synthesis of prostaglandins, which are mediators of inflammation, pain, and fever. This results in decreased inflammation, analgesia, and antipyresis.

2. Pharmacokinetics:

a. **Absorption**: Ibuprofen is rapidly absorbed from the gastrointestinal tract, with peak plasma concentrations occurring within 1-2 hours after oral administration.
b. **Distribution**: It is widely distributed throughout the body and is highly bound to plasma proteins.
c. **Metabolism**: Ibuprofen is metabolized in the liver to inactive metabolites.
d. **Excretion**: The metabolites are excreted primarily through the urine.

3. Uses:

a. **Pain Relief**: Used to manage mild to moderate pain, such as headaches, toothaches, menstrual cramps, and musculoskeletal pain.
b. **Anti-inflammatory**: Effective in reducing inflammation in conditions such as arthritis and other inflammatory disorders.
c. **Antipyretic**: Used to reduce fever in various conditions.

4. Dosage:

a. **Adults**: Typically dosed at 200 to 400 mg every 4 to 6 hours as needed, with a maximum daily dose of 1200 mg for over-the-counter use and up to 2400 mg for prescription use.

b. **Pediatrics**: Dosage is based on weight, usually 5 to 10 mg/kg every 6 to 8 hours, not to exceed 40 mg/kg per day.

5. Side Effects:

a. **Common**: Gastrointestinal disturbances such as nausea, dyspepsia, and diarrhea. Drowsiness and dizziness can also occur.

b. **Severe**: Risk of gastrointestinal bleeding, ulceration, renal impairment, and cardiovascular effects, especially with long-term use.

6. Toxicity and Management:

a. **Signs of Toxicity**: Symptoms of overdose include nausea, vomiting, abdominal pain, and gastrointestinal bleeding.

b. **Management**: Supportive care is generally recommended. Activated charcoal may be used if ingestion is recent. Gastric lavage and intravenous fluids may be necessary in severe cases.

E. Warfarin:

1. Mechanism of Action:

a. **Anticoagulant**: Warfarin is an oral anticoagulant that works by inhibiting vitamin K epoxide reductase, an enzyme crucial for recycling vitamin K. Vitamin K is necessary for the synthesis of several clotting factors (II, VII, IX, and X) and anticoagulant proteins C and S.

b. **Clotting Factor Synthesis**: By reducing vitamin K availability, warfarin decreases the production of functional clotting factors, leading to prolonged bleeding times and reduced risk of clot formation.

2. Pharmacokinetics:

a. **Absorption**: Warfarin is rapidly absorbed from the gastrointestinal tract. Its bioavailability is almost complete.

b. **Distribution**: It is extensively bound to plasma proteins (primarily albumin), leading to high plasma protein binding (about 99%).

c. **Metabolism**: Warfarin is metabolized in the liver by cytochrome P450 enzymes, primarily CYP2C19 and CYP2C9. It has two enantiomers with different potencies: R-warfarin (more potent) and S-warfarin.

d. **Excretion**: It is excreted primarily in the urine as metabolites.

3. Uses:

a. **Venous Thromboembolism**: Used to prevent and treat deep vein thrombosis (DVT) and pulmonary embolism (PE).

b. **Stroke Prevention**: Used in patients with atrial fibrillation to prevent stroke.

c. **Post-Surgical**: Used to prevent clot formation in patients who have undergone certain types of surgeries, such as hip or knee replacement.

4. Dosage:

a. **Initial Dose**: Typically 5 to 10 mg per day, adjusted based on INR (International Normalized Ratio) levels.

b. **Maintenance Dose**: Adjusted based on INR, with usual maintenance doses ranging from 2 to 10 mg per day.

5. Side Effects:

a. **Common**: Bleeding complications, including easy bruising, nosebleeds, and gum bleeding.

b. **Severe**: Risk of major bleeding, including gastrointestinal bleeding and intracranial hemorrhage.

6. Toxicity and Management:

a. **Signs of Toxicity**: Symptoms include bleeding, bruising, and in severe cases, hemorrhagic stroke.

b. **Management**: For minor bleeding, dose adjustment or discontinuation may be sufficient. For major bleeding, vitamin K (oral or intravenous) is administered to reverse the effects. Prothrombin complex concentrates or fresh frozen plasma may be used in severe cases.

7. Drug Interactions:

a. **Inhibitors**: Certain drugs (e.g., antibiotics like metronidazole, antifungals like fluconazole) can increase warfarin levels and bleeding risk.

b. **Inducers**: Drugs like rifampin can reduce warfarin effectiveness by increasing its metabolism.

Multiple-Choice Questions (MCQs)

1. What is the definition of posology?
   a) The study of drug interactions
   b) The science of drug dosage
   c) The study of drug side effects
   d) The development of new drugs
2. Which of the following factors does NOT typically affect drug dosage?
   a) Age
   b) Body weight
   c) Eye color
   d) Renal function
3. What is a loading dose?
   a) A dose given to maintain therapeutic drug levels
   b) An initial higher dose to quickly achieve therapeutic levels
   c) A dose adjusted based on patient response
   d) A single dose administered to achieve an effect
4. Which method of dosage calculation is commonly used in oncology?
   a) Weight-based dosing
   b) Fixed dosing
   c) Age-based dosing
   d) Body surface area (BSA) dosing

5. What is the primary consideration when calculating pediatric doses?
    a) Skin color
    b) Body weight
    c) Eye color
    d) Hair length
6. Which of the following is a type of chemical incompatibility?
    a) Precipitation
    b) Phase separation
    c) Degradation reactions
    d) Viscosity changes
7. What is the therapeutic window?
    a) The time frame for drug administration
    b) The range of drug concentrations that are effective without being toxic
    c) The ideal temperature for drug storage
    d) The time needed for a drug to take effect
8. Which administration route is associated with the fastest onset of action?
    a) Oral
    b) Intramuscular
    c) Intravenous
    d) Subcutaneous
9. What does "titration" refer to in the context of drug dosing?
    a) Increasing the dose to achieve the highest possible concentration
    b) Adjusting the dose based on patient response and tolerance
    c) Administering a single, large dose of medication
    d) Reducing the dose until no therapeutic effect is observed
10. What is a common side effect of acetaminophen when taken in excessive doses?
    a) Kidney failure

b) Liver damage
c) Heart failure
d) Lung damage

11. How is methotrexate primarily excreted from the body?
a) Through the lungs
b) Through the skin
c) Through the urine
d) Through bile

12. Which drug is a beta-lactam antibiotic that inhibits bacterial cell wall synthesis?
a) Ibuprofen
b) Warfarin
c) Amoxicillin
d) Acetaminophen

13. Which of the following drugs is classified as a nonsteroidal anti-inflammatory drug (NSAID)?
a) Methotrexate
b) Azithromycin
c) Ibuprofen
d) Heparin

14. Which drug requires monitoring of the International Normalized Ratio (INR) for safe dosing?
a) Warfarin
b) Acetaminophen
c) Insulin
d) Azithromycin

15. Which of the following drugs is administered to manage blood glucose levels in patients with diabetes?
a) Methotrexate

b) Insulin

c) Warfarin

d) Heparin

16. Which drug is often used in combination with clavulanic acid to overcome bacterial resistance?

a) Acetaminophen

b) Methotrexate

c) Amoxicillin

d) Ibuprofen

17. What is the primary action of heparin?

a) Pain relief

b) Antibiotic action

c) Anticoagulation

d) Anti-inflammatory effect

18. Which drug is commonly used to treat sexually transmitted infections like chlamydia?

a) Warfarin

b) Azithromycin

c) Heparin

d) Insulin

19. What is a common side effect of ibuprofen?

a) Jaundice

b) Constipation

c) Gastrointestinal disturbances

d) Blurred vision

20. Which of the following drugs is used in the acute management of diabetic ketoacidosis?

a) Warfarin

b) Heparin

c) Insulin

d) Azithromycin

Short Answer Type Questions (Subjective)

1. Define posology and explain its importance in pharmacology.
2. What factors influence the dosage of a drug?
3. Describe the role of pharmacokinetics in determining drug dosage.
4. Explain the concept of a therapeutic window and its significance in drug therapy.
5. How is a loading dose different from a maintenance dose? Provide an example.
6. What are the common methods of calculating pediatric drug doses?
7. Discuss the significance of body surface area (BSA) dosing in chemotherapy.
8. What is titration in the context of drug dosing, and why is it important?
9. How does renal function affect drug dosage?
10. Describe the pharmacokinetics of acetaminophen, including its absorption, metabolism, and excretion.
11. Explain how amoxicillin works as an antibiotic.
12. What are the potential side effects of methotrexate, and how is its toxicity managed?
13. How does ibuprofen exert its anti-inflammatory and analgesic effects?
14. What are the uses of warfarin, and why is monitoring INR important in patients taking this drug?
15. Discuss the mechanisms of action and therapeutic uses of insulin.
16. What are the common side effects of heparin, and how is heparin-induced thrombocytopenia managed?
17. How does azithromycin work to treat bacterial infections?

18. What factors should be considered when calculating drug dosages for geriatric patients?
19. Explain the importance of adjusting drug doses in patients with liver disease.
20. How can drug interactions affect the efficacy and safety of drug therapy?

Long Answer Type Questions (Subjective)

1. Discuss the various factors that affect drug dosage and explain how they influence posology.
2. Describe the different methods used to calculate drug dosages in pediatric patients and provide examples for each.
3. Explain the pharmacokinetics and pharmacodynamics of warfarin, including its uses, side effects, and management of overdose.
4. Discuss the classification of posology based on dosage calculation methods, therapeutic context, and dosage regimen.
5. Describe the pharmacological properties, uses, side effects, and toxicity management of acetaminophen.
6. Explain the mechanism of action, pharmacokinetics, and clinical applications of methotrexate in cancer therapy.
7. Discuss the role of insulin in the management of diabetes, including the different types of insulin and their administration.
8. Explain the significance of monitoring and dose adjustment in patients receiving anticoagulants like heparin and warfarin.
9. Describe the pharmacokinetics, mechanism of action, and therapeutic uses of azithromycin, and discuss its side effects and drug interactions.
10. Discuss the challenges and strategies in managing drug dosages for patients with multiple comorbidities, focusing on the importance of individualized therapy.

Answer Key for 20 MCQs

1. (b) The science of drug dosage
2. (c) Eye color
3. (b) An initial higher dose to quickly achieve therapeutic levels
4. (d) Body surface area (BSA) dosing
5. (b) Body weight
6. (c) Degradation reactions
7. (b) The range of drug concentrations that are effective without being toxic
8. (c) Intravenous
9. (b) Adjusting the dose based on patient response and tolerance
10. (b) Liver damage
11. (c) Through the urine
12. (c) Amoxicillin
13. (c) Ibuprofen
14. (a) Warfarin
15. (b) Insulin
16. (c) Amoxicillin
17. (c) Anticoagulation
18. (b) Azithromycin
19. (c) Gastrointestinal disturbances
20. (c) Insulin

CHAPTER – 5

PHARMACEUTICAL CALCULATIONS

INTRODUCTION:

Pharmaceutical calculations are essential for pharmacists and healthcare professionals to ensure accurate dosage and safe administration of medications. Here's a detailed introduction:

1. Importance of Pharmaceutical Calculations

Accurate pharmaceutical calculations are crucial for:

a. **Ensuring Safety:** Avoiding medication errors and overdoses.
b. **Effective Treatment:** Delivering the correct dose for therapeutic efficacy.
c. **Regulatory Compliance:** Adhering to standards and guidelines.

2. Basic Mathematical Skills

Pharmaceutical calculations rely on fundamental mathematical skills:

a. **Arithmetic:** Addition, subtraction, multiplication, and division.
b. **Fractions and Decimals:** Converting and manipulating fractions and decimals.
c. **Ratios and Proportions:** Understanding relationships between quantities.

3. Units of Measurement

Different units are used in pharmaceutical calculations:

a. **Volume:** Milliliters (mL), liters (L)
b. **Weight:** Milligrams (mg), grams (g), micrograms (mcg)

c. **Concentration:** Percentage (%), ratio (e.g., 1:1000), molarity (M)

4. Conversions

Conversion between units is often necessary:

a. **Metric System Conversions:** mg to g, mL to L.

b. **Volume Conversions:** 1 L = 1000 mL, 1 mL = 20 drops (approximate).

c. **Weight Conversions:** 1 g = 1000 mg, 1 mg = 1000 mcg.

5. Dosage Calculations

Key formulas and methods include:

a. **Desired Over Have (DOH) Formula:**

$$\text{Dose to Administer} = \left(\frac{\text{Desired Dose}}{\text{Have Dose}}\right) \times \text{Quantity}$$

Example: If you need 250 mg of a drug and the stock is 500 mg/5 mL, you calculate:

$$\text{Volume} = \left(\frac{250}{500}\right) \times 5 = 2.5\ \text{mL}$$

b. **Alligation Method:** Used for mixing solutions of different concentrations.

6. Calculating Dosages

Dosages can be calculated based on:

a. **Body Weight or Surface Area:**

$$\text{Dose} = \text{Body Weight (kg)} \times \text{Dose per kg}$$

Example: A patient weighs 70 kg, and the dose is 10 mg/kg:

$$\text{Total Dose} = 70 \times 10 = 700\ \text{mg}$$

b. **Infusion Rates:** Calculating drip rates for intravenous medications.

$$\text{Drip Rate} = \left(\frac{\text{Volume (mL)}}{\text{Time (min)}}\right) \times \text{Drop Factor}$$

Example:

$$\text{Drip Rate} = \left(\frac{500}{240}\right) \times 20 \approx 41.67 \text{ gtt/min}$$

7. Drug Concentration

Understanding and calculating drug concentration:

a. **Percentage Solutions:**

$$\text{Percentage} = \left(\frac{\text{Solute}}{\text{Solution}}\right) \times 100$$

Example: A 5% solution has 5 grams of solute per 100 mL of solution.

b. **Ratio Strengths:** Expressed as 1: X. Example: A 1:1000 solution has 1 part of drug in 1000 parts of solution.

8. Calculating Compound Formulas

When compounding medications, accurate calculations are necessary for:

a. **Ingredient Amounts:** Measuring precise quantities for mixing.
b. **Final Volume and Concentration:** Ensuring the final product meets required specifications.

9. Practical Tips

a. **Double-Check Calculations:** Always verify calculations to minimize errors.
b. **Use Tools:** Calculators and computer software can assist in complex calculations.

c. **Stay Updated:** Be aware of changes in guidelines or units of measurement.

WEIGHTS AND MEASURES – IMPERIAL & METRIC SYSTEM

In pharmaceutical calculations, understanding weights and measures in both the Imperial and Metric systems is crucial for accurate medication preparation and administration. Here's a detailed breakdown:

1. Metric System

The Metric System is widely used in pharmaceuticals due to its simplicity and ease of conversion. It is based on powers of ten, making calculations straightforward.

Common Metric Units:

a. **Mass**:
   i. **Grams (g)**: Basic unit of mass.
   ii. **Milligrams (mg)**: 1 g=1000 mg.
   iii. **Micrograms (µg)**:1 mg=1000 µg.

b. **Volume**:
   i. **Liters (L)**: Basic unit of volume.
   ii. **Milliliters (mL)**: 1 L=1000 mL.
   iii. **Microliters (µL)**:1 mL=1000 µL.

c. **Concentration**:
   i. **Percent (%):** For solutions, it indicates the amount of solute per 100 parts of solution (e.g., 5% solution means 5 grams of solute per 100 mL of solution).
   ii. **Molarity (M):** Moles of solute per liter of solution (e.g., 1 M solution has 1 mole of solute per liter).

Conversions:

a. **Mass**: 1 g=1000 mg , 1 mg=1000 µg.

b. **Volume**:1 L=1000 mL1 , 1 mL=1000 µL.

2. Imperial System

The Imperial System is less commonly used in pharmaceuticals but still important in certain contexts, particularly in the US. It uses a variety of units for mass and volume.

Common Imperial Units:

a. **Mass**:
   i. **Ounces (oz)**: Basic unit of mass.
   ii. **Pounds (lb)**: 1 lb=16 oz.
   iii. **Grains (gr)**: 1 grain ≈ 64.8 mg.

b. **Volume**:
   i. **Teaspoons (tsp)**: 1 teaspoon ≈ 5 mL.
   ii. **Tablespoons (tbsp)**: 1 tablespoon = 3 teaspoons ≈ 15 mL.
   iii. **Fluid Ounces (fl oz)**: 1 fluid ounce ≈ 30 mL.
   iv. **Pints (pt)**: 1 pint = 16 fluid ounces ≈ 480 mL.
   v. **Quarts (qt)**: 1 quart = 2 pints ≈ 960 mL.
   vi. **Gallons (gal)**: 1 gallon = 4 quarts ≈ 3.8 L.

Conversions:

a. **Mass**: 1 lb=16 oz , 1 oz=28.35 g (for practical use).
b. **Volume**: 1 fl oz=29.5735 mL, 1 pint=473.176 mL, 1 quart=946.352 , 1 gallon=3.78541 L.

3. Practical Considerations

a. **Accuracy**: The Metric System is preferred in pharmaceuticals for its precision and ease of use. Conversions within the Metric System are simple (multiples of 10).
b. **Application**: While the Metric System is standard for most pharmaceutical calculations, knowledge of the Imperial System is useful in contexts where it is still used or required.
c. **Conversions**: When converting between systems, use conversion factors carefully to avoid errors. Double-check calculations to ensure accuracy.

CALCULATIONS INVOLVING PERCENTAGE SOLUTIONS WITH EXAMPLE

Calculating percentage solutions is a fundamental skill in pharmaceutical calculations. Percentage solutions describe the concentration of a solute in a solution. Here's a detailed guide on how to perform these calculations with examples.

1. Types of Percentage Solutions

a. **Percentage by Weight (w/w%)**: The weight of solute per 100 grams of solution.

b. **Percentage by Volume (v/v%)**: The volume of solute per 100 milliliters of solution.

c. **Percentage by Weight/Volume (w/v%)**: The weight of solute per 100 milliliters of solution.

2. Basic Formulae

a. **w/w%**: \text{w/w%} = \left(\frac{\text{Weight of Solute}}{\text{Total Weight of Solution}} \right) \times 100

b. **v/v%**: \text{v/v%} = \left(\frac{\text{Volume of Solute}}{\text{Total Volume of Solution}} \right) \times 100

c. **w/v%**: \text{w/v%} = \left(\frac{\text{Weight of Solute}}{\text{Volume of Solution}} \right) \times 100

3. Example Calculations

Example 1: Preparing a 10% w/v Solution

Problem: Prepare 100 mL of a 10% w/v sodium chloride (NaCl) solution.

Solution:

1. **Calculate the weight of NaCl needed:**

    a. **w/v% formula**: \text{w/v%} = \left(\frac{\text{Weight of Solute}}{\text{Volume of Solution}} \right) \times 100

    b. Rearranging for Weight of Solute: \text{Weight of Solute} = \frac{\text{w/v%} \times \text{Volume of Solution}}{100}

c. Substituting values:

$$\text{Weight of Solute} = \frac{10 \times 100 \text{ mL}}{100} = 10 \text{ g}$$

2. **Prepare the solution:**
    a. Weigh 10 grams of NaCl.
    b. Dissolve it in enough water to make the total volume 100 mL.

Example 2: Calculating the Concentration of a 25% w/w Solution

Problem: You have 150 grams of a solution that is 25% w/w ethanol. How much ethanol is in the solution?

Solution:

1. **Calculate the weight of ethanol:**
    a. **w/w% formula**: \text{w/w%} = \left(\frac{\text{Weight of Solute}}{\text{Total Weight of Solution}} \right) \times 100
    b. Rearranging for Weight of Solute: \text{Weight of Solute} = \frac{\text{w/w%} \times \text{Total Weight of Solution}}{100}
    c. Substituting values:

$$\text{Weight of Solute} = \frac{25 \times 150 \text{ g}}{100} = 37.5 \text{ g}$$

Example 3: Preparing a 5% v/v Solution

Problem: Prepare 200 mL of a 5% v/v alcohol solution.

Solution:

1. **Calculate the volume of alcohol needed:**
    a. **v/v% formula**: \text{v/v%} = \left(\frac{\text{Volume of Solute}}{\text{Total Volume of Solution}} \right) \times 100
    b. Rearranging for Volume of Solute: \text{Volume of Solute} = \frac{\text{v/v%} \times \text{Total Volume of Solution}}{100}
    c. Substituting values:

$$\text{Volume of Solute} = \frac{5 \times 200 \text{ mL}}{100} = 10 \text{ mL}$$

2. **Prepare the solution:**

a. Measure 10 mL of alcohol.

b. Add it to a container and dilute with enough water to make the total volume 200 mL.

4. Additional Considerations

a. **Accuracy**: Ensure precise measurements of solutes and solvents to maintain the intended concentration.

b. **Mixing**: Always mix thoroughly to ensure the solute is completely dissolved and the solution is homogeneous.

c. **Units**: Be consistent with units, especially when converting between weight and volume or between different percentage types.

CALCULATIONS INVOLVING ALLEGATION WITH EXAMPLE

Allegation is a method used in pharmaceutical calculations to determine the proportions of different solutions to achieve a desired concentration. This technique is especially useful when preparing mixtures from solutions of different concentrations. It is commonly applied in compounding and pharmacy practice.

1. Basic Concept of Allegation

Allegation involves the following steps:

1. **Identify the concentrations** of the solutions you are mixing.
2. **Determine the desired concentration** of the final mixture.
3. **Use the Allegation Method** to calculate the proportions of each solution needed.

2. Allegation Method

There are two types of allegations: **allegation medica** (for mixtures of solutions) and **allegation forte** (for mixtures involving solid and liquid).

Allegation Medica (Mixtures of Solutions)

Steps:

1. **Write Down the Concentrations:**

    a. Let's denote:

i. Solution A: Concentration CA
ii. Solution B: Concentration CB
iii. Desired Concentration: CD

2. **Calculate the Differences:**
    a. Find the difference between each concentration and the desired concentration:
        i. Difference for Solution A: DA=CB−CD
        ii. Difference for Solution B: DB=CD−CA
3. **Determine the Ratio:**
    a. The ratio of Solution A to Solution B is given by DA to DB.

Example Calculation:

Problem: You need to prepare 1 liter of a 15% solution of NaCl by mixing a 10% NaCl solution and a 20% NaCl solution.

Solution:

1. **Identify Concentrations:**
    a. Solution A (10% NaCl)
    b. Solution B (20% NaCl)
    c. Desired Concentration: 15%
2. **Calculate the Differences:**
    a. DA=20%−15%=5%
    b. DB=15%−10%=5%
3. **Determine the Ratio:**
    a. The ratio of Solution A to Solution B is 5:55:55:5 or 1:11:11:1.
4. **Prepare the Mixture:**
    a. Mix equal volumes of 10% and 20% NaCl solutions to make 1 liter of 15% NaCl solution.
5. For 1 liter:
    a. Volume of 10% solution =

$\frac{1}{2}$ liter $= 500$ mL

b. Volume of 20% solution =

$\frac{1}{2}$ liter $= 500$ mL

Allegation Forte (Mixing Solid and Liquid)

Steps:

1. **Identify the Concentrations:**
   a. Solid Solution: Concentration CS
   b. Liquid Solution: Concentration CL
   c. Desired Concentration: CD
2. **Calculate the Ratios:**
   a. Find the amount of each required to achieve the desired concentration, using the formula:

$$\text{Amount of Solid} = \frac{C_L - C_D}{C_L - C_S} \times \text{Total Amount}$$

$$\text{Amount of Liquid} = \frac{C_D - C_S}{C_L - C_S} \times \text{Total Amount}$$

Example Calculation:

Problem: You need to prepare 500 grams of a 5% solution of NaCl. You have a 10% NaCl solution and pure water (0% NaCl).

Solution:

1. **Identify Concentrations:**
   a. Solid (Pure NaCl): 100%
   b. Liquid (10% NaCl): 10%
   c. Desired Concentration: 5%
2. **Calculate the Amounts:**

a. Use the formula to determine the proportion of the 10% solution needed: \text{Amount of 10% Solution} = \frac{5 - 0}{10 - 0} \times 500 = 250 \text{ grams}

b. Amount of pure water needed:

$$\text{Amount of Pure Water} = 500 - 250 = 250 \text{ grams}$$

3. **Prepare the Mixture:**

   a. Mix 250 grams of 10% NaCl solution with 250 grams of pure water to obtain 500 grams of a 5% NaCl solution.

3. Additional Considerations

a. **Accuracy:** Ensure precise measurements and mixing to achieve the desired concentration.

b. **Homogeneity:** Mix thoroughly to ensure a uniform solution.

CALCULATIONS INVOLVING PROOF SPIRIT WITH EXAMPLE

Proof spirit is a measure of the alcohol content in a solution, commonly used in pharmacology and pharmacy. It is expressed in degrees proof, where proof spirit refers to a solution with 100 degrees proof, which is equivalent to 50% alcohol by volume.

1. Understanding Proof Spirit

a. **Degrees Proof**: The term "proof" is a measure of alcohol content. In the UK system, 100 degrees proof is equivalent to 50% alcohol by volume (ABV). In the US system, 100 proof is also 50% alcohol by volume.

b. **Proof Spirit**: A spirit with 100 degrees proof. It is used as a reference standard in calculations.

2. Conversion of Proof to Alcohol Content

To convert proof degrees to alcohol content (ABV), use the following formulas:

a. **UK Proof System**:

$$\text{ABV (\%)} = \frac{\text{Proof Degrees}}{2}$$

b. **US Proof System**:

$$\text{ABV (\%)} = \frac{\text{Proof Degrees}}{2}$$

For example, 120 proof is equivalent to 60% alcohol by volume.

3. Calculations Involving Proof Spirit

Example 1: Preparing a Specific Proof Solution

Problem: You need to prepare 1 liter of a 40% alcohol solution from 100 degrees proof spirit.

Solution:

1. **Identify Concentrations:**
    a. Proof Spirit (100 degrees proof) = 50% alcohol by volume
    b. Desired Concentration = 40% alcohol by volume
2. **Calculate the Volume of Proof Spirit Required:**
    a. Use the concept of dilution to calculate the volume of 100 degrees proof spirit required.

C1V1=C2V2

Where:

b. C1 = concentration of the stock solution (50%)
c. V1 = volume of the stock solution needed
d. C2 = desired concentration (40%)
e. V2 = total volume of the final solution (1 liter or 1000 mL)

3. Rearranging the formula to solve for V1:

$$V_1 = \frac{C_2 V_2}{C_1}$$

Substituting the values:

$$V_1 = \frac{40 \times 1000}{50} = 800 \text{ mL}$$

4. **Prepare the Solution:**

a. Measure 800 mL of 100 degrees proof spirit.

b. Dilute with water to make a total volume of 1 liter.

Example 2: Determining the Proof of a Solution

Problem: You have a solution containing 40% alcohol by volume. What is its proof in the US system?

Solution:

1. **Convert Alcohol Content to Proof:**

    a. Use the conversion formula for US proof:

$$\text{Proof Degrees} = 2 \times \text{ABV } (\%)$$

b. Substituting the values:

$$\text{Proof Degrees} = 2 \times 40 = 80 \text{ degrees proof}$$

4. Practical Considerations

a. **Accuracy**: Ensure precise measurement of volumes to achieve the desired concentration.

b. **Mixing**: Thoroughly mix the solutions to ensure uniformity.

c. **Labeling**: Clearly label prepared solutions with their alcohol content and proof for proper usage.

5. Additional Formulas for Calculations

a. **Dilution Formula**: C1V1=C2V2

b. **Volume of Solvent Needed**:

$$V_{\text{solvent}} = V_{\text{final}} - V_{\text{solute}}$$

CALCULATIONS INVOLVING ISOTONIC SOLUTIONS BASED ON FREEZING POINT WITH EXAMPLE

Isotonic solutions are solutions that have the same osmotic pressure as bodily fluids, such as blood. In pharmaceutical calculations, isotonicity is crucial for ensuring that intravenous solutions do not cause cell damage due to osmotic pressure differences.

1. Understanding Isotonic Solutions

a. **Isotonicity**: Solutions are isotonic if they have the same osmotic pressure as a reference solution (usually physiological saline or blood plasma).

b. **Freezing Point Depression**: One common method to determine isotonicity is based on freezing point depression, which is the lowering of the freezing point of a solution compared to the pure solvent.

2. Freezing Point Depression Formula

The freezing point depression can be used to calculate the concentration of solutes needed to make a solution isotonic. The formula is:

$$\Delta T_f = i \cdot K_f \cdot m$$

Where:

a. ΔTf = Freezing point depression (difference between the freezing point of the pure solvent and the solution)

b. i = Van't Hoff factor (number of particles the solute dissociates into)

c. Kf = Cryoscopic constant (freezing point depression constant) of the solvent

d. m = Molality of the solution (moles of solute per kilogram of solvent)

For physiological solutions, the freezing point depression is typically around 0.52°C for a 1 molal solution (for water).

3. Preparing an Isotonic Solution

To prepare an isotonic solution based on freezing point depression:

a. **Determine the Freezing Point Depression Required:**

   i. For physiological isotonicity, ΔTf is generally -0.52°C.

b. **Calculate the Amount of Solute Required:**

   i. Use the freezing point depression formula rearranged to solve for molality (m):

$$m = \frac{\Delta T_f}{i \cdot K_f}$$

For water (Kf=1.86°C·kg/mol), and assuming i=1 (for non-dissociating solutes):

$$m = \frac{0.52}{1.86} \approx 0.28 \text{ mol/kg}$$

c. **Calculate the Mass of Solute Required:**

   i. To prepare 1 liter of an isotonic solution, the molality needs to be converted to molarity. For water, the density is approximately 1 kg/L, so the molality in mol/kg is approximately the molarity in mol/L.

d. If the molar mass of the solute is M:

$$\text{Mass of Solute} = m \times M \times \text{Volume}$$

Example for Sodium Chloride (NaCl) with a molar mass of 58.44 g/mol:

$$\text{Mass of NaCl} = 0.28 \text{ mol/L} \times 58.44 \text{ g/mol} \approx 16.3 \text{ g}$$

e. **Prepare the Solution:**

   i. Dissolve 16.3 grams of NaCl in enough water to make the final volume 1 liter.

4. Example Calculation: Preparing an Isotonic Solution

Problem: Prepare 500 mL of an isotonic sodium chloride solution (NaCl) for intravenous use.

Solution:

a. **Determine Freezing Point Depression:**

   i. ΔTf=0.52°C (for isotonicity)

b. **Calculate the Molality:**

   i. For NaCl (i=2, as it dissociates into Na+ and Cl−):

$$m = \frac{0.52}{2 \times 1.86} \approx 0.14 \text{ mol/kg}$$

c. **Calculate the Amount of NaCl Required:**

   i. The molarity is approximately 0.14 mol/L.

   ii. For 500 mL (0.5 L):

$$\text{Moles of NaCl} = 0.14 \text{ mol/L} \times 0.5 \text{ L} = 0.07 \text{ mol}$$

   iii. Mass of NaCl required:

$$\text{Mass of NaCl} = 0.07 \text{ mol} \times 58.44 \text{ g/mol} \approx 4.1 \text{ g}$$

d. **Prepare the Solution:**

   i. Dissolve 4.1 grams of NaCl in enough water to make the total volume 500 mL.

5. Practical Considerations

a. **Accuracy**: Accurate measurements are crucial to ensure the solution is isotonic and safe for use.

b. **Mixing**: Ensure complete dissolution of the solute.

c. **Verification**: In clinical practice, verify isotonicity with appropriate methods if precision is critical.

CALCULATIONS INVOLVING MOLECULAR WEIGHT WITH EXAMPLE

Molecular weight (or molecular mass) is a fundamental concept in pharmaceutical calculations. It is the mass of a molecule of a compound, measured in atomic mass units (amu) or grams per mole (g/mol). Molecular weight is essential for preparing solutions, dosing medications, and understanding drug interactions.

1. Understanding Molecular Weight

a. **Definition**. Molecular weight is the sum of the atomic weights of all atoms in a molecule. It is calculated by adding up the atomic weights of each element in the compound according to its number of atoms.

b. **Units**: Molecular weight is expressed in grams per mole (g/mol).

2. Calculating Molecular Weight

Steps to Calculate Molecular Weight:

a. **Identify the Chemical Formula**: Determine the molecular formula of the compound. For example, the molecular formula of aspirin is $C_9H_8O_4$.

b. **Find Atomic Weights**: Use the periodic table to find the atomic weights of each element. For instance:

  i. Carbon (C) = 12.01 amu

  ii. Hydrogen (H) = 1.008 amu

  iii. Oxygen (O) = 16.00 amu

c. **Calculate Molecular Weight**: Multiply the atomic weight of each element by the number of atoms of that element in the molecule, and sum the results.

Example Calculation:

Problem: Calculate the molecular weight of aspirin ($C_9H_8O_4$).

Solution:

a. **Identify the Chemical Formula**: $C_9H_8O_4$

b. **Find Atomic Weights**:

  i. Carbon (C) = 12.01 amu

  ii. Hydrogen (H) = 1.008 amu

  iii. Oxygen (O) = 16.00 amu

c. **Calculate Molecular Weight**:

  i. Carbon: 9 atoms$\times$12.01 amu=108.09amu

  ii. Hydrogen: 8 atoms$\times$1.008 amu=8.064 amu

  iii. Oxygen: 4 atoms$\times$16.00 amu=64.00amu

  iv. Total Molecular Weight: 108.09+8.064+64.00=180.154amu

d. So, the molecular weight of aspirin is approximately 180.15 g/mol.

3. Example Calculations in Pharmaceutical Contexts

Example 1: Preparing a Solution

Problem: Prepare 500 mL of a 0.2 M solution of aspirin. What is the mass of aspirin needed?

Solution:

a. **Determine Molecular Weight**: From the previous calculation, the molecular weight of aspirin is 180.15 g/mol.

b. **Calculate Moles Required**:

   i. Molarity (M) = Moles of solute / Volume of solution (L)

   ii. Rearranging to find moles: Moles = Molarity × Volume

c. For a 0.2 M solution and 500 mL (0.5 L):

$$\text{Moles of Aspirin} = 0.2\ \text{mol/L} \times 0.5\ \text{L} = 0.1\ \text{mol}$$

d. **Calculate Mass Required**:

   i. Mass = Moles × Molecular Weight

$$\text{Mass of Aspirin} = 0.1\ \text{mol} \times 180.15\ \text{g/mol} = 18.015\ \text{g}$$

So, 18.015 grams of aspirin are needed to prepare 500 mL of a 0.2 M solution.

Example 2: Dosing Calculation

Problem: A patient needs a dose of 250 mg of a drug with a molecular weight of 150 g/mol. How many moles of the drug is this?

Solution:

a. **Convert Mass to Moles**:

   i. Moles = Mass / Molecular Weight

b. For 250 mg (0.250 g) and a molecular weight of 150 g/mol:

$$\text{Moles} = \frac{0.250\ \text{g}}{150\ \text{g/mol}} = 0.00167\ \text{mol}$$

So, 250 mg of the drug corresponds to 0.00167 moles.

4. Practical Considerations

a. **Precision**: Accurate molecular weight calculations are crucial for preparing correct dosages and solutions.
b. **Conversion**: Ensure proper conversion between units (e.g., grams to milligrams) and volume units (liters to milliliters) as needed.
c. **Consistency**: Use consistent units throughout calculations to avoid errors.

Multiple-Choice Questions (MCQs)

1. What is the basic unit of mass in the Metric System?
    a) Grams (g)
    b) Pounds (lb)
    c) Ounces (oz)
    d) Liters (L)
2. How many milligrams are there in 1 gram?
    a) 10 mg
    b) 100 mg
    c) 1000 mg
    d) 10,000 mg
3. What is the concentration of a 1:1000 solution?
    a) 1%
    b) 0.1%
    c) 0.01%
    d) 0.001%
4. How many moles of solute are there in a 1 molal solution?
    a) 1 mole
    b) 2 moles
    c) 0.5 moles
    d) 10 moles
5. Which method is used for mixing solutions of different concentrations to achieve a desired concentration?

a) Dilution
b) Alligation
c) Titration
d) Fermentation

6. In pharmaceutical calculations, what is the unit of volume for liquids in the Metric System?
    a) Ounces
    b) Milliliters
    c) Grains
    d) Pounds
7. How many teaspoons are approximately equal to 1 fluid ounce?
    a) 2 tsp
    b) 3 tsp
    c) 5 tsp
    d) 6 tsp
8. What is the freezing point depression constant (Kf) of water?
    a) 1.86°C·kg/mol
    b) 0.52°C·kg/mol
    c) 3.86°C·kg/mol
    d) 2.86°C·kg/mol
9. What is the molecular weight of aspirin?
    a) 180.15 g/mol
    b) 108.09 g/mol
    c) 150.00 g/mol
    d) 58.44 g/mol
10. What is the proof spirit concentration in the US system equivalent to 50% alcohol by volume?
    a) 50 proof
    b) 75 proof

c) 100 proof

d) 120 proof

11. Which of the following is used to calculate the volume of a solvent required in dilution?

a) Allegation

b) C1V1 = C2V2

c) Ratio Strength

d) Proof Calculation

12. What does "Molarity" measure in a solution?

a) Mass per unit volume

b) Moles of solute per liter of solution

c) Grams per mole

d) Volume per unit mass

13. What is the percentage concentration of a solution with 5 grams of solute in 100 mL of solution?

a) 0.5%

b) 5%

c) 50%

d) 0.05%

14. How many mL are in 1 liter?

a) 10 mL

b) 100 mL

c) 500 mL

d) 1000 mL

15. What is the desired concentration in an alligation problem involving a 10% and a 20% solution to make a final 15% solution?

a) 10%

b) 20%

c) 15%

d) 5%

16. What does the freezing point depression method determine?

a) Molecular Weight
b) Isotonicity
c) Molarity
d) Alcohol Content

17. In which unit is the proof spirit measured in the UK system?

a) Degrees proof
b) Moles
c) Grams per mole
d) Milliliters

18. What is the concentration of a 10% w/v sodium chloride solution?

a) 10 grams of NaCl in 100 mL of solution
b) 10 grams of NaCl in 10 mL of solution
c) 10 grams of NaCl in 1 liter of solution
d) 10 grams of NaCl in 1 mL of solution

19. What is the volume of alcohol needed to prepare 200 mL of a 5% v/v solution?

a) 5 mL
b) 10 mL
c) 15 mL
d) 20 mL

20. What is the standard freezing point depression for isotonic solutions?

a) 0.52°C
b) 0.32°C
c) 1.00°C
d) 0.12°C

Short Answer Type Questions (Subjective)

1. Explain the importance of pharmaceutical calculations in ensuring patient safety.
2. Describe the process of converting milligrams to grams with an example.
3. What are the different types of percentage solutions used in pharmaceutical calculations?
4. Explain the concept of molality and how it is used in pharmaceutical calculations.
5. Describe the alligation method and its application in mixing solutions.
6. How do you calculate the volume of a solution needed to prepare a specific concentration?
7. What is the significance of the freezing point depression in preparing isotonic solutions?
8. How do you calculate the molecular weight of a compound?
9. Explain the concept of proof spirit and its use in pharmaceutical calculations.
10. What is the difference between the Metric and Imperial systems in pharmaceutical calculations?
11. Describe the steps to prepare a 10% w/v sodium chloride solution.
12. How do you calculate the dosage of a drug based on body weight?
13. Explain the significance of molarity in preparing pharmaceutical solutions.
14. How do you calculate the amount of solute required for a specific solution concentration?
15. What is the importance of accurate measurements in pharmaceutical compounding?
16. Describe the process of converting fluid ounces to milliliters.
17. Explain the concept of ratio strength in pharmaceutical calculations.
18. What is the role of atomic weights in calculating molecular weights?
19. How do you prepare a 5% v/v alcohol solution?

20. Describe the practical considerations when preparing an isotonic solution.

Long Answer Type Questions (Subjective)

1. Discuss the importance of accurate pharmaceutical calculations and the potential consequences of errors.
2. Explain the process of preparing percentage solutions with detailed examples for w/w%, v/v%, and w/v% solutions.
3. Describe the alligation method in detail and provide examples of its use in pharmacy practice.
4. How do you calculate drug dosages based on body weight and surface area? Provide examples.
5. Explain the concept of proof spirit and how it is used to prepare alcoholic solutions in pharmacy.
6. Discuss the process of calculating isotonic solutions based on freezing point depression, including an example.
7. Describe the steps involved in calculating the molecular weight of a compound and its application in pharmaceutical calculations.
8. Explain the differences between the Metric and Imperial systems in pharmaceutical calculations and the importance of conversions.
9. Discuss the role of molarity and molality in pharmaceutical calculations and provide examples of their application.
10. How do you ensure accuracy and precision in pharmaceutical compounding? Discuss practical tips and tools.

Answer Key for MCQs

1. (a) Grams (g)
2. (c) 1000 mg
3. (d) 0.1%
4. (a) 1 mole

5. (b) Alligation
6. (b) Milliliters
7. (b) 6 tsp
8. (a) 1.86°C·kg/mol
9. (a) 180.15 g/mol
10. (c) 100 proof
11. (b) $C1V1 = C2V2$
12. (b) Moles of solute per liter of solution
13. (b) 5%
14. (d) 1000 mL
15. (c) 15%
16. (b) Isotonicity
17. (a) Degrees proof
18. (a) 10 grams of NaCl in 100 mL of solution
19. (b) 10 mL
20. (a) 0.52°C

CHAPTER – 6

POWDERS

INTRODUCTION:

Powders are a fundamental dosage form in pharmaceuticals, consisting of finely ground particles of active pharmaceutical ingredients (APIs) and excipients. Here's a detailed introduction to powders:

1. Definition and Types

a. **Definition:** Powders are solid particles with a size typically ranging from a few micrometers to millimeters. They can be composed of a single substance or a mixture of substances.

b. **Types:**

i. **Granular Powders:** Coarse particles with a size range from 0.1 to 2 mm, often used in bulk drugs and excipients.

ii. **Fine Powders:** Very small particles, usually less than 100 micrometers in diameter, used in tablets, capsules, and suspensions.

iii. **Pulverized Powders:** Extremely fine particles used for specific pharmaceutical applications and formulations.

2. Preparation Methods

a. **Mechanical Methods:**

i. **Grinding:** Using mills or grinders to break down larger particles into finer ones.

ii. **Sieving:** Separating particles based on size using a series of mesh screens

b. **Chemical Methods:**

i. **Precipitation:** Forming powders from a solution by altering conditions like temperature or pH.

ii. **Sublimation:** Transitioning a solid directly into a gas and then back into a solid powder form.

3. Properties of Powders

a. **Particle Size Distribution:** Affects the powder's solubility, absorption, and flow properties.

b. **Particle Shape:** Impacts the powder's flowability and compactness.

c. **Density:** Both bulk density and tapped density are important for determining the powder's volume and dosage.

d. **Flowability:** The ease with which powders can move, important for manufacturing processes and tablet formation.

4. Applications in Pharmaceuticals

a. **Tablets:** Powders are compressed into tablet form, allowing for controlled release and dosage.

b. **Capsules:** Powders are encapsulated in gelatin or other materials, offering convenience and precise dosing.

c. **Oral Solutions and Suspensions:** Powders are reconstituted with a liquid to create a solution or suspension for oral administration.

d. **Topical Formulations:** Powders are applied directly to the skin or mixed into ointments and creams.

5. Challenges in Powder Formulation

a. **Uniformity:** Ensuring consistent particle size and distribution to maintain efficacy and safety.

b. **Stability:** Powders must be stable over time, maintaining their potency and quality.

c. **Flow Characteristics:** Powders must flow well during manufacturing to ensure uniformity and efficient production.

6. Quality Control

a. **Powder Characteristics:** Tests for particle size, density, and flow properties.

b. **Assay:** Determining the concentration of the active ingredient in the powder.
c. **Uniformity Testing:** Ensuring each dose contains the same amount of active ingredient.

7. Regulatory Considerations

a. **Standards and Specifications:** Compliance with pharmacopeial standards (e.g., USP, EP) for powder quality.
b. **Labeling Requirements:** Accurate labeling for dosage, administration, and storage instructions.

DEFINITION OF POWDER

In the context of pharmaceuticals, the term **"powder"** refers to a dosage form consisting of finely divided solid particles. These particles are typically ground or crushed into a fine state and can be composed of a single substance or a blend of multiple substances. Powders are an essential component in drug formulation and delivery. Here's a detailed look at the definition and characteristics of powders in pharmaceuticals:

Definition

a. **Powder:** A pharmaceutical powder is a dry, solid substance composed of fine particles that can be used for oral, topical, or inhalation applications. Powders are created through the mechanical or chemical reduction of substances into a fine particulate form.

Characteristics of Pharmaceutical Powders

1. **Particle Size:**
    a. Powders can vary in particle size from coarse to very fine. Particle size influences the powder's dissolution rate, bioavailability, and overall effectiveness.
    b. Fine powders, with particles typically less than 100 micrometers, are often used in formulations that require rapid dissolution.

2. **Particle Shape:**
    a. The shape of particles can be irregular or more spherical, affecting the powder's flowability and compressibility.
    b. Uniform particle shape can contribute to more consistent drug release and dosing.
3. **Density:**
    a. **Bulk Density:** The mass of the powder per unit volume, including void spaces between particles. It affects the powder's volume and weight for dosing purposes.
    b. **Tapped Density:** The mass of the powder per unit volume after tapping or vibration, providing insight into the powder's compactness and potential to settle.
4. **Flow Properties:**
    a. Flowability refers to how easily the powder moves or flows. Good flow properties are crucial for consistent filling in capsules and tablets.
    b. Powders with poor flow properties can cause issues during manufacturing, such as inconsistent tablet weight or capsule filling.
5. **Solubility:**
    a. The ability of the powder to dissolve in a solvent is critical for oral powders and suspensions. Solubility affects the drug's bioavailability and therapeutic efficacy.
6. **Hygroscopicity:**
    a. Some powders can absorb moisture from the air, which can affect their stability and performance. Hygroscopic powders need proper storage to maintain their quality.
7. **Stability:**
    a. Powders should remain stable over time, with no significant changes in their chemical composition or physical properties.

Stability testing ensures that the powder maintains its intended effectiveness and safety throughout its shelf life.

Applications

1. **Oral Powders:** Used for reconstitution into solutions or suspensions for oral administration. They provide flexibility in dosing and can be used for drugs that are unstable in liquid form.
2. **Topical Powders:** Applied directly to the skin for localized treatment of conditions like fungal infections or dermatological issues.
3. **Inhalation Powders:** Designed for delivery to the lungs, such as in inhalers for respiratory conditions. They need to be finely ground to ensure proper aerosolization and deposition in the respiratory tract.

Preparation Methods

1. **Mechanical Grinding:** Using mills or grinders to reduce particle size.
2. **Sieving:** Separating particles by size through mesh screens.
3. **Chemical Processes:** Precipitation and sublimation methods to create powders with specific properties.

CLASSIFICATION OF POWDER

Powders in pharmaceuticals can be classified based on several criteria, including their composition, purpose, and the method of preparation. Here's a detailed classification of powders:

1. Classification by Composition

a. **Simple Powders:**

i. **Single-Substance Powders:** Contain only one active pharmaceutical ingredient (API). Example: A powder of pure acetaminophen.

ii. **Bulk Powders:** Typically contain one API and may be used for oral or topical administration. Example: Magnesium sulfate powder for oral use.

b. **Compound Powders:**

i. **Mixtures of Multiple Substances:** Combine two or more APIs or a combination of APIs and excipients. Example: A powder blend of antibiotics and excipients for oral use.

ii. **Pharmaceutical Mixtures:** Formulated to produce a specific therapeutic effect by combining various ingredients. Example: Powders used in compounding pharmacies to prepare custom formulations.

2. Classification by Purpose

a. **Oral Powders:**

i. **Effervescent Powders:** Contain ingredients that release gas when dissolved in water, aiding in faster dissolution. Example: Vitamin C effervescent powders.

ii. **Immediate Release Powders:** Designed to dissolve quickly upon ingestion. Example: Laxatives in powder form.

iii. **Sustained Release Powders:** Provide a controlled release of the drug over time. Example: Certain extended-release formulations.

b. **Topical Powders:**

i. **Dusting Powders:** Applied to the skin to treat conditions like fungal infections or to provide a protective barrier. Example: Talcum powder.

ii. **Medicated Powders:** Contain active ingredients for treatment of skin conditions. Example: Powdered antifungal agents.

c. **Inhalation Powders:**

i. **Dry Powder Inhalers (DPIs):** Designed for direct inhalation into the lungs. Example: Inhaled corticosteroids or bronchodilators.

3. Classification by Method of Preparation

a. **Mechanical Powders:**

i. **Ground Powders:** Produced by grinding or milling substances to reduce particle size. Example: Ground aspirin powder.
ii. **Sieved Powders:** Separated by size using sieves or screens. Example: Powders used in tablet formulations.

b. **Chemical Powders:**

i. **Precipitated Powders:** Created by chemical reactions that form solid particles from a solution. Example: Precipitated calcium carbonate.
ii. **Sublimed Powders:** Formed by sublimation, where a solid transitions directly to a gas and then back to a solid form. Example: Sublimed sulfur.

4. Classification by Particle Size

a. **Coarse Powders:** Particles with larger sizes, typically greater than 100 micrometers. Example: Coarse powdered substances used in certain bulk formulations.
b. **Fine Powders:** Particles smaller than 100 micrometers, often used in tablets and capsules for better dissolution. Example: Fine powdered APIs for oral medications.
c. **Ultrafine Powders:** Extremely small particles, often less than 10 micrometers, used for specialized applications such as inhalation therapies.

5. Classification by Flow Properties

a. **Free-Flowing Powders:** Powders that flow easily, which are important for consistent manufacturing processes. Example: Powdered sugar or salt used in food and pharmaceutical applications.
b. **Cohesive Powders:** Powders that tend to clump together, which can affect their flowability and handling. Example: Certain pharmaceutical powders that require special processing to ensure uniformity.

6. Classification by Stability

a. **Stable Powders:** Powders that maintain their quality and effectiveness over time under normal storage conditions. Example: Many dry powders for oral reconstitution.

b. **Hygroscopic Powders:** Powders that absorb moisture from the air, potentially affecting their stability and effectiveness. Example: Some antibiotic powders.

ADVANTAGES OF POWDER

Powders in pharmaceuticals can be classified based on several criteria, including their composition, purpose, and the method of preparation. Here's a detailed classification of powders:

1. Classification by Composition

a. **Simple Powders:**

  i. **Single-Substance Powders:** Contain only one active pharmaceutical ingredient (API). Example: A powder of pure acetaminophen.

  ii. **Bulk Powders:** Typically contain one API and may be used for oral or topical administration. Example: Magnesium sulfate powder for oral use.

b. **Compound Powders:**

  i. **Mixtures of Multiple Substances:** Combine two or more APIs or a combination of APIs and excipients. Example: A powder blend of antibiotics and excipients for oral use.

  ii. **Pharmaceutical Mixtures:** Formulated to produce a specific therapeutic effect by combining various ingredients. Example: Powders used in compounding pharmacies to prepare custom formulations.

2. Classification by Purpose

a. **Oral Powders:**

i. **Effervescent Powders:** Contain ingredients that release gas when dissolved in water, aiding in faster dissolution. Example: Vitamin C effervescent powders.

ii. **Immediate Release Powders:** Designed to dissolve quickly upon ingestion. Example: Laxatives in powder form.

iii. **Sustained Release Powders:** Provide a controlled release of the drug over time. Example: Certain extended-release formulations.

b. **Topical Powders:**

i. **Dusting Powders:** Applied to the skin to treat conditions like fungal infections or to provide a protective barrier. Example: Talcum powder.

ii. **Medicated Powders:** Contain active ingredients for treatment of skin conditions. Example: Powdered antifungal agents.

c. **Inhalation Powders:**

i. **Dry Powder Inhalers (DPIs):** Designed for direct inhalation into the lungs. Example: Inhaled corticosteroids or bronchodilators.

3. Classification by Method of Preparation

a. **Mechanical Powders:**

i. **Ground Powders:** Produced by grinding or milling substances to reduce particle size. Example: Ground aspirin powder.

ii. **Sieved Powders:** Separated by size using sieves or screens. Example: Powders used in tablet formulations.

b. **Chemical Powders:**

i. **Precipitated Powders:** Created by chemical reactions that form solid particles from a solution. Example: Precipitated calcium carbonate.

ii. **Sublimed Powders:** Formed by sublimation, where a solid transitions directly to a gas and then back to a solid form. Example: Sublimed sulfur.

4. Classification by Particle Size

a. **Coarse Powders:** Particles with larger sizes, typically greater than 100 micrometers. Example: Coarse powdered substances used in certain bulk formulations.

b. **Fine Powders:** Particles smaller than 100 micrometers, often used in tablets and capsules for better dissolution. Example: Fine powdered APIs for oral medications.

c. **Ultrafine Powders:** Extremely small particles, often less than 10 micrometers, used for specialized applications such as inhalation therapies.

5. Classification by Flow Properties

a. **Free-Flowing Powders:** Powders that flow easily, which are important for consistent manufacturing processes. Example: Powdered sugar or salt used in food and pharmaceutical applications.

b. **Cohesive Powders:** Powders that tend to clump together, which can affect their flowability and handling. Example: Certain pharmaceutical powders that require special processing to ensure uniformity.

6. Classification by Stability

a. **Stable Powders:** Powders that maintain their quality and effectiveness over time under normal storage conditions. Example: Many dry powders for oral reconstitution.

b. **Hygroscopic Powders:** Powders that absorb moisture from the air, potentially affecting their stability and effectiveness. Example: Some antibiotic powders.

DISADVANTAGES OF POWDER

Powders, despite their versatility and wide range of applications in pharmaceuticals, have several disadvantages. Here’s a detailed look at these drawbacks:

1. Handling and Storage Challenges

a. **Dust Generation:** Powders can produce dust when handled or transferred, which can pose a risk of inhalation and contamination. Dust generation can also lead to loss of product and environmental issues.
b. **Hygroscopicity:** Some powders are hygroscopic and absorb moisture from the air, leading to clumping, degradation, or changes in potency. This requires careful storage in moisture-proof containers.
c. **Bulkiness:** Powders can be bulky and require more space for storage compared to liquid forms, which may impact storage and transportation logistics.

2. Dosing and Accuracy Issues

a. **Inconsistent Dosing:** Accurate dosing can be challenging with powders, especially if they are not evenly mixed or if the particle size distribution is not uniform. This can lead to variability in the amount of active ingredient administered.
b. **Measurement Difficulties:** Ensuring precise dosing of powders often requires special equipment like weighing scales or measuring devices, which can be less convenient than pre-measured liquid doses.

3. Stability and Shelf Life Concerns

a. **Chemical Instability:** Powders may be chemically unstable and susceptible to reactions with environmental factors like light, oxygen, or moisture. This instability can lead to reduced efficacy or the formation of harmful degradation products.
b. **Physical Instability:** Powders can experience changes in physical properties over time, such as caking or agglomeration, which can affect their performance and ease of use.

4. Formulation and Processing Issues

a. **Flowability Problems:** Powders with poor flow properties can be difficult to process and handle during manufacturing. This can lead to problems like inconsistent filling of capsules or tablets.

b. **Powder Size and Distribution:** Achieving and maintaining a consistent particle size and distribution can be challenging. Variations in particle size can affect the powder's solubility, dissolution rate, and bioavailability.

5. **User Acceptance and Compliance**
   a. **Palatability:** Powders can have an unpleasant taste or texture, making them less acceptable to some patients, particularly children and elderly individuals.
   b. **Difficult Administration:** Some powders require mixing with liquids or other substances before use, which can be inconvenient and lead to errors in dosage or preparation.
6. **Manufacturing and Quality Control**
   a. **Complexity in Manufacturing:** The production of powders often involves multiple steps, including grinding, blending, and sieving, which can be complex and time-consuming.
   b. **Quality Control:** Ensuring uniformity and quality in powder formulations requires rigorous quality control measures to verify particle size, density, and content uniformity.
7. **Environmental and Safety Concerns**
   a. **Environmental Impact:** Dust from powders can contribute to environmental pollution and require measures to control emissions and minimize exposure.
   b. **Safety Risks:** Inhalation of fine powders can pose respiratory risks and may require additional safety precautions in handling and manufacturing processes.

SIMPLE & COMPOUND POWDERS

Official Preparations:

Official preparations in pharmaceutical powders refer to standardized formulations that are officially recognized and listed in pharmacopeias. These preparations are designed to ensure consistency, safety, and efficacy in their use. Here's a detailed look at official preparations for simple and compound powders:

1. Simple Powders

Definition: Simple powders contain a single active pharmaceutical ingredient (API) or a single substance, often combined with excipients to improve handling or stability.

Official Preparations:

a. **Powdered Medications:**

   i. **Aspirin Powder:** Used for pain relief and anti-inflammatory purposes. It is prepared by grinding acetylsalicylic acid to a fine powder.

   ii. **Calcium Carbonate Powder:** Commonly used as a dietary supplement for calcium. It is prepared by grinding calcium carbonate to a specific particle size.

b. **Powdered Excipients:**

   i. **Lactose Powder:** Used as a filler or binder in tablet formulations. It is prepared by grinding lactose to the desired particle size.

   ii. **Starch Powder:** Used as a binder or disintegrant in tablets and capsules. It is prepared by grinding starch.

2. Compound Powders

Definition: Compound powders consist of a mixture of two or more substances, which may include APIs and excipients, combined to achieve a specific therapeutic effect or to facilitate the preparation of dosage forms.

Official Preparations:

a. **Bulk Powder Formulations:**

   i. **Magnesium Sulfate Powder:** Often used as a laxative or for other therapeutic purposes. It is prepared by blending magnesium sulfate with excipients as necessary.

ii. **Antacid Powders:** Combinations of substances like calcium carbonate, magnesium hydroxide, and aluminum hydroxide are used to neutralize stomach acid and relieve heartburn.

b. **Powder Mixtures:**

i. **Pulvis Cinnamomi (Cinnamon Powder):** A powdered preparation of cinnamon used in traditional medicine and as a flavoring agent.

ii. **Pulvis Ipecacuanhae (Ipecac Powder):** Used as an emetic agent, prepared from the powdered root of the ipecacuanha plant.

c. **Pharmaceutical Compounds:**

i. **Powdered Antibiotics:** Such as powdered penicillin or tetracycline, which are prepared by grinding the antibiotics and mixing with suitable excipients for oral or topical use.

ii. **Effervescent Powders:** Contains acids (e.g., citric acid) and bases (e.g., sodium bicarbonate) that react to produce carbon dioxide when dissolved in water, providing a fizzy drink. Example: Effervescent aspirin powder.

General Characteristics and Considerations:

a. **Standardization:** Official preparations are standardized to ensure uniformity in composition, particle size, and potency, as specified in pharmacopeias like the USP (United States Pharmacopeia) or BP (British Pharmacopoeia).

b. **Preparation Methods:** Involves precise grinding, mixing, and blending techniques to ensure the correct particle size and uniform distribution of active ingredients and excipients.

c. **Labeling and Storage:** Official preparations must be labeled according to pharmacopeial requirements and stored under conditions that maintain their stability and efficacy.

Dusting Powders:

Dusting powders are a specific type of powder preparation designed for topical application. They are used to treat various skin conditions or provide protective or soothing effects. Dusting powders can be classified into simple and compound types based on their composition and use. Here's a detailed look at these preparations:

1. Simple Dusting Powders

Definition: Simple dusting powders consist of a single active ingredient or substance and are primarily used for their therapeutic or protective properties on the skin.

Examples:

a. **Talc Powder:**

    i. **Composition:** Pure talc (magnesium silicate).

    ii. **Use:** Talc is used for its absorbent properties, helping to reduce moisture and friction. Commonly used in personal care products like baby powder.

    iii. **Preparation:** Talc is finely ground and sifted to ensure a smooth texture and to prevent clumping.

b. **Zinc Oxide Powder:**

    i. **Composition:** Pure zinc oxide.

    ii. **Use:** Used as a protective agent and to treat minor skin irritations, diaper rash, and sunburn. It acts as a skin barrier and has mild astringent properties.

    iii. **Preparation:** Zinc oxide is finely milled to ensure a fine, smooth powder that can be evenly applied.

2. Compound Dusting Powders

Definition: Compound dusting powders contain a mixture of two or more substances, combining their properties to enhance therapeutic effects or to treat specific conditions.

Examples:

a. **Anti-Fungal Dusting Powder:**
   i. **Composition:** A combination of antifungal agents such as miconazole or clotrimazole with excipients like talc or starch.
   ii. **Use:** Used to treat fungal infections of the skin, such as athlete's foot or ringworm. The antifungal agents work to eliminate the infection, while the excipients help to keep the powder dry and easy to apply.
   iii. **Preparation:** The active antifungal ingredient is blended with a base powder, ensuring uniform distribution and consistency.

b. **Medicated Dusting Powder:**
   i. **Composition:** A combination of active ingredients like menthol or camphor with a base powder such as talc or starch.
   ii. **Use:** Provides cooling and soothing effects for conditions like pruritus (itching) or minor skin irritation. Menthol and camphor provide relief through their counterirritant properties.
   iii. **Preparation:** Active ingredients are mixed thoroughly with the base powder to ensure even distribution and effectiveness.

General Characteristics and Considerations:

a. **Particle Size:** Dusting powders are typically finely milled to ensure a smooth texture and to minimize irritation when applied to the skin. The particle size is crucial for ensuring even application and effectiveness.
b. **Absorbency:** Many dusting powders are designed to absorb moisture and reduce friction, making them useful for preventing skin irritation and discomfort.
c. **Safety:** Dusting powders should be formulated to avoid respiratory hazards, particularly when used in large quantities or in environments where dust inhalation could be a concern.

d. **Application:** Dusting powders are usually applied directly to the skin in a thin, even layer. Proper application techniques are important to ensure effectiveness and minimize potential side effects.

Dusting powders, both simple and compound, are important in pharmaceutical and personal care contexts for their therapeutic, protective, and soothing properties. They must be carefully formulated and prepared to ensure their efficacy and safety for topical use.

Effervescent powders:

Effervescent powders are a specific type of powder formulation designed to release gas when dissolved in water, producing a fizzy or effervescent effect. This property can aid in the rapid dissolution of the powder and improve the palatability of the resulting solution. Here's a detailed look at effervescent powders, including their simple and compound types:

1. Simple Effervescent Powders

Definition: Simple effervescent powders consist of a single active ingredient or a basic mixture of effervescent components that react to produce carbon dioxide when dissolved in water.

Examples:

a. **Sodium Bicarbonate Powder:**
   i. **Composition:** Sodium bicarbonate (baking soda) as the primary ingredient.
   ii. **Use:** Often used in antacid formulations to neutralize stomach acid. It reacts with acids in the stomach to produce carbon dioxide, which can relieve discomfort.
   iii. **Preparation:** Sodium bicarbonate is finely ground and blended to ensure even distribution in the powder.

b. **Citric Acid Powder:**
   i. **Composition:** Pure citric acid.

ii. **Use:** Commonly used in combination with bicarbonates in effervescent formulations. It reacts with bicarbonates to produce carbon dioxide and has a tart flavor that can enhance the taste of the solution.

iii. **Preparation:** Citric acid is finely milled to a specific particle size to ensure it reacts effectively with other components.

2. Compound Effervescent Powders

Definition: Compound effervescent powders are more complex formulations that combine multiple active ingredients with effervescent agents. They are designed to provide specific therapeutic effects or to enhance the sensory experience of the powder.

Examples:

a. **Effervescent Vitamin C Powder:**

i. **Composition:** Vitamin C (ascorbic acid) combined with sodium bicarbonate and citric acid.

ii. **Use:** Provides a source of vitamin C with the added benefit of effervescence, which can make the powder more pleasant to drink and facilitate faster dissolution.

iii. **Preparation:** The vitamin C is blended with the effervescent agents (sodium bicarbonate and citric acid) to ensure uniform distribution and reaction.

b. **Effervescent Pain Relievers:**

i. **Composition:** Active ingredients like acetaminophen or ibuprofen combined with effervescent agents (e.g., citric acid, sodium bicarbonate).

ii. **Use:** Provides pain relief with the added benefit of effervescence, which can improve the taste and aid in faster dissolution. This formulation helps in quick absorption of the medication.

iii. **Preparation:** The active drug is mixed with effervescent agents and any necessary excipients to create a stable, uniform powder that produces a fizzy solution when dissolved.

General Characteristics and Considerations:

a. **Reaction Mechanism:** Effervescent powders typically contain a combination of an acid (e.g., citric acid) and a base (e.g., sodium bicarbonate). When dissolved in water, these components react to produce carbon dioxide gas, which creates the effervescent effect.

b. **Taste and Palatability:** The effervescent reaction often masks the taste of the active ingredient, making the solution more palatable, especially for drugs or supplements with unpleasant flavors.

c. **Storage and Stability:** Effervescent powders must be stored in airtight containers to prevent premature reaction and loss of effervescence. Exposure to moisture can cause the powder to react and lose its effervescent properties.

d. **Preparation:** Proper mixing and blending of effervescent components are crucial to ensure a uniform reaction and effective dissolution. The powder must be finely milled to ensure that the reaction occurs uniformly when the powder is dissolved.

Effervescent powders offer a unique advantage in drug delivery and supplement formulations by enhancing solubility, masking unpleasant tastes, and providing a more enjoyable experience for the user.

Efflorescent Powders:

Efflorescent powders are a specific category of powders that exhibit a tendency to lose water of crystallization or moisture when exposed to the air. This property can affect the stability, handling, and effectiveness of the powder. Here's a detailed look at efflorescent powders, including their simple and compound types:

1. Simple Efflorescent Powders

Definition: Simple efflorescent powders consist of a single substance that has the property of efflorescence, meaning it loses water of crystallization when exposed to the air.

Examples:

a. **Sodium Carbonate (Soda Ash):**

   i. **Composition:** Sodium carbonate, often in its decahydrate form (sodium carbonate decahydrate).

   ii. **Efflorescent Property:** Sodium carbonate decahydrate loses water upon exposure to air, converting to anhydrous sodium carbonate.

   iii. **Use:** Used in various industrial processes and as a cleaning agent. Its efflorescent nature requires careful handling to prevent changes in its chemical composition.

b. **Calcium Chloride:**

   i. **Composition:** Calcium chloride, often in its hexahydrate form (calcium chloride hexahydrate).

   ii. **Efflorescent Property:** Calcium chloride hexahydrate loses water to become anhydrous calcium chloride.

   iii. **Use:** Commonly used as a desiccant and in de-icing applications. It needs to be stored in airtight containers to prevent efflorescence and maintain its effectiveness.

2. Compound Efflorescent Powders

Definition: Compound efflorescent powders are mixtures of substances where one or more components have efflorescent properties. These powders can be formulated to provide specific therapeutic or functional effects but require careful handling due to their tendency to lose moisture.

Examples:

a. **Efflorescent Antiseptic Powders:**

i. **Composition:** A mixture of active antiseptic agents (e.g., zinc sulfate) and excipients. Zinc sulfate can be efflorescent, especially in its heptahydrate form.
ii. **Use:** Used for treating skin infections and wounds. The formulation must be carefully managed to avoid changes in the potency due to moisture loss.
iii. **Preparation:** The active ingredient and excipients are blended in a controlled environment to minimize exposure to moisture and prevent premature efflorescence.

b. **Efflorescent Electrolyte Powders:**

i. **Composition:** A combination of electrolytes such as sodium chloride and potassium chloride, where potassium chloride can be efflorescent.
ii. **Use:** Used in rehydration solutions and electrolyte replenishment. The powder needs to be stored in moisture-proof packaging to maintain its stability and effectiveness.
iii. **Preparation:** The electrolytes are mixed with other components and stored in airtight containers to prevent moisture loss and ensure proper function.

General Characteristics and Considerations:

a. **Efflorescence:** This refers to the loss of water of crystallization from a substance when it is exposed to air. It can lead to a change in the powder's physical properties and effectiveness.
b. **Storage:** Efflorescent powders must be stored in airtight and moisture-proof containers to prevent exposure to air and maintain their intended properties.
c. **Handling:** Careful handling is necessary to avoid exposure to moisture and ensure that the powder retains its intended chemical and physical properties.

d. **Stability:** The stability of efflorescent powders can be compromised if they are not stored properly. Manufacturers must ensure that the formulation is robust enough to handle the potential effects of efflorescence.

Efflorescent powders, whether simple or compound, require special attention to their storage and handling to maintain their stability and effectiveness. Their tendency to lose moisture can affect their application and use in pharmaceutical and industrial contexts.

Hygroscopic Powders:

Hygroscopic powders are those that have the ability to absorb moisture from the air. This property can affect their stability, handling, and effectiveness. Here's a detailed look at hygroscopic powders, including both simple and compound types:

1. Simple Hygroscopic Powders

Definition: Simple hygroscopic powders consist of a single substance that has a tendency to attract and retain moisture from the environment.

Examples:

a. **Calcium Chloride:**

   i. **Composition:** Typically used in its anhydrous form or as a hexahydrate.

   ii. **Hygroscopic Property:** Calcium chloride is highly hygroscopic and absorbs moisture from the air, which can lead to clumping and a change in its physical form.

   iii. **Use:** Commonly used as a drying agent and in de-icing applications. It must be stored in airtight containers to prevent moisture absorption.

b. **Sodium Hydroxide:**

   i. **Composition:** Often used in its solid form.

ii. **Hygroscopic Property:** Sodium hydroxide is hygroscopic and absorbs moisture from the air, which can cause it to become caustic and lose effectiveness.

iii. **Use:** Used in various industrial applications and chemical processes. Proper storage is essential to maintain its stability.

2. Compound Hygroscopic Powders

Definition: Compound hygroscopic powders consist of a mixture of substances, where one or more of the components have hygroscopic properties. These compounds require careful formulation and handling to prevent issues related to moisture absorption.

Examples:

a. **Electrolyte Replacement Powders:**

i. **Composition:** May contain a combination of hygroscopic substances like potassium chloride and sodium chloride.

ii. **Hygroscopic Property:** These electrolytes can absorb moisture, which can affect their dissolution and stability.

iii. **Use:** Used for rehydration solutions and electrolyte replenishment. The powders are typically formulated and packaged to minimize moisture exposure.

b. **Pharmaceutical Powders for Oral Rehydration:**

i. **Composition:** Typically include a mix of salts and sugars (e.g., glucose, sodium chloride, potassium chloride).

ii. **Hygroscopic Property:** The components of these powders are often hygroscopic and can absorb moisture, affecting their effectiveness and ease of use.

iii. **Use:** Used to treat dehydration. The powders are often packaged in moisture-proof sachets to maintain their efficacy.

General Characteristics and Considerations:

a. **Moisture Absorption:** Hygroscopic powders attract and hold moisture from the air, which can lead to clumping, caking, or dissolution of the powder, potentially affecting its performance.

b. **Storage:** Hygroscopic powders should be stored in airtight, moisture-proof containers to prevent exposure to atmospheric humidity. Packaging should include desiccants or moisture-absorbing materials to protect the powder.

c. **Handling:** Careful handling is required to avoid exposure to moisture during processing, packaging, and usage. Precautions may include working in controlled environments or using moisture-resistant equipment.

d. **Formulation Adjustments:** To mitigate the effects of hygroscopy, formulations may include stabilizers or moisture control agents that help maintain the powder's integrity and performance.

Hygroscopic powders, whether simple or compound, require special attention to storage, handling, and formulation to ensure their stability and effectiveness. Proper measures must be taken to manage their moisture-absorbing properties and to preserve their intended use and quality.

Eutectic Mixtures:

Eutectic mixtures in pharmaceutical powders refer to combinations of two or more substances that, when mixed, form a eutectic system. This system has a lower melting point than the individual components. Here's a detailed look at eutectic mixtures, including simple and compound powders:

1. Simple Eutectic Mixtures

Definition: Simple eutectic mixtures consist of two or more substances that, when combined, create a mixture with a melting point lower than that of the individual substances.

Examples:

a. **Camphor and Menthol:**
   i. **Composition:** A mixture of camphor and menthol.
   ii. **Eutectic Property:** Camphor and menthol form a eutectic mixture with a melting point lower than either substance individually. This is useful for creating a solid formulation that is more easily meltable or dispersed.
   iii. **Use:** Used in topical preparations like ointments and creams for their soothing and aromatic properties.

b. **Lidocaine and Benzocaine:**
   i. **Composition:** A combination of local anesthetics, lidocaine and benzocaine.
   ii. **Eutectic Property:** These two substances form a eutectic mixture that has a lower melting point than either drug alone, which can be beneficial for creating a stable, solid dosage form.
   iii. **Use:** Often used in topical anesthetics and pain relief creams.

2. Compound Eutectic Mixtures

Definition: Compound eutectic mixtures are more complex formulations that include multiple components, some of which may form eutectic mixtures with others. These mixtures can enhance the properties of the final powder.

Examples:

a. **Eutectic Mixtures in Analgesic Powders:**
   i. **Composition:** A combination of multiple analgesic agents, such as aspirin and acetaminophen, which may form eutectic mixtures with other excipients.
   ii. **Eutectic Property:** The mixture may have a lower melting point and improved solubility compared to individual components, aiding in the formulation of powders or tablets.

iii. **Use:** Used in analgesic powders or tablets to improve dissolution rates and therapeutic efficacy.

b. **Eutectic Mixtures in Antibiotic Powders:**

i. **Composition:** Antibiotics combined with excipients that may form eutectic systems.

ii. **Eutectic Property:** The formulation can achieve a lower melting point, enhancing the powder's stability and solubility.

iii. **Use:** Used in powdered formulations for oral or topical administration, improving drug delivery and effectiveness.

General Characteristics and Considerations:

a. **Melting Point Depression:** Eutectic mixtures have a melting point lower than the melting points of the individual substances. This can affect the physical properties of the powder, such as flowability and stability.

b. **Preparation:** Creating eutectic mixtures requires precise blending and mixing of the components to ensure that the eutectic system is formed and maintains its properties.

c. **Stability:** Eutectic mixtures can be more prone to changes in physical form, such as liquefaction, if not stored properly. This requires careful handling and packaging to prevent issues like caking or clumping.

d. **Pharmaceutical Applications:** Eutectic mixtures can be advantageous in pharmaceutical formulations for improving solubility, dissolution rates, and the overall effectiveness of the drug delivery system.

Multiple Choice Questions (MCQs)

1. What is the typical size range of pharmaceutical powders?

A) 1 to 10 millimetres

B) 0.1 to 2 millimetres

C) 10 to 50 micrometres

D) 1 to 5 centimetres

2. Which of the following is a type of powder with particles smaller than 100 micrometres?

   A) Granular Powders

   B) Coarse Powders

   C) Fine Powders

   D) Pulverized Powders

3. What process involves reducing larger particles into finer ones by grinding or milling?

   A) Precipitation

   B) Sublimation

   C) Sieving

   D) Grinding

4. Which method is used to separate particles based on size using mesh screens?

   A) Grinding

   B) Sublimation

   C) Sieving

   D) Precipitation

5. What type of powder is designed to be inhaled directly into the lungs?

   A) Oral Powders

   B) Topical Powders

   C) Inhalation Powders

   D) Effervescent Powders

6. Which property of powders affects their solubility, absorption, and flow characteristics?

   A) Particle Size Distribution

   B) Colour

   C) Odour

D) Taste

7. Which powder property refers to the ease with which powders can move or flow?
   A) Density
   B) Solubility
   C) Hygroscopicity
   D) Flowability
8. What type of powders are designed for topical application to treat skin conditions like fungal infections?
   A) Oral Powders
   B) Effervescent Powders
   C) Dusting Powders
   D) Inhalation Powders
9. What is a major challenge in powder formulation related to ensuring each dose contains the same amount of active ingredient?
   A) Solubility
   B) Stability
   C) Uniformity
   D) Flowability
10. What is the property of hygroscopic powders?
   A) They are resistant to moisture absorption
   B) They absorb moisture from the air
   C) They release moisture when heated
   D) They change colour when exposed to light
11. Which of the following is a type of effervescent powder?
   A) Dusting Powder
   B) Medicated Powder
   C) Electrolyte Replacement Powder
   D) Sodium Bicarbonate Powder

12. What is the key characteristic of eutectic mixtures?

A) They have a higher melting point than their individual components

B) They are resistant to moisture absorption

C) They form a mixture with a lower melting point than the individual substances

D) They dissolve slowly in water

13. What is the primary disadvantage of efflorescent powders?

A) They are difficult to grind

B) They lose moisture and change form when exposed to air

C) They are toxic

D) They are highly explosive

14. What is a common use of effervescent powders in pharmaceuticals?

A) To treat skin infections

B) To enhance the palatability of oral solutions

C) To prevent moisture absorption

D) To form solid tablets

15. Which type of powder is commonly used in de-icing applications due to its hygroscopic properties?

A) Sodium Hydroxide

B) Calcium Chloride

C) Zinc Oxide

D) Magnesium Sulfate

16. What is the significance of flowability in powder formulation?

A) It determines the color of the powder

B) It affects the powder's ability to absorb moisture

C) It influences the ease of handling and processing during manufacturing

D) It increases the stability of the powder

17. What is the purpose of stability testing in powder formulation?

A) To ensure the powder has a pleasant taste

B) To determine the powder's effectiveness in treating infections

C) To assess the chemical and physical stability over time

D) To improve the powder's solubility

18. What type of powder mixture is formed when camphor and menthol are combined?

A) Hygroscopic Mixture

B) Efflorescent Mixture

C) Eutectic Mixture

D) Effervescent Mixture

19. Which powder is commonly used for its cooling and soothing properties in topical formulations?

A) Talc Powder

B) Effervescent Powder

C) Sodium Bicarbonate Powder

D) Zinc Oxide Powder

20. What is the main challenge when handling hygroscopic powders?

A) Ensuring the powder remains stable in light

B) Preventing moisture absorption during storage

C) Avoiding dust generation

D) Maintaining uniform particle size

Short Answer Type Questions (Subjective)

1. Define pharmaceutical powders and list their types based on particle size.
2. Explain the process of grinding and its significance in powder preparation.
3. Describe the importance of particle size distribution in powders.
4. What are effervescent powders, and how are they prepared?
5. Discuss the challenges associated with the formulation of hygroscopic powders.

6. What is a eutectic mixture? Provide an example.
7. How does flowability affect the manufacturing process of powders?
8. What is the significance of stability testing in the quality control of powders?
9. Describe the difference between simple and compound dusting powders.
10. How does hygroscopicity impact the storage and handling of pharmaceutical powders?
11. What are efflorescent powders, and what challenges do they present?
12. How can particle shape influence the flowability and compressibility of powders?
13. Explain the role of density in determining the dosage of powders.
14. What are oral powders, and how are they typically administered?
15. Describe the preparation method for an effervescent analgesic powder.
16. How do effervescent powders enhance the palatability of oral medications?
17. Discuss the regulatory considerations in the formulation of pharmaceutical powders.
18. Explain how hygroscopic powders are packaged to prevent moisture absorption.
19. What are the advantages of using topical powders in pharmaceutical formulations?
20. How are compound powders used in the preparation of custom pharmaceutical formulations?

Long Answer Type Questions (Subjective)

1. Discuss the different types of pharmaceutical powders, including their preparation methods, properties, and applications.
2. Explain the challenges in formulating and handling hygroscopic and efflorescent powders, and suggest strategies to mitigate these challenges.
3. Describe the process of creating and evaluating a eutectic mixture in pharmaceutical formulations. Provide examples of its applications.

4. Discuss the role of particle size, shape, and distribution in the effectiveness and stability of pharmaceutical powders.
5. Explain the significance of flowability in the manufacturing of powders and how it can be measured and improved.
6. Describe the regulatory considerations and quality control measures necessary for the production of pharmaceutical powders.
7. Discuss the advantages and disadvantages of using effervescent powders in pharmaceutical applications, with examples.
8. Explain how stability testing is conducted for powders and its importance in ensuring the shelf life and efficacy of pharmaceutical products.
9. Compare and contrast simple and compound powders, providing examples of each and their respective uses in pharmaceuticals.
10. Discuss the formulation, storage, and application challenges of efflorescent and hygroscopic powders, and how these can impact pharmaceutical product quality.

Answer Key for MCQs

1. B) 0.1 to 2 millimeters
2. C) Fine Powders
3. D) Grinding
4. C) Sieving
5. C) Inhalation Powders
6. A) Particle Size Distribution
7. D) Flowability
8. C) Dusting Powders
9. C) Uniformity
10. B) They absorb moisture from the air
11. D) Sodium Bicarbonate Powder

12.C) They form a mixture with a lower melting point than the individual substances

13.B) They lose moisture and change form when exposed to air

14.B) To enhance the palatability of oral solutions

15.B) Calcium Chloride

16.C) It influences the ease of handling and processing during manufacturing

17.C) To assess the chemical and physical stability over time

18.C) Eutectic Mixture

19.A) Talc Powder

20.B) Preventing moisture absorption during storage

CHAPTER – 7

LIQUID DOSAGE FORMS

INTRODUCTION:

Liquid dosage forms are medications dissolved or suspended in liquid vehicles. They are often preferred for their ease of administration, particularly in cases where swallowing pills is difficult or impossible. Here's a detailed introduction to liquid dosage forms:

1. Types of Liquid Dosage Forms

a. **Solutions**:

   i. **Definition**: Homogeneous mixtures of one or more solutes dissolved in a solvent.

   ii. **Types**:

      1. **Oral Solutions**: Intended for ingestion, such as cough syrups and electrolyte solutions.
      2. **Injectable Solutions**: Sterile solutions administered via injection.
      3. **Topical Solutions**: Applied to the skin or mucous membranes, such as antiseptics and astringents.

b. **Suspensions**:

   i. **Definition**: Heterogeneous mixtures in which solid particles are dispersed throughout a liquid.

   ii. **Types**:

      1. **Oral Suspensions**: Used when the drug is not soluble in water or has poor stability in solution. Examples include antibiotics and antacids.

2. **Injectable Suspensions**: Sterile suspensions used for injectable medications.
3. **Topical Suspensions**: Applied to the skin for localized treatment.

c. **Emulsions**:

i. **Definition**: Mixtures of two immiscible liquids (usually oil and water) where one liquid is dispersed in the other.

ii. **Types**:

1. **Oral Emulsions**: Often used to administer oily medications or nutrients.
2. **Topical Emulsions**: Used in creams and lotions for skin application.

d. **Syrups**:

i. **Definition**: Concentrated solutions of sugar in water or another aqueous liquid, often used to mask the taste of medicines.

ii. **Types**:

1. **Medicated Syrups**: Contain therapeutic agents along with a sweetening agent.
2. **Non-Medicated Syrups**: Used as flavoring agents or excipients.

e. **Elixirs**:

i. **Definition**: Clear, sweetened hydroalcoholic solutions containing one or more active ingredients.

ii. **Types**:

1. **Oral Elixirs**: Used for both medicinal and non-medicinal purposes, such as in some cough preparations and tonics.

f. **Tinctures**:

i. **Definition**. Alcoholic or hydroalcoholic solutions containing plant extracts or chemical substances.

ii. **Types**:

1. **Herbal Tinctures**: Made from plant materials, used in herbal medicine.
2. **Pharmacopoeial Tinctures**: Standardized tinctures used in pharmaceutical preparations.

2. Advantages of Liquid Dosage Forms

a. **Ease of Swallowing**: Ideal for children, elderly patients, or those who have difficulty swallowing tablets or capsules.
b. **Flexible Dosing**: Allows for more precise dosage adjustments compared to tablets or capsules.
c. **Rapid Onset of Action**: Liquid forms can be absorbed more quickly in the gastrointestinal tract.
d. **Immediate Availability**: Useful for drugs that are unstable or poorly absorbed in solid form.

3. Challenges of Liquid Dosage Forms

a. **Stability Issues**: Liquids can be more susceptible to chemical degradation and microbial contamination.
b. **Taste**: Unpleasant taste can be a problem, particularly with oral solutions.
c. **Storage and Handling**: Some liquids require special storage conditions and handling to maintain their efficacy.
d. **Dosing Accuracy**: Requires careful measurement to ensure correct dosing.

4. Formulation Considerations

a. **Solvent Choice**: The solvent should be compatible with the active ingredient and suitable for the intended route of administration.

b. **Preservatives**: Added to prevent microbial growth and extend shelf life.
c. **Flavoring and Sweetening Agents**: Used to improve palatability.
d. **pH Adjustment**: Necessary to ensure drug stability and solubility.
e. **Viscosity Modifiers**: Adjustments may be made to ensure proper flow and consistency.

DEFINITION OF LIQUID DOSAGE FORMS

Liquid dosage forms are pharmaceutical preparations in which the active drug ingredient is dissolved or suspended in a liquid vehicle. These forms are designed to be administered in a liquid state and are used to deliver medication through various routes such as oral, topical, intravenous, or other parenteral methods.

Key Characteristics:

1. **Homogeneity or Heterogeneity:** Liquid dosage forms can be either homogeneous (solutions) or heterogeneous (suspensions and emulsions). Solutions are uniform throughout, whereas suspensions contain undissolved particles dispersed in a liquid, and emulsions are mixtures of two immiscible liquids.
2. **Flexibility in Dosing:** Liquid forms allow for precise adjustment of doses, which is particularly useful in pediatric and geriatric medicine where dose requirements may vary.
3. **Ease of Administration:** They are often preferred for patients who have difficulty swallowing solid dosage forms, such as young children or elderly patients.
4. **Rapid Absorption:** Liquids can be absorbed more quickly by the body compared to solids since the drug is already in a dissolved state.

Common Types of Liquid Dosage Forms:

1. **Solutions:** Clear, homogeneous mixtures of solute and solvent. Examples include oral solutions, injectables, and eye drops.

2. **Suspensions:** Heterogeneous mixtures where solid particles are dispersed throughout a liquid. They need to be shaken before use to ensure uniformity. Examples include some antibiotics and antacids.
3. **Emulsions:** Mixtures of two immiscible liquids (like oil and water) stabilized by emulsifiers. Used in various forms, including oral, topical, and injectable products.
4. **Syrups:** Concentrated solutions of sugars or sugar substitutes used to mask the taste of drugs and provide a pleasant flavor. Examples include cough syrups.
5. **Elixirs:** Clear, sweetened solutions containing alcohol, which aids in dissolving drugs and can enhance flavor. They are less viscous than syrups.
6. **Tinctures:** Alcoholic or hydroalcoholic solutions used primarily for their preservative properties and ease of administration, often in herbal medicine.
7. **Colloids:** Solutions containing particles that are larger than molecules but still small enough to remain suspended, such as certain intravenous fluids.

Benefits:

1. **Precise Dosage:** Allows for accurate measurement and adjustment of doses.
2. **Ease of Use:** Suitable for patients who have difficulty with solid forms.
3. **Faster Onset:** Can be absorbed more quickly compared to solids.

Challenges:

1. **Stability:** Liquid forms can be less stable than solids, requiring special formulation to prevent degradation.
2. **Preservation:** May require preservatives to prevent microbial growth.
3. **Taste Masking:** Sweeteners and flavorings are often added to improve palatability, which can affect drug stability.

ADVANTAGES OF LIQUID DOSAGE FORMS

1. **Ease of Administration:**
    a. **For Difficult-to-Swallow Patients:** Ideal for individuals who have difficulty swallowing tablets or capsules, such as young children, elderly patients, or those with certain medical conditions.
    b. **Flexible Dosing:** Allows for precise dosing, which can be particularly useful for pediatric and geriatric patients where dose adjustments are often needed.
2. **Rapid Absorption:**
    a. **Pre-Dissolved Drug:** The drug is already in a dissolved form, which can lead to faster absorption compared to solid dosage forms that need to dissolve in the gastrointestinal tract.
    b. **Immediate Effect:** This can be beneficial for medications that need to act quickly.
3. **Adjustable Dosage:**
    a. **Customizable Doses:** Liquid forms allow for easy adjustment of doses, which is useful in situations where dose titration is required.
    b. **Accurate Measurement:** Precise measurement of doses is possible with appropriate measuring devices.
4. **Flexibility in Administration Routes:**
    a. **Oral:** Can be used for oral administration, making them suitable for a wide range of conditions and patients.
    b. **Topical:** Can be applied to the skin for localized treatment.
    c. **Parenteral:** Certain liquid forms are designed for intravenous, intramuscular, or subcutaneous injection.
5. **Masking Unpleasant Tastes:**
    a. **Flavoring Agents:** Liquid forms, such as syrups and elixirs, can be flavored to mask the unpleasant taste of medications, improving patient compliance.
6. **Enhanced Bioavailability:**

a. **Improved Solubility:** Liquids can improve the solubility and absorption of drugs that are poorly soluble in solid form.
b. **Reduced Gastrointestinal Irritation:** Some drugs may cause less gastrointestinal irritation when administered in a liquid form.

7. **Convenience and Versatility:**
   a. **Ease of Use:** Simple to administer, especially when compared to some complex dosage forms.
   b. **Adaptable Formulations:** Can be formulated to include additional components such as preservatives, stabilizers, and flavorings to enhance efficacy and patient acceptance.
8. **Application for Specialized Needs:**
   a. **Special Populations:** Suitable for patients who require medications in small, adjustable doses or those who need medications delivered via non-oral routes.
   b. **Emergency Situations:** Liquids can be used in emergency situations where rapid drug administration is crucial.

Liquid dosage forms offer numerous advantages, making them an essential component in pharmacotherapy. They provide flexibility in administration, rapid onset of action, and the ability to cater to various patient needs, though they also come with specific challenges that need to be managed during formulation and use.

DISADVANTAGES OF LIQUID DOSAGE FORMS

1. **Stability Issues:**
   a. **Chemical Degradation:** Liquid formulations can be prone to chemical degradation over time, such as hydrolysis or oxidation, which can affect the drug's efficacy and safety.
   b. **Microbial Contamination:** Liquids are susceptible to microbial contamination, necessitating the use of preservatives or strict hygiene measures during manufacturing and storage.

2. **Shorter Shelf Life:**
    a. **Limited Storage:** Liquid dosage forms generally have a shorter shelf life compared to solid forms, due to their susceptibility to changes in stability and the potential for microbial growth.
3. **Dosage Accuracy and Measurement:**
    a. **Risk of Inaccurate Dosing:** Improper measurement can lead to dosing errors. It requires accurate measuring devices (e.g., droppers, syringes) to ensure correct dosage.
    b. **Variability:** Measuring liquids can introduce variability, especially if the liquid is not uniform or if the measuring device is not calibrated correctly.
4. **Taste and Palatability:**
    a. **Unpleasant Taste:** Some medications in liquid form can have a very unpleasant taste, which can be difficult to mask, particularly in children or sensitive adults.
    b. **Flavorings and Sweeteners:** While flavorings and sweeteners are used to improve taste, they can also affect the stability and efficacy of the medication.
5. **Bulk and Weight:**
    a. **Volume and Storage:** Liquid dosage forms often require larger packaging and can be bulkier compared to solid forms, which can be less convenient for storage and transportation.
    b. **Weight:** Heavier than solid forms, which can be an issue in terms of logistics and patient compliance.
6. **Potential for Leakage and Spillage:**
    a. **Risk of Leakage:** Liquid forms are more likely to leak or spill, especially if the packaging is not robust or properly sealed.

b. **Handling and Transportation:** Increased risk of spills during handling and transportation, which can lead to waste and potential contamination.

7. **Formulation Challenges:**
    a. **Complexity:** Developing stable and effective liquid formulations can be more complex and costly compared to solid forms, requiring specialized equipment and techniques.
    b. **Preservation:** The need for preservatives to prevent microbial growth can complicate formulation and may not be suitable for all patients.
8. **Storage Conditions:**
    a. **Temperature Sensitivity:** Some liquid formulations require specific storage conditions (e.g., refrigeration) to maintain stability, which can limit their convenience and shelf life.
9. **Compliance and Acceptance:**
    a. **Patient Preferences:** Some patients may prefer solid dosage forms or may find liquids less convenient or less desirable to take regularly.

EXCIPIENTS USED IN FORMULATION OF LIQUID DOSAGE FORMS

Excipients are inactive substances used alongside the active drug ingredient in liquid dosage forms to aid in the preparation, stability, and delivery of the medication. Each excipient serves a specific purpose to ensure the effectiveness and usability of the final product. Here are the key types of excipients used in liquid dosage forms:

1. Solvents and Vehicles

a. **Water:** The most common solvent used in oral solutions, injections, and eye drops. It is used for its ability to dissolve a wide range of substances.

b. **Alcohol:** Used in elixirs and tinctures to dissolve both water-soluble and alcohol-soluble substances. Common types include ethanol and isopropyl alcohol.
c. **Glycerin (Glycerol):** A viscous liquid used to enhance the solubility of some drugs and provide a sweet taste. It also has preservative properties.
d. **Propylene Glycol:** Used as a solvent in oral, topical, and injectable formulations, especially when alcohol is not desirable.

2. Preservatives

a. **Parabens:** Such as methylparaben and propylparaben, used to prevent microbial growth in products that are exposed to air and moisture.
b. **Phenylmercuric Nitrate:** Used in some eye and ear drops to prevent microbial contamination.
c. **Sodium Benzoate:** Commonly used in syrups and other aqueous solutions to inhibit bacterial growth.

3. Sweeteners and Flavoring Agents

a. **Sucrose (Table Sugar):** Used in syrups to provide sweetness and mask unpleasant tastes.
b. **High-Fructose Corn Syrup:** A liquid sweetener used in syrups and elixirs.
c. **Artificial Sweeteners:** Such as aspartame, saccharin, and sucralose, used in formulations for diabetics or to reduce caloric intake.
d. **Flavorings:** Natural or artificial flavors (e.g., vanilla, citrus) are added to improve the palatability of the medication.

4. Stabilizers and Thickeners

a. **Gums:** Such as xanthan gum, guar gum, and alginate, used to stabilize suspensions and emulsions by increasing viscosity.
b. **Cellulose Derivatives:** Such as hydroxyethyl cellulose (HEC) or hydroxypropyl methylcellulose (HPMC), used as thickening agents and stabilizers.

c. **Pectin:** Used in syrups and suspensions to enhance viscosity and stability.

5. Surfactants and Emulsifiers

a. **Polysorbates:** Such as Polysorbate 80 (Tween 80), used to stabilize emulsions and enhance the solubility of drugs.

b. **Sodium Lauryl Sulfate:** A surfactant used to aid in the dissolution of drugs and stabilize emulsions.

6. Buffers

a. **Citric Acid and Sodium Citrate:** Used to maintain the pH of the formulation within a specific range to ensure drug stability and enhance solubility.

b. **Phosphate Buffers:** Commonly used to adjust and stabilize the pH in injectable solutions.

7. Chelating Agents

a. **EDTA (Ethylenediaminetetraacetic Acid):** Used to bind metal ions and prevent their interaction with the drug or excipients, which can cause degradation.

8. Colorants

a. **Dyes:** Used to provide color to the liquid dosage form, which can be important for aesthetic reasons and to distinguish between different formulations.

9. Anti-Oxidants

a. **Ascorbic Acid (Vitamin C):** Used to prevent oxidation of drugs that are sensitive to oxygen.

b. **BHA (Butylated Hydroxyanisole) and BHT (Butylated Hydroxytoluene):** Synthetic antioxidants used to prevent the oxidation of drugs and excipients.

10. Miscellaneous Agents

a. **Alcohols:** Such as ethanol and isopropyl alcohol, used in certain formulations for their solvent properties and to enhance stability.
b. **Salts:** Such as sodium chloride or potassium chloride, used to adjust the tonicity of solutions, especially for injectable forms.

Each excipient plays a crucial role in the formulation of liquid dosage forms, affecting the stability, efficacy, safety, and overall quality of the medication. The selection and concentration of these excipients must be carefully balanced to ensure the desired properties and performance of the final product.

SOLUBILITY ENHANCEMENT TECHNIQUES

Enhancing the solubility of drugs in liquid dosage forms is crucial for ensuring their efficacy and bioavailability. Many drugs have poor solubility, which can limit their therapeutic effectiveness. Various techniques are employed to improve solubility and ensure optimal performance. Here are some common techniques:

1. Use of Solvents and Co Solvents

a. **Solvents:** Selecting an appropriate solvent can significantly enhance solubility. Common solvents include water, ethanol, and glycerin. The choice depends on the drug's chemical properties and the desired dosage form.
b. **Co-Solvents:** Adding co-solvents, such as propylene glycol or polyethylene glycol, can improve the solubility of drugs that are poorly soluble in water alone. Co-solvents work by reducing the polarity of the solvent mixture, facilitating the dissolution of the drug.

2. Formulation of Solutions

a. **Saturation Solutions:** Preparing solutions at a concentration that is close to the saturation point of the drug can enhance solubility. This technique often involves adjusting temperature or using solvents to achieve higher drug concentrations.

3. Particle Size Reduction

a. **Micronization:** Reducing the particle size of the drug increases the surface area available for dissolution. Techniques such as milling or grinding are used to achieve micronized particles.
b. **Nanosuspensions:** Formulating drugs as nanosuspensions involves dispersing drug particles in a liquid medium at a nanometer scale, which greatly enhances solubility and dissolution rates.

4. Use of Surfactants and Solubilizers

a. **Surfactants:** Agents like Polysorbates (e.g., Tween 80) or sodium lauryl sulfate reduce surface tension and improve wetting, which enhances the solubility of hydrophobic drugs.
b. **Solubilizers:** Compounds such as cyclodextrins form inclusion complexes with drugs, increasing their solubility. Cyclodextrins have a hydrophobic cavity that can encapsulate drug molecules.

5. Formation of Complexes

a. **Cyclodextrin Complexation:** Cyclodextrins are cyclic oligosaccharides that can encapsulate hydrophobic drug molecules, improving their solubility and stability.
b. **Salt Formation:** Converting the drug into a salt form (e.g., sodium or potassium salt) can enhance solubility, particularly for drugs with poor aqueous solubility.

6. pH Adjustment

a. **Buffer Systems:** Adjusting the pH of the solution to the optimal range can improve the solubility of weakly acidic or basic drugs. Buffer systems maintain a stable pH environment, which can enhance solubility and drug stability.

7. Use of Complex Formulations

a. **Lipid-Based Formulations:** Incorporating lipids, such as oils or liposomes, can enhance the solubility of lipophilic drugs. Lipid-based formulations can improve drug absorption and bioavailability.

b. **Micellar Solutions:** Micelles formed by surfactants can solubilize hydrophobic drugs by encapsulating them in their hydrophobic core.

8. Hydrotropy

a. **Hydrotropes:** Compounds like urea, sodium benzoate, and alcohols can increase the solubility of poorly soluble drugs by disrupting the structure of water and increasing solubilization capacity.

9. Use of Solid Dispersions

a. **Solid Dispersions:** The drug is dispersed in a solid matrix (e.g., with polymers) to enhance its dissolution rate. When this matrix is dissolved in a liquid, the drug's solubility can be improved.

10. Temperature Adjustment

a. **Heat:** Increasing the temperature can enhance the solubility of certain drugs by reducing the viscosity of the solvent and increasing the dissolution rate. However, care must be taken to avoid degradation of temperature-sensitive drugs.

11. Supercritical Fluid Technology

a. **Supercritical Fluids:** Using supercritical fluids (e.g., supercritical carbon dioxide) can enhance solubility by creating a unique environment that improves drug solubilization and processing.

CLASSIFICATION:

Liquid dosage forms are classified based on their composition, intended use, and the state of the drug within the formulation. Here's a detailed classification with examples for each type:

1. Solutions

a. **Definition:** Homogeneous mixtures where the drug is completely dissolved in a solvent.

b. **Examples:**

i. **Oral Solutions:** E.g., acetaminophen oral solution (Tylenol®).

ii. **Injectable Solutions:** E.g., normal saline (0.9% sodium chloride) for intravenous use.

iii. **Eye Drops:** E.g., artificial tears (Systane®).

2. Suspensions

a. **Definition:** Heterogeneous mixtures in which solid particles are dispersed throughout a liquid medium. The particles do not dissolve but are suspended.

b. **Examples:**

i. **Oral Suspensions:** E.g., amoxicillin oral suspension (Amoxil®).

ii. **Topical Suspensions:** E.g., calamine lotion for skin irritation.

iii. **Injectable Suspensions:** E.g., penicillin G benzathine suspension for intramuscular injection.

3. Emulsions

a. **Definition:** Mixtures of two immiscible liquids (such as oil and water) stabilized by emulsifying agents.

b. **Examples:**

i. **Oral Emulsions:** E.g., some nutritional supplements like Ensure®.

ii. **Topical Emulsions:** E.g., hydrocortisone cream (Cortizone®).

iii. **Injectable Emulsions:** E.g., intravenous fat emulsion (Intralipid®) used for parenteral nutrition.

4. Syrups

a. **Definition:** Concentrated solutions of sugar or sugar substitutes in water, used to mask unpleasant tastes and improve palatability.

b. **Examples:**

i. **Cough Syrups:** E.g., dextromethorphan cough syrup (Robitussin®).

ii. **Antibiotic Syrups:** E.g., cephalexin syrup (Keflex®).

5. Elixirs

a. **Definition:** Clear, sweetened solutions containing alcohol, which can dissolve both alcohol-soluble and water-soluble substances.

b. **Examples:**

   i. **Cough Elixirs:** E.g., diphenhydramine elixir (Benadryl®).

   ii. **Antihistamine Elixirs:** E.g., brompheniramine elixir.

6. Tinctures

a. **Definition:** Alcoholic or hydroalcoholic solutions of drugs, often used for their preservative qualities and ease of administration.

b. **Examples:**

   i. **Herbal Tinctures:** E.g., echinacea tincture.

   ii. **Pharmaceutical Tinctures:** E.g., tincture of iodine (used as a disinfectant).

7. Colloids

a. **Definition:** Solutions containing particles larger than molecules but still small enough to remain suspended throughout the liquid.

b. **Examples:**

   i. **Intravenous Colloids:** E.g., hydroxyethyl starch (HES) solutions used for volume expansion.

   ii. **Topical Colloids:** E.g., colloidal oatmeal in skin care products.

8. Gels

a. **Definition:** Semi-solid systems where the drug is dispersed in a gel matrix. Gels have a consistency between liquid and solid.

b. **Examples:**

   i. **Topical Gels:** E.g., benzoyl peroxide gel (for acne treatment).

   ii. **Oral Gels:** E.g., oral numbing gels (for mouth sores).

9. Aerosols

a. **Definition:** Liquids dispersed in a fine mist or spray, often used for inhalation or topical application.

b. **Examples:**

i. **Inhalers:** E.g., albuterol inhalation aerosol (Proventil®).

ii. **Topical Aerosols:** E.g., antifungal spray (Tinactin®).

10. Suspension Emulsions

a. **Definition:** Systems that combine features of both suspensions and emulsions, with suspended particles in an emulsion base.

b. **Examples:**

i. **Oral Suspension Emulsions:** E.g., certain antibiotic formulations for pediatric use.

A. Acetaminophen Oral Solution:

Definition: Acetaminophen (also known as paracetamol) oral solution is a liquid form of the medication used to relieve pain and reduce fever.

Pharmacological Considerations:

1. **Mechanism of Action:**
    a. **Central Action:** Acetaminophen primarily acts in the central nervous system (CNS), where it is believed to inhibit prostaglandin synthesis, particularly in the brain. This inhibition leads to analgesic (pain-relieving) and antipyretic (fever-reducing) effects.

    b. **Peripherally:** The exact mechanism in peripheral tissues is less well understood but may involve reducing the production of prostaglandins.
2. **Absorption:**
    a. **Oral Bioavailability:** Acetaminophen is rapidly absorbed from the gastrointestinal tract. The oral solution form provides an immediate and consistent release of the drug compared to solid forms like tablets.

    b. **Peak Plasma Concentration:** Achieved approximately 30 minutes to 1 hour after ingestion, depending on the formulation and presence of food.

3. **Distribution:**
    a. **Plasma Protein Binding:** Approximately 20-50% of acetaminophen is bound to plasma proteins, with the remainder being free and active in the bloodstream.
    b. **Crosses Blood-Brain Barrier:** Effective at reaching therapeutic levels in the central nervous system, which is crucial for its analgesic and antipyretic effects.
4. **Metabolism:**
    a. **Liver Metabolism:** Primarily metabolized in the liver. Acetaminophen is conjugated with glucuronic acid and sulfate to form non-toxic metabolites.
    b. **Minor Pathway:** A small portion is metabolized via the cytochrome P450 enzyme system to a highly reactive metabolite (N-acetyl-p-benzoquinone imine), which is normally detoxified by glutathione.
5. **Excretion:**
    a. **Renal Excretion:** Metabolites are excreted primarily through the urine. About 85-95% of the drug is eliminated in the urine within 24 hours.
6. **Clinical Uses:**
    a. **Pain Relief:** Effective for mild to moderate pain, including headaches, muscle aches, and arthritis.
    b. **Fever Reduction:** Commonly used to reduce fever in children and adults.
7. **Dosage and Administration:**
    a. **Dosing:** Typically dosed every 4-6 hours as needed, with maximum daily doses limited to avoid toxicity (e.g., 4 grams per day for adults).

b. **Administration:** The liquid form allows for easy adjustment of doses, particularly useful for pediatric patients.

8. **Adverse Effects:**
    a. **Hepatotoxicity:** High doses or prolonged use can lead to liver damage, especially in patients with pre-existing liver conditions or those consuming alcohol.
    b. **Allergic Reactions:** Rarely, allergic reactions may occur, including rash or swelling.

B. Normal Saline:

Definition: Normal saline is a sterile solution of 0.9% sodium chloride (NaCl) in water, used for intravenous administration.

Pharmacological Considerations:

1. **Composition and Properties:**
    a. **Isotonic Solution:** Normal saline is isotonic with respect to blood plasma, meaning it has the same osmotic pressure, which helps maintain fluid balance in the body without causing shifts in fluid between the intravascular and extravascular spaces.
2. **Mechanism of Action:**
    a. **Fluid Replacement:** Used to replace lost fluids and electrolytes. The sodium chloride in the solution helps restore and maintain normal electrolyte balance.
    b. **Hydration:** Provides hydration to patients who are dehydrated or in need of fluid resuscitation.
3. **Absorption and Distribution:**
    a. **Intravenous Administration:** Once infused into the bloodstream, normal saline rapidly distributes throughout the extracellular fluid compartment.

b. **Volume Expansion:** Increases blood volume and can improve circulation and perfusion.

4. **Clinical Uses:**
   a. **Fluid Resuscitation:** Used in cases of hypovolemia, dehydration, or shock to restore blood volume and blood pressure.
   b. **Diluent:** Serves as a diluent for other intravenous medications.
   c. **Irrigation:** Used for irrigation during surgical procedures or wound care.
5. **Dosage and Administration:**
   a. **Dosage:** Administered based on the patient's needs and clinical condition, often in variable volumes (e.g., 500 mL to several liters per day).
   b. **Administration:** Administered via intravenous infusion using standard infusion sets.
6. **Adverse Effects:**
   a. **Fluid Overload:** Excessive use can lead to fluid overload, especially in patients with heart, kidney, or liver issues.
   b. **Electrolyte Imbalance:** Although normal saline is isotonic, prolonged use in large volumes can still affect electrolyte balance.
7. **Precautions:**
   a. **Monitoring:** Patients receiving normal saline should be monitored for signs of fluid overload, electrolyte imbalances, and other adverse effects.

C. Artificial Tears (Systane®):

Definition: Artificial tears are lubricating eye drops designed to relieve dry eye symptoms and provide moisture to the ocular surface.

Pharmacological Considerations:

1. **Mechanism of Action:**

a. **Lubrication:** Artificial tears work by forming a protective layer on the surface of the eye, which helps to reduce friction during blinking and improve comfort.
b. **Moisturization:** They provide moisture to the eye, which helps to soothe dryness and irritation. This is especially useful for patients with insufficient natural tear production.

2. **Composition:**
   a. **Main Ingredients:** Artificial tears commonly contain lubricants such as polyvinyl alcohol, hydroxypropyl methylcellulose, or carboxymethylcellulose. These compounds act as hydrophilic polymers that mimic natural tears.
   b. **Osmolarity and pH:** Formulations are designed to match the osmolarity and pH of natural tears to minimize irritation and discomfort.
3. **Administration and Absorption:**
   a. **Topical Application:** Artificial tears are applied directly to the eye as eye drops. They are designed for local action on the ocular surface rather than systemic absorption.
   b. **Duration of Action:** The effects are typically short-lived, requiring repeated applications throughout the day for sustained relief.
4. **Clinical Uses:**
   a. **Dry Eye Relief:** Used to alleviate symptoms of dry eye syndrome, which can be caused by various factors such as environmental conditions, medications, or underlying conditions.
   b. **Post-Surgical Care:** Helps to soothe the eyes following surgical procedures like LASIK or cataract surgery.
5. **Adverse Effects:**
   a. **Mild Irritation:** Some patients may experience transient stinging or irritation upon application.

b. **Allergic Reactions:** Rarely, patients may develop allergic reactions to the preservatives or other components in the formulation.

6. **Precautions:**

a. **Preservatives:** Some formulations contain preservatives (e.g., benzalkonium chloride) that may cause irritation with frequent use. Preservative-free options are available for patients with sensitive eyes or who use artificial tears frequently.

D. Amoxicillin Oral Suspension (Amoxil®):

Definition: Amoxicillin oral suspension is a liquid antibiotic used to treat various bacterial infections. It is a form of amoxicillin, a penicillin-type antibiotic.

Pharmacological Considerations:

1. **Mechanism of Action:**

a. **Inhibition of Cell Wall Synthesis:** Amoxicillin works by inhibiting bacterial cell wall synthesis. It binds to penicillin-binding proteins (PBPs) located on the bacterial cell membrane, disrupting cell wall formation, leading to bacterial cell lysis and death.

b. **Broad-Spectrum Activity:** Effective against a range of Gram-positive and some Gram-negative bacteria.

2. **Absorption:**

a. **Oral Bioavailability:** Amoxicillin is well absorbed from the gastrointestinal tract, with bioavailability of approximately 75-90%.

b. **Peak Plasma Concentration:** Achieved within 1-2 hours after oral administration, depending on the formulation and presence of food.

3. **Distribution:**
    a. **Tissue Penetration:** Distributed widely throughout the body, including in the lungs, skin, and urinary tract. It does not cross the blood-brain barrier effectively but reaches therapeutic levels in the middle ear and sinuses.
4. **Metabolism:**
    a. **Minimal Metabolism:** Amoxicillin is not extensively metabolized in the liver. It is mostly excreted unchanged in the urine.
5. **Excretion:**
    a. **Renal Excretion:** About 60-70% of the administered dose is excreted unchanged in the urine within 6-8 hours. Dosage adjustments may be necessary in patients with renal impairment.
6. **Clinical Uses:**
    a. **Infections:** Used to treat a variety of bacterial infections, including respiratory tract infections, ear infections, sinusitis, and urinary tract infections.
    b. **Pediatric Use:** Commonly used in children due to its palatable liquid formulation.
7. **Dosage and Administration:**
    a. **Dosing:** Typically dosed every 8-12 hours, depending on the infection and severity. Dosage is adjusted based on the age, weight, and renal function of the patient.
    b. **Administration:** The liquid form allows for precise dosing, which is particularly useful for pediatric patients or those with difficulty swallowing tablets.
8. **Adverse Effects:**
    a. **Gastrointestinal Distress:** Common side effects include nausea, vomiting, and diarrhea.

b. **Allergic Reactions:** Potential for allergic reactions, such as rash, urticaria, or, in severe cases, anaphylaxis.
c. **Superinfection:** Prolonged use may lead to superinfection with resistant organisms.

9. **Precautions:**
   a. **Allergy History:** Caution in patients with a history of penicillin allergy.
   b. **Drug Interactions:** May interact with other medications, including anticoagulants and certain diuretics, affecting their efficacy.

Examples:

1. **Amoxil®:** A brand of amoxicillin oral suspension that is used for treating infections in both adults and children.

Calamine Lotion:

Definition: Calamine lotion is a topical preparation used to relieve itching, irritation, and discomfort caused by various skin conditions. It typically contains calamine (a combination of zinc oxide and ferric oxide) as its active ingredient.

Pharmacological Considerations:

1. **Mechanism of Action:**
   a. **Astringent Effect:** Calamine acts as an astringent, which means it helps to tighten the skin and reduce secretions, thereby providing relief from itching and irritation.
   b. **Protective Barrier:** It forms a protective barrier on the skin, which can help to soothe the affected area and prevent further irritation.
2. **Composition:**
   a. **Active Ingredients:** Calamine is a mixture of zinc oxide and ferric oxide. Zinc oxide has soothing, anti-inflammatory, and antimicrobial properties, while ferric oxide contributes to the characteristic color and additional soothing effects.

b. **Additional Components:** Calamine lotion may also contain other ingredients such as water, glycerin, or minor amounts of other compounds to improve the lotion's texture and application properties.

3. **Administration and Absorption:**
    a. **Topical Application:** Applied directly to the skin. The lotion is designed for external use only and is not absorbed systemically.
    b. **Duration of Action:** The lotion provides localized relief and is usually applied multiple times a day as needed.
4. **Clinical Uses:**
    a. **Itching and Irritation:** Commonly used for conditions like insect bites, chickenpox, poison ivy, and sunburn to relieve itching and discomfort.
    b. **Dry Skin:** Can be used to soothe dry, irritated skin.
5. **Adverse Effects:**
    a. **Skin Irritation:** May cause mild irritation or dryness in some individuals, particularly with frequent use.
    b. **Allergic Reactions:** Rarely, patients may experience allergic reactions or sensitivity to the lotion.
6. **Precautions:**
    a. **Avoid Contact with Eyes:** Should be applied carefully to avoid contact with the eyes and mucous membranes.
    b. **Use in Children:** Generally considered safe for use in children but should be used according to directions to avoid overuse.

Multiple-Choice Questions (MCQs)

1. What is a solution in the context of liquid dosage forms?
    a) A suspension of solid particles in a liquid
    b) A homogeneous mixture of solutes dissolved in a solvent

c) A mixture of two immiscible liquids

d) A concentrated solution of sugar in water

2. Which of the following is an example of an oral solution?

a) Injectable saline

b) Amoxicillin oral suspension

c) Acetaminophen oral solution

d) Hydrocortisone cream

3. What is the primary advantage of liquid dosage forms in pediatric medicine?

a) Longer shelf life

b) Easier swallowing

c) Better taste

d) Less microbial contamination

4. Which of the following is a common solvent used in liquid dosage forms?

a) Water

b) Calcium carbonate

c) Magnesium sulfate

d) Sodium bicarbonate

5. What is the main disadvantage of liquid dosage forms compared to solid forms?

a) Faster onset of action

b) More susceptible to microbial contamination

c) Easier to administer

d) Enhanced bioavailability

6. What is a suspension?

a) A mixture where solid particles are dispersed in a liquid

b) A solution with no solid particles

c) A concentrated sugar solution

d) A mixture of oil and water

7. Which of the following is a type of emulsifier used in liquid dosage forms?

a) Propylene glycol
b) Sodium chloride
c) Polysorbate 80
d) Glycerin

8. What is the purpose of using preservatives in liquid dosage forms?
    a) To enhance flavor
    b) To prevent microbial growth
    c) To increase viscosity
    d) To improve solubility

9. Which of the following is a disadvantage of using syrups as a liquid dosage form?
    a) Difficult to swallow
    b) Difficult to measure dosage accurately
    c) Can have a very unpleasant taste
    d) May require refrigeration

10. What is the role of glycerin in liquid dosage forms?
    a) To act as a solvent
    b) To increase the pH
    c) To provide a bitter taste
    d) To reduce viscosity

11. Which of the following is a type of liquid dosage form that uses alcohol as a solvent?
    a) Syrup
    b) Suspension
    c) Elixir
    d) Emulsion

12. What is the purpose of using thickening agents like xanthan gum in liquid dosage forms?
    a) To stabilize the solution

b) To reduce the amount of active ingredient

c) To enhance the flavor

d) To improve solubility

13. Which liquid dosage form is typically used for patients who have difficulty swallowing solid dosage forms?

a) Tincture

b) Oral solution

c) Topical cream

d) Injectable solution

14. Which type of excipient is used to adjust the pH of a liquid dosage form?

a) Preservatives

b) Sweeteners

c) Buffers

d) Solvents

15. What is the primary reason for adding flavoring agents to liquid dosage forms?

a) To enhance the therapeutic effect

b) To improve palatability

c) To increase shelf life

d) To stabilize the active ingredient

16. What is an emulsion in the context of liquid dosage forms?

a) A mixture of solid particles in a liquid

b) A mixture of two immiscible liquids

c) A concentrated sugar solution

d) A suspension with a thickener

17. Which of the following is an example of a medication commonly formulated as a suspension?

a) Amoxicillin oral suspension

b) Acetaminophen oral solution

c) Normal saline

d) Tincture of iodine

18. What is the advantage of using elixirs as a liquid dosage form?

a) They have a long shelf life

b) They are easy to measure accurately

c) They are alcohol-free

d) They are usually flavorless

19. Which of the following techniques is used to enhance the solubility of poorly soluble drugs?

a) Increasing particle size

b) Using hydrotropes

c) Decreasing the solvent concentration

d) Removing preservatives

20. What is a potential disadvantage of using normal saline as a liquid dosage form?

a) It may cause fluid overload in some patients

b) It is not isotonic with blood plasma

c) It has a short shelf life

d) It is not suitable for intravenous administration

Short Answer Type Questions (Subjective)

1. Define liquid dosage forms and explain their significance in pharmacotherapy.
2. What are the advantages and disadvantages of using liquid dosage forms compared to solid forms?
3. Explain the difference between a solution and a suspension in liquid dosage forms.
4. Describe the role of preservatives in liquid dosage forms and give examples.

5. How does the particle size reduction technique enhance the solubility of drugs in liquid dosage forms?
6. What are emulsions, and how are they classified in liquid dosage forms?
7. Discuss the importance of solvent selection in the formulation of liquid dosage forms.
8. How do excipients like glycerin and propylene glycol contribute to the formulation of liquid dosage forms?
9. What is the purpose of using thickening agents in liquid dosage forms, and how do they work?
10. How does the use of flavoring agents improve patient compliance with liquid dosage forms?
11. Explain the role of surfactants and emulsifiers in stabilizing emulsions.
12. What are the challenges associated with the stability of liquid dosage forms?
13. Describe the pharmacokinetics of acetaminophen when administered as an oral solution.
14. What factors should be considered when selecting a preservative for a liquid dosage form?
15. Explain the process of solubility enhancement using co-solvents.
16. What are the advantages of using syrups as a liquid dosage form, and what are the potential drawbacks?
17. Discuss the significance of pH adjustment in liquid dosage forms.
18. How do cyclodextrins enhance the solubility of poorly soluble drugs in liquid dosage forms?
19. Describe the formulation considerations for preparing a suspension.
20. Explain the role of normal saline as a liquid dosage form in clinical practice.

Long Answer Type Questions (Subjective)

1. Discuss the different types of liquid dosage forms, including their definitions, examples, advantages, and disadvantages

2. Explain the role of excipients in the formulation of liquid dosage forms, with a focus on solvents, preservatives, and stabilizers.
3. Describe the challenges and strategies involved in ensuring the stability and shelf life of liquid dosage forms.
4. Discuss the pharmacological considerations and clinical uses of acetaminophen oral solution, including its mechanism of action, absorption, and adverse effects.
5. Explain the various techniques used to enhance the solubility of poorly soluble drugs in liquid dosage forms.
6. Discuss the importance of pH adjustment, preservatives, and flavoring agents in the formulation of liquid dosage forms.
7. Describe the classification and formulation of emulsions in liquid dosage forms, including the role of surfactants and emulsifiers.
8. Explain the advantages and challenges of using liquid dosage forms in pediatric and geriatric patients.
9. Discuss the formulation, pharmacokinetics, and clinical applications of normal saline as a liquid dosage form.
10. Describe the process and considerations for formulating a suspension, including the use of stabilizers, thickeners, and particle size reduction.

Answer Key for 20 MCQs

1. (b) A homogeneous mixture of solutes dissolved in a solvent
2. (c) Acetaminophen oral solution
3. (b) Easier swallowing
4. (a) Water
5. (b) More susceptible to microbial contamination
6. (a) A mixture where solid particles are dispersed in a liquid
7. (c) Polysorbate 80
8. (b) To prevent microbial growth

9. (c) Can have a very unpleasant taste

10.(a) To act as a solvent

11.(c) Elixir

12.(a) To stabilize the solution

13.(b) Oral solution

14.(c) Buffers

15.(b) To improve palatability

16.(b) A mixture of two immiscible liquids

17.(a) Amoxicillin oral suspension

18.(a) They have a long shelf life

19.(b) Using hydrotropes

20.(a) It may cause fluid overload in some patients

CHAPTER – 8

MONOPHASIC LIQUIDS

INTRODUCTION:

Monophasic liquids are a type of liquid dosage form used in pharmaceuticals. They consist of a single homogeneous phase, meaning they are uniform in composition throughout. Here's a detailed introduction:

Monophasic Liquids

1. Definition: Monophasic liquids are solutions, suspensions, or emulsions where only one phase is continuous. Unlike biphasic or multiparticulate systems, there is no separation into distinct layers or phases.

2. Types of Monophasic Liquids:

a. **Solutions:** These are clear liquids where a solute (such as a drug) is completely dissolved in a solvent. The solute particles are distributed at the molecular or ionic level. Examples include saline solutions, sugar solutions, and medicinal syrups.

b. **Suspensions:** These are heterogeneous mixtures where solid particles are dispersed in a liquid medium. The particles are not dissolved but are suspended throughout the liquid. Over time, suspensions may settle, so they often need to be shaken before use. Examples include antibiotic suspensions.

c. **Emulsions:** These are mixtures of two immiscible liquids where one is dispersed in the other. Emulsions can be oil-in-water (O/W) or water-in-oil (W/O). They are stabilized by emulsifying agents. Examples include some topical creams and oral emulsions.

3. Characteristics:

a. **Uniformity:** Monophasic liquids are homogeneous, meaning the solute or dispersed phase is evenly distributed throughout the liquid.

b. **Clarity:** Solutions are typically clear, while suspensions and emulsions may appear cloudy or opaque.

c. **Stability:** The stability of monophasic liquids depends on the formulation. Solutions are generally stable, while suspensions and emulsions may require proper storage and shaking.

4. Advantages:

a. **Ease of Administration:** Monophasic liquids are easy to administer, especially for those who have difficulty swallowing tablets or capsules.

b. **Rapid Onset of Action:** Solutions often provide a faster onset of action compared to solid dosage forms, as the drug is already dissolved.

c. **Customizable Dosage:** The dosage can be easily adjusted by measuring out the liquid.

5. Disadvantages:

a. **Short Shelf Life:** Some monophasic liquids, particularly suspensions and emulsions, have a shorter shelf life and may require preservatives to prevent microbial growth.

b. **Need for Proper Storage:** Some formulations may need specific storage conditions to maintain stability.

6. Formulation Considerations:

a. **Solubility:** Ensuring that the drug is soluble or properly suspended in the chosen solvent or carrier.

b. **Viscosity:** Adjusting the viscosity to achieve the desired consistency and ease of administration.

c. **Preservation:** Adding preservatives to prevent microbial contamination and extend shelf life.

Monophasic liquids are a versatile and commonly used form of medication that can be tailored to meet various therapeutic needs. Their formulation requires careful consideration of stability, solubility, and patient compliance factors.

GARGLES

Gargles are a type of monophasic liquid preparation used primarily for oral hygiene and therapeutic purposes. They are designed to be used by swishing or gargling in the mouth and throat. Here's a detailed look at the definitions and preparations of gargles:

Definitions:

1. Gargles:

a. Gargles are liquid formulations intended for oral use, primarily for the purpose of cleansing, soothing, or providing localized treatment to the mouth and throat. They are not meant to be swallowed but rather to be used in a gargling or swishing action.

2. Characteristics:

a. **Homogeneity:** Gargles are typically monophasic liquids, meaning they have a uniform composition without any separate phases.

b. **Function:** They can provide a range of effects including antimicrobial action, anti-inflammatory effects, or simply freshening breath.

Preparations of Gargles:

1. **Formulation:** Gargles are formulated to include active ingredients, solvents, and additional agents that provide the desired effect. Common components include:

a. **Active Ingredients:** These can be antiseptics (like chlorhexidine), analgesics (like benzocaine), anti-inflammatory agents (like hydrocortisone), or astringents.

b. **Solvent:** The primary solvent is usually water or an aqueous solution of alcohol or glycerin.

c. **Buffering Agents:** To maintain the pH balance and stability of the gargle.

d. **Flavoring Agents:** For palatability, such as mint or fruit flavors.

e. **Sweeteners:** To improve taste, if needed.

f. **Preservatives:** To prevent microbial growth and extend shelf life, especially in aqueous preparations.

2. **Preparation Methods:**
   a. **Simple Solution:** Dissolve the active ingredients in water or an appropriate solvent. For example, a salt solution can be made by dissolving sodium chloride in water.
   b. **Syrup-Based Gargles:** Prepare a syrup base using water, sugars, and thickeners. The active ingredients are then added to this base.
   c. **Alcohol-Based Gargles:** Combine active ingredients with ethanol or isopropyl alcohol and water. These are less common due to the potential for irritation and unpleasant taste.
   d. **Emulsions:** For gargles containing oily substances or active ingredients, an emulsion may be prepared using emulsifiers to keep the oil evenly dispersed in the water phase.
3. **Quality Control:**
   a. **Sterility:** Ensure that the preparation process and final product are free from microbial contamination, especially if the gargle is intended for therapeutic use.
   b. **Stability Testing:** Check that the formulation maintains its efficacy and stability throughout its shelf life.
   c. **pH Testing:** Verify that the pH of the gargle is appropriate for both efficacy and patient comfort.
4. **Usage Instructions:**
   a. **Dosage:** Typically, gargles are used in a specific volume, such as 15-30 mL per use.
   b. **Frequency:** The recommended frequency of use is usually specified, such as 2 3 times a day.
   c. **Application:** The liquid should be swished around the mouth and gargled in the throat, then spat out

5. **Examples:**

   a. **Saline Gargle:** A simple solution of sodium chloride (salt) in water, used for soothing sore throats.

   b. **Antiseptic Gargle:** Contains chlorhexidine or cetylpyridinium chloride for reducing oral bacteria.

   c. **Herbal Gargle:** May include extracts of plants like sage or chamomile for their soothing properties.

Gargles are an effective way to manage oral and throat conditions, and their preparation involves ensuring that the formulation is safe, effective, and pleasant for the user.

MOUTHWASHES

Mouthwashes are another common form of monophasic liquid used for oral hygiene and therapeutic purposes. They are intended for use in the mouth and throat to improve oral health. Here's a detailed overview of mouthwashes, including definitions and preparations:

Definitions:

1. Mouthwashes:

   a. Mouthwashes are liquid preparations designed to be swished around the mouth and then expelled. They are used for a variety of purposes, including freshening breath, reducing oral bacteria, and treating conditions like gingivitis or sore throats.

2. Characteristics:

   a. **Monophasic Liquids:** Mouthwashes are typically monophasic, meaning they consist of a single, uniform phase without separation into layers or distinct phases.

   b. **Function:** They can have antimicrobial, antiseptic, anti-inflammatory, or cosmetic effects, depending on their formulation.

Preparations of Mouthwashes:

1. **Formulation Components:**

a. **Active Ingredients:** The choice of active ingredients depends on the desired effect:

   i. **Antiseptics/Antimicrobials:** Ingredients like chlorhexidine, cetylpyridinium chloride, or essential oils (e.g., eucalyptol, thymol) to combat bacteria.

   ii. **Fluoride:** To help prevent tooth decay.

   iii. **Astringents:** Such as zinc sulfate, for tightening tissues.

   iv. **Anti-inflammatory Agents:** Like hydrocortisone, for reducing inflammation.

b. **Solvents:** The primary solvent is usually water, but alcohol (ethanol) or glycerin may also be used.

c. **Flavoring Agents:** To improve taste and make the mouthwash more palatable, such as mint, cinnamon, or fruit flavors.

d. **Sweeteners:** To enhance flavor, with options like sorbitol or xylitol.

e. **Colorants:** Optional, to provide visual appeal, though they are not essential.

f. **Preservatives:** To extend shelf life and prevent microbial contamination, such as sodium benzoate.

2. **Preparation Methods:**

   a. **Simple Solution:** Dissolve the active ingredients in water or an aqueous solvent. This method is used for formulations where the ingredients are readily soluble.

   b. **Alcohol-Based Mouthwashes:** Combine active ingredients with ethanol and water. Alcohol-based mouthwashes often have antimicrobial properties and are used for their antiseptic effects. Care must be taken to balance the concentration of alcohol to avoid irritation.

   c. **Alcohol-Free Formulations:** Use glycerin or other non alcoholic solvents, making them suitable for those sensitive to alcohol or for use in children.

d. **Concentrated Formulations:** Prepare a concentrated solution that can be diluted with water before use. This is less common but allows for easier storage and use.

3. **Quality Control:**
   a. **Sterility:** Ensure the preparation process is clean and that the final product is free from microbial contamination.
   b. **Stability Testing:** Verify that the formulation maintains its efficacy, appearance, and safety over its intended shelf life.
   c. **pH Testing:** Ensure that the pH is appropriate for oral use and does not cause irritation.
4. **Usage Instructions:**
   a. **Dosage:** Typically, a specific volume is used per application, such as 20-30 mL.
   b. **Frequency:** Instructions generally recommend using mouthwash 1-2 times a day, or as directed by a healthcare professional.
   c. **Application:** Swish the liquid around the mouth for 30 seconds to 1 minute, ensuring it reaches all areas, then spit it out. Do not swallow.
5. **Examples:**
   a. **Antiseptic Mouthwash:** Contains chlorhexidine or cetylpyridinium chloride, used for reducing oral bacteria and treating gingivitis.
   b. **Fluoride Mouthwash:** Contains fluoride to help prevent tooth decay.
   c. **Herbal Mouthwash:** Includes natural extracts like aloe vera, tea tree oil, or chamomile for their soothing and anti-inflammatory properties.
   d. **Cosmetic Mouthwash:** Focuses on freshening breath with mint flavors and sometimes includes alcohol for its antimicrobial effects.

Mouthwashes play a key role in maintaining oral hygiene and addressing various dental and oral health issues. Their preparation involves careful consideration of ingredients and their effects to ensure effectiveness and safety for the user.

THROAT PAINT, EARDROPS

Throat Paints and **Eardrops** are specialized forms of monophasic liquids designed for specific therapeutic applications. Here's a detailed overview of each:

Throat Paints:

1. Definition:

a. Throat paints are liquid preparations used to treat localized conditions in the throat, such as sore throat, inflammation, or infection. They are applied directly to the mucous membranes of the throat.

2. Characteristics:

a. **Monophasic Liquid:** Throat paints are typically single-phase liquids, meaning they are uniform and do not separate into different layers.

b. **Application:** They are applied topically to the throat, usually with a brush or swab.

3. Preparation:

a. **Active Ingredients:**

   i. **Antiseptics:** Such as iodine or phenol, for their antimicrobial properties.

   ii. **Local Anesthetics:** Such as benzocaine or lidocaine, to provide temporary pain relief.

   iii. **Anti-inflammatory Agents:** Such as corticosteroids or non-steroidal anti-inflammatory drugs (NSAIDs), to reduce inflammation.

b. **Solvent:** Typically water or alcohol (ethanol), which acts as a carrier for the active ingredients.

c. **Thickening Agents:** To ensure the paint adheres to the throat mucosa, such as glycerin or natural gums.

d. **Flavoring Agents:** Sometimes added to improve taste, though not always necessary.

e. **Colorants:** May be included to help with visualization during application, though not essential for efficacy.

4. Preparation Methods:

a. **Simple Solution:** Dissolve the active ingredients in water or alcohol. Adjust viscosity with thickening agents to ensure proper application and adherence.

b. **Suspension:** For ingredients that are not fully soluble, create a suspension with appropriate stabilizers to keep the particles evenly dispersed.

5. Quality Control:

a. **Sterility:** Ensure that the preparation process is sterile to avoid contamination.

b. **Viscosity Testing:** Check that the paint has the correct consistency for effective application.

c. **Stability Testing:** Ensure that the paint maintains its efficacy and stability over time.

6. Usage Instructions:

a. **Dosage:** Apply a small amount of throat paint to the affected area as directed, usually 2-3 times a day.

b. **Application:** Use a sterile brush or swab to apply the paint directly to the throat.

Eardrops:

1. Definition:

a. Eardrops are liquid preparations used for the treatment of ear conditions such as infections, inflammation, or wax buildup. They are administered directly into the ear canal.

2. Characteristics:

a. **Monophasic Liquid:** Eardrops are typically single-phase liquids that do not separate into layers.

b. **Application:** Administered by placing drops directly into the ear canal.

3. Preparation:

a. **Active Ingredients:**

i. **Antibiotics:** Such as neomycin or polymyxin B, for treating bacterial infections.

ii. **Anti-inflammatory Agents:** Such as corticosteroids, to reduce inflammation.

iii. **Cerumenolytics:** Such as carbamide peroxide, for softening and removing earwax.

iv. **Antiseptics:** Such as hydrogen peroxide or alcohol, for cleaning and preventing infections.

b. **Solvent:** Usually a combination of water and an organic solvent like ethanol or glycerin. Some formulations may use oil (such as olive oil) as a base for certain purposes.

c. **Preservatives:** To prevent microbial growth, especially in aqueous formulations.

d. **pH Adjusters:** To maintain the pH balance suitable for the ear canal.

4. Preparation Methods:

a. **Simple Solution:** Dissolve the active ingredients in a suitable solvent. Ensure the solution is sterile and adjust the pH as needed.

b. **Suspension:** For insoluble ingredients, create a suspension with appropriate stabilizers to ensure even dispersion of particles.

c. **Oily Formulations:** Mix active ingredients with oil or oil-based solvents for applications where oil is preferred.

5. Quality Control:

a. **Sterility:** Ensure that the preparation process is clean to avoid contamination.

b. **pH Testing:** Verify that the eardrop solution has a pH that is compatible with the ear canal.
c. **Stability Testing:** Confirm that the formulation remains effective and safe over time.

6. Usage Instructions:

a. **Dosage:** Typically, a few drops are administered into the ear canal, usually 1-2 times a day or as directed.
b. **Application:** Tilt the head to one side and place the prescribed number of drops into the ear canal. Hold the head tilted for a few minutes to ensure the drops reach the affected area.

NASAL DROPS

Nasal Drops are a type of monophasic liquid designed for application into the nasal passages. They are used to treat various nasal and sinus conditions. Here's a detailed overview of nasal drops, including definitions and preparations:

Definitions:

1. Nasal Drops:

a. Nasal drops are liquid formulations administered into the nostrils to deliver medication directly to the nasal mucosa. They are used to treat conditions such as nasal congestion, allergic rhinitis, and nasal infections.

2. Characteristics:

a. **Monophasic Liquid:** Nasal drops are typically uniform in composition, without separation into different phases.
b. **Administration:** They are applied using a dropper or nozzle designed for nasal delivery.

Preparations of Nasal Drops:

1. **Formulation Components:**

a. **Active Ingredients:**

i. **Decongestants:** Such as oxymetazoline or phenylephrine, to reduce nasal congestion by constricting blood vessels.
ii. **Antihistamines:** Such as azelastine or levocabastine, to relieve symptoms of allergic rhinitis.
iii. **Saline Solutions:** For moisturizing and flushing out nasal passages.
iv. **Corticosteroids:** Such as fluticasone or mometasone, for reducing inflammation in chronic conditions.
v. **Antibiotics:** For treating bacterial infections (though less common due to the risk of resistance).

b. **Solvents:**
   i. **Water:** The most common solvent, used in aqueous nasal drops.
   ii. **Saline:** A salt solution that mimics the body's natural fluids.
   iii. **Glycerin or Propylene Glycol:** May be used to enhance viscosity or moisturize.
c. **Preservatives:** To prevent microbial growth, such as benzalkonium chloride.
d. **pH Adjusters:** To ensure the solution is compatible with the nasal mucosa.

2. **Preparation Methods:**
   a. **Simple Solution:** Dissolve the active ingredients in water or saline. This method is commonly used for aqueous nasal drops.
   b. **Oily Formulations:** For some specific treatments, an oil-based carrier might be used, though this is less common for nasal drops due to potential irritation and difficulty in spreading.
   c. **Suspension:** If the active ingredient is not fully soluble, prepare a suspension with appropriate stabilizers to keep the particles evenly dispersed.
3. **Quality Control:**

a. **Sterility:** Ensure that the preparation process is sterile to avoid contamination and infection.
b. **pH Testing:** Verify that the pH is suitable for nasal mucosa to prevent irritation.
c. **Viscosity Testing:** Ensure the solution has the correct viscosity to flow easily from the dropper and coat the nasal passages effectively.
d. **Stability Testing:** Confirm that the formulation remains effective and safe over its shelf life.

4. **Usage Instructions:**
   a. **Dosage:** Typically, a few drops are administered into each nostril as needed. Dosage may vary depending on the medication and condition being treated.
   b. **Application:** Tilt the head back slightly or keep it upright, insert the dropper into the nostril, and squeeze the prescribed number of drops. Gently breathe in through the nose to help the drops reach the nasal passages.
5. **Examples:**
   a. **Decongestant Nasal Drops:** Contain active ingredients like oxymetazoline or phenylephrine to relieve nasal congestion.
   b. **Saline Nasal Drops:** Simple saline solutions used to moisturize and flush out the nasal passages.
   c. **Antihistamine Nasal Drops:** Contain antihistamines like azelastine for treating allergic symptoms.
   d. **Corticosteroid Nasal Drops:** Contain corticosteroids like fluticasone for reducing inflammation in chronic rhinitis or sinusitis.

Nasal drops are designed to provide targeted relief for nasal conditions, and their preparation requires careful consideration of the active ingredients, solvents, and other components to ensure they are effective and safe for nasal use.

ENEMAS

Enemas are liquid preparations administered into the rectum to treat a variety of conditions affecting the lower gastrointestinal tract. They are used for purposes such as relieving constipation, administering medications, or preparing the bowel for diagnostic procedures. Here's a detailed overview of enemas, including definitions and preparations:

Definitions:

1. Enemas:

a. Enemas are liquid solutions or suspensions delivered into the rectum via the anus. They are used to achieve therapeutic effects locally within the colon or for systemic absorption of medications.

2. Characteristics:

a. **Monophasic Liquid:** Enemas are typically monophasic, meaning they are uniform and do not separate into distinct phases.

b. **Administration:** They are administered using a rectal applicator or enema bulb designed for rectal delivery.

Preparations of Enemas:

1. **Formulation Components:**

a. **Active Ingredients:**

i. **Laxatives:** Such as sodium phosphate, bisacodyl, or glycerin to stimulate bowel movements.

ii. **Anti-inflammatory Agents:** Such as corticosteroids (e.g., hydrocortisone) for treating conditions like ulcerative colitis.

iii. **Antiseptics or Antibiotics:** For treating localized infections or inflammation.

iv. **Saline:** For its osmotic effect to draw water into the colon, which helps to soften stool and promote bowel movements.

b. **Solvents:**

    i. **Water:** The primary solvent used in most enemas, sometimes with added salts or buffering agents.
    ii. **Saline:** A salt solution for osmotic action.
    iii. **Glycerin:** Used to provide lubrication and osmotic effect.
  c. **Buffering Agents:** To maintain the appropriate pH of the solution.
  d. **Preservatives:** To prevent microbial growth and ensure the solution remains stable over time.

2. **Preparation Methods:**
   a. **Simple Solution:** Dissolve the active ingredients in water or saline. This is the most common method for preparing enemas, especially for osmotic or stimulant types.
   b. **Suspension:** If the active ingredient is not fully soluble, prepare a suspension with appropriate stabilizers to keep the particles evenly dispersed.
   c. **Oily Formulations:** For certain types of enemas, such as those intended to soften hard stool, use an oil-based solution like mineral oil.
3. **Quality Control:**
   a. **Sterility:** Ensure that the preparation process and final product are free from microbial contamination, especially since enemas are administered into the rectum.
   b. **pH Testing:** Verify that the pH is appropriate for rectal mucosa to prevent irritation.
   c. **Viscosity Testing:** Ensure the enema has the correct consistency for easy administration and effective distribution.
   d. **Stability Testing:** Confirm that the formulation maintains its efficacy and safety over its shelf life.
4. **Usage Instructions:**

a. **Dosage:** The volume of the enema is usually specified, commonly ranging from 60 to 500 mL depending on the type and purpose of the enema.
b. **Application:** Lie on your side with knees drawn up or assume a position as directed. Insert the enema nozzle or applicator into the rectum and administer the solution. Retain the enema for the prescribed time before evacuating.

5. **Examples:**
   a. **Saline Enemas:** Contain a saline solution used to soften stool and induce bowel movements. Often used for constipation relief.
   b. **Glycerin Enemas:** Use glycerin to lubricate and stimulate bowel movements. Typically used for mild constipation.
   c. **Medication Enemas:** Contain corticosteroids or other therapeutic agents to treat inflammatory bowel conditions such as ulcerative colitis.
   d. **Oil Enemas:** Use oils like mineral oil to soften hard stool and ease its passage.

SYRUPS

Syrups are a type of monophasic liquid used primarily as a vehicle for delivering medications or as a sweetener and flavoring agent in various formulations. They are characterized by their viscous, sweet consistency. Here's a detailed overview of syrups, including definitions and preparations:

Definitions:

1. **Syrups:**
   a. Syrups are concentrated solutions of sugars or sugar substitutes in water or other liquids. They are often used to deliver medications in a palatable form and can also be used for their own flavoring and sweetening properties.

2. **Characteristics:**

a. **Monophasic Liquid:** Syrups are typically monophasic, meaning they are uniform in composition without any separate phases.
b. **Consistency:** They have a viscous consistency due to the high concentration of sugars or other sweetening agents.
c. **Sweetness:** The sweetness of syrups makes them suitable for masking the taste of medications.

Preparations of Syrups:

1. **Formulation Components:**
   a. **Sweetening Agents:**
      i. **Sucrose:** The most common sweetener used in syrups, providing both sweetness and viscosity.
      ii. **Glucose or Fructose:** Sometimes used in combination with sucrose or as alternatives to modify sweetness and texture.
      iii. **Sugar Substitutes:** Such as sorbitol, xylitol, or stevia for sugar-free formulations.
   b. **Solvent:**
      i. **Water:** The primary solvent used to dissolve the sugars and other components.
   c. **Flavoring Agents:** To enhance the taste of the syrup, such as fruit extracts, essential oils, or synthetic flavors.
   d. **Colorants:** Optional, used to provide visual appeal if needed.
   e. **Preservatives:** To prevent microbial growth and extend shelf life, such as sodium benzoate or potassium sorbate.
   f. **Thickening Agents:** Sometimes used to adjust viscosity, such as xanthan gum or guar gum.

2. **Preparation Methods:**
   a. **Simple Syrup Preparation:**

i. **Dissolve Sugar:** Heat water and dissolve sucrose (or other sugars) to achieve a concentrated solution. The concentration of sugar typically ranges from 60% to 85% by weight.

ii. **Cool and Adjust:** Allow the syrup to cool and adjust the final volume as necessary. Optionally, add flavoring agents or preservatives.

b. **Medicinal Syrups:**

i. **Dissolve Active Ingredients:** Dissolve or suspend active pharmaceutical ingredients in the syrup base. Ensure the active ingredients are fully dissolved or uniformly dispersed.

ii. **Add Other Components:** Mix in any additional ingredients such as flavorings, colorants, or preservatives.

c. **Sugar-Free Syrups:**

i. **Use Sugar Substitutes:** Prepare the syrup using sugar substitutes and adjust the sweetness and viscosity as needed.

3. **Quality Control:**

a. **Consistency Testing:** Ensure the syrup has the appropriate viscosity for easy administration and stable formulation.

b. **pH Testing:** Verify that the pH is suitable for the syrup's stability and safety.

c. **Microbial Testing:** Ensure that the syrup is free from microbial contamination, particularly if it contains preservatives.

d. **Stability Testing:** Confirm that the syrup maintains its efficacy, taste, and appearance over its shelf life.

4. **Usage Instructions:**

a. **Dosage:** Syrups are typically measured using a dosing spoon or cup, with the dosage varying depending on the intended use, whether for medication or as a sweetener.

b. **Administration:** For medicinal syrups, follow the dosage instructions provided by a healthcare professional or included on the label.

5. **Examples:**

a. **Medicinal Syrups:** Used to deliver medications such as cough suppressants (e.g., dextromethorphan syrup), expectorants, or antibiotics.

b. **Flavoring Syrups:** Used in cooking and baking or as a sweetener in beverages, such as vanilla syrup or fruit-flavored syrups.

c. **Sugar-Free Syrups:** Formulated with sugar substitutes for individuals who need to avoid sugar for health reasons, such as diabetic patients.

Syrups are versatile formulations used both in medicine and as sweeteners. Their preparation requires careful consideration of the sweetening agents, solvents, and additional components to ensure they are effective, stable, and pleasant for the user.

ELIXIRS

Elixirs are a type of monophasic liquid used primarily for medicinal purposes. They are clear, sweetened solutions that often contain a combination of alcohol, water, and active pharmaceutical ingredients. Here's a detailed overview of elixirs, including their definitions and preparations:

Definitions:

1. Elixirs:

a. Elixirs are liquid preparations that contain one or more active ingredients dissolved or suspended in a mixture of alcohol and water. They are used to deliver medication in a palatable form and are often used for their therapeutic properties.

2. Characteristics:

a. **Monophasic Liquid:** Elixirs are typically uniform in composition without separation into distinct phases.

b. **Alcohol Content:** They usually contain a significant amount of alcohol, which serves as a solvent and preservative.

c. **Sweetness:** Elixirs often include sweetening agents to mask the taste of the active ingredients and make the medication more palatable.

Preparations of Elixirs:

1. **Formulation Components:**
   a. **Active Ingredients:**
      i. **Pharmaceutical Agents:** The primary therapeutic substances included in the elixir, such as antihistamines, cough suppressants, or other medications.
   b. **Solvents:**
      i. **Alcohol:** Ethanol is commonly used as the primary solvent due to its ability to dissolve both hydrophilic and lipophilic substances and its preservative properties. Alcohol content typically ranges from 5% to 20% by volume.
      ii. **Water:** Used in combination with alcohol to adjust the solvent properties and dissolve the active ingredients.
   c. **Sweetening Agents:**
      i. **Syrups or Sugar:** To enhance the flavor and mask the taste of the active ingredients. Examples include sucrose syrup or high fructose corn syrup.
   d. **Flavoring Agents:**
      i. **Natural or Artificial Flavors:** Such as fruit extracts, mint, or vanilla to improve taste.
   e. **Colorants:** Optional, used to give the elixir a pleasant appearance.
   f. **Preservatives:**
      i. **Antimicrobial Agents:** Such as sodium benzoate or potassium sorbate, to prevent microbial growth and extend shelf life.

2. **Preparation Methods:**
   a. **Simple Solution:**

   i. **Dissolve Active Ingredients:** Mix the active ingredients with alcohol and water to form a homogeneous solution. The concentration of alcohol and water should be adjusted to ensure that the active ingredients are properly dissolved.

b. **Syrup Addition:**
   i. **Combine with Syrup:** Mix the active ingredients and solvents with a syrup or sweetening agent to achieve the desired sweetness and viscosity.

c. **Flavoring and Color Addition:**
   i. **Incorporate Flavorings and Colorants:** Add these components to enhance the taste and appearance of the elixir. Mix thoroughly to ensure uniformity.

3. **Quality Control:**
   a. **Uniformity:** Ensure that the elixir is homogenous and that the active ingredients are evenly distributed throughout the solution.
   b. **Alcohol Content Testing:** Verify that the alcohol concentration is within the specified range for both efficacy and safety.
   c. **pH Testing:** Ensure that the pH is appropriate for the stability and safety of the elixir.
   d. **Microbial Testing:** Confirm that the elixir is free from microbial contamination, especially due to the presence of alcohol.
   e. **Stability Testing:** Ensure that the elixir maintains its efficacy, taste, and appearance over its shelf life.

4. **Usage Instructions:**
   a. **Dosage:** Administer the elixir according to the prescribed dosage, usually measured using a dropper or dosing cup.
   b. **Administration:** Take the elixir orally, following any specific instructions regarding whether it should be taken with or without food.

5. **Examples:**

a. **Cough Elixirs:** Contain active ingredients like dextromethorphan or codeine for cough suppression.
b. **Antihistamine Elixirs:** Include antihistamines such as diphenhydramine for allergy relief.
c. **Digestive Elixirs:** Used to aid digestion or relieve symptoms of gastrointestinal discomfort.

Elixirs are effective for delivering medication in a palatable liquid form, with the alcohol and sweeteners aiding in the dissolution and flavoring of the active ingredients. Proper formulation and quality control are crucial to ensure their efficacy and safety.

LINIMENTS

Liniments are topical preparations used for their soothing, analgesic, or anti-inflammatory effects. They are typically applied to the skin to relieve muscle and joint pain. Liniments can be monophasic or biphasic, but here's a detailed overview of monophasic liniments, including their definitions and preparations:

Definitions:

1. Liniments:

a. Liniments are liquid preparations intended for external application to the skin. They are used to relieve pain, inflammation, or stiffness in muscles and joints.

2. Characteristics:

a. **Monophasic Liquid:** Monophasic liniments are uniform in composition, meaning they do not separate into different phases.
b. **Application:** Applied directly to the skin and usually massaged in to enhance absorption.
c. **Consistency:** Typically less viscous than ointments but may be more viscous than simple solutions, depending on the formulation.

Preparations of Liniments:

1. **Formulation Components:**
   a. **Active Ingredients:**
      i. **Analgesics:** Such as menthol, methyl salicylate, or capsaicin, which provide pain relief.
      ii. **Anti-inflammatory Agents:** Such as non-steroidal anti-inflammatory drugs (NSAIDs) like diclofenac or ketoprofen.
      iii. **Counterirritants:** Such as camphor or eucalyptus oil, which produce a sensation of warmth or cooling to relieve pain.
   b. **Solvents and Carriers:**
      i. **Alcohol:** Often used as a solvent for the active ingredients and to provide a cooling effect. Examples include ethanol or isopropyl alcohol.
      ii. **Water:** Sometimes used in combination with alcohol to adjust the solvent properties and viscosity.
      iii. **Oils:** Such as mineral oil or vegetable oils, which may be used to enhance skin absorption and provide emollient properties.
   c. **Emulsifiers or Stabilizers:** To maintain uniform dispersion of active ingredients in the liquid phase.
   d. **Colorants and Fragrance:** Optional, used to improve appearance and scent, though not essential for the efficacy of the liniment.
2. **Preparation Methods:**
   a. **Simple Solution:**
      i. **Dissolve Active Ingredients:** Dissolve the active ingredients in alcohol or a mixture of alcohol and water. Ensure that all components are completely dissolved to achieve a homogeneous solution.
   b. **Emulsified Liniments:**

    i. **Combine Ingredients:** For liniments containing oils, mix the oils with alcohol and water, using emulsifiers to maintain a stable solution.

c. **Mixing and Adjustment:**
    i. **Incorporate Additives:** Add any colorants or fragrances if desired, and mix thoroughly to ensure uniformity.

3. **Quality Control:**
    a. **Uniformity:** Ensure that the liniment is homogeneous and that the active ingredients are evenly distributed throughout the solution.
    b. **Viscosity Testing:** Verify that the liniment has the appropriate consistency for easy application and effective distribution on the skin.
    c. **pH Testing:** Ensure the pH is suitable for topical application to prevent skin irritation.
    d. **Microbial Testing:** Confirm that the liniment is free from microbial contamination, especially if it contains water or other potentially susceptible ingredients.
    e. **Stability Testing:** Ensure that the liniment maintains its efficacy, consistency, and appearance over its shelf life.
4. **Usage Instructions:**
    a. **Dosage:** Apply a small amount of liniment to the affected area as directed, usually several times a day.
    b. **Application:** Gently massage the liniment into the skin until absorbed. Avoid applying to broken or irritated skin and avoid contact with the eyes and mucous membranes.
5. **Examples:**
    a. **Menthol Liniments:** Contain menthol for its cooling and analgesic effects, often used for muscle and joint pain relief.
    b. **Methyl Salicylate Liniments:** Contain methyl salicylate (wintergreen oil) for its counterirritant and analgesic properties.

c. **Capsaicin Liniments:** Contain capsaicin, derived from chili peppers, used for its pain-relieving effects by depleting substance P.

Liniments are effective for providing localized relief from muscle and joint pain through their active ingredients and solvent systems. Proper formulation and quality control are essential to ensure their safety and efficacy for topical use.

LOTIONS

Lotions are topical monophasic liquids used for their moisturizing, soothing, or therapeutic effects on the skin. They are often used to treat or manage conditions such as dryness, irritation, or minor skin conditions. Here's a detailed overview of lotions, including their definitions and preparations:

Definitions:

1. Lotions:

a. Lotions are fluid emulsions that contain a mixture of water and other ingredients, often including oils or other active compounds. They are applied to the skin to deliver active ingredients or to provide hydration and relief.

2. Characteristics:

a. **Monophasic Liquid:** Monophasic lotions are uniform and homogeneous, meaning they do not separate into different phases.

b. **Consistency:** Typically less viscous than creams or ointments, providing a light and easily spreadable texture.

c. **Application:** Applied to the skin, often for hydration or to deliver medication.

Preparations of Lotions:

1. **Formulation Components:**

a. **Active Ingredients:**

i. **Medications:** Such as corticosteroids, antihistamines, or antibiotics for treating skin conditions.

ii. **Moisturizers:** Ingredients like glycerin, hyaluronic acid, or dimethicone for hydration.

iii. **Anti-inflammatory Agents:** Such as calamine or colloidal oatmeal.

b. **Solvents:**

i. **Water:** The primary solvent in most lotions, providing the base and hydration.

c. **Oils and Emollients:**

i. **Oils:** Such as mineral oil, sunflower oil, or squalane, used to provide moisture and improve skin feel.

ii. **Emollients:** Such as petrolatum or lanolin to soften and smooth the skin.

d. **Emulsifiers:** To stabilize the mixture of water and oils and ensure a consistent product. Examples include cetyl alcohol or polysorbates.

e. **Thickeners:** To adjust the viscosity of the lotion and enhance its texture, such as xanthan gum or carbomers.

f. **Preservatives:** To prevent microbial growth and extend shelf life, such as parabens or phenoxyethanol.

g. **Colorants and Fragrances:** Optional, used for aesthetic purposes and to enhance the sensory experience.

2. **Preparation Methods:**

a. **Emulsion Preparation:**

i. **Combine Ingredients:** Mix the oil phase (oils, emulsifiers) with the water phase (water, thickeners). Heat if necessary to dissolve the ingredients completely.

ii. **Emulsification:** Use high-shear mixing or homogenization to blend the oil and water phases into a uniform emulsion.

   iii. **Cooling and Addition:** Cool the mixture and add any heat-sensitive ingredients like fragrances or preservatives.

b. **Simple Solution:**
   i. **Dissolve Active Ingredients:** In cases where the lotion does not require emulsification, dissolve active ingredients directly in water or a water-based solution.

3. **Quality Control:**
   a. **Uniformity:** Ensure that the lotion is homogeneous and that active ingredients are evenly distributed.
   b. **Viscosity Testing:** Verify that the lotion has the appropriate consistency for easy application and spreadability.
   c. **pH Testing:** Ensure the pH is suitable for the skin to avoid irritation or adverse effects.
   d. **Microbial Testing:** Confirm that the lotion is free from microbial contamination, especially if it contains water.
   e. **Stability Testing:** Ensure that the lotion maintains its efficacy, consistency, and appearance over its shelf life.

4. **Usage Instructions:**
   a. **Dosage:** Apply a thin layer of lotion to the affected area as needed, usually several times a day.
   b. **Application:** Gently rub or massage the lotion into the skin until absorbed. Avoid applying to broken or irritated skin unless specifically directed.

5. **Examples:**
   a. **Moisturizing Lotions:** Contain ingredients like glycerin or hyaluronic acid to provide hydration and soothe dry skin.
   b. **Anti-inflammatory Lotions:** Include agents like corticosteroids or calamine to reduce inflammation and relieve itching.

c. **Therapeutic Lotions:** Used for specific skin conditions, such as acne lotions containing salicylic acid or benzoyl peroxide.

Lotions are versatile and widely used formulations for skin care and treatment. Their preparation involves careful consideration of emulsifiers, active ingredients, and other components to ensure effectiveness, stability, and user satisfaction.

Multiple-Choice Questions (MCQs)

1. Which of the following is a characteristic of monophasic liquids?
   A) Biphasic composition
   B) Presence of multiple phases
   C) Uniform composition throughout
   D) Separation into distinct layers
2. What type of monophasic liquid is characterized by a solute completely dissolved in a solvent?
   A) Suspension
   B) Emulsion
   C) Solution
   D) Lotion
3. Which of the following is NOT a type of monophasic liquid?
   A) Emulsion
   B) Suspension
   C) Solution
   D) Ointment
4. What is the primary use of gargles?
   A) To be swallowed for systemic effects
   B) For cleansing and soothing the throat
   C) For nasal congestion relief
   D) As a topical pain reliever

5. Which active ingredient is commonly found in antiseptic gargles?

    A) Benzocaine

    B) Hydrocortisone

    C) Chlorhexidine

    D) Methyl salicylate

6. Mouthwashes are typically:

    A) Biphasic liquids

    B) Monophasic liquids

    C) Suspensions

    D) Solid dosage forms

7. Which solvent is most commonly used in mouthwashes?

    A) Glycerin

    B) Water

    C) Alcohol

    D) Mineral oil

8. Which preparation is directly applied to the mucous membranes of the throat?

    A) Mouthwash

    B) Throat Paint

    C) Elixir

    D) Nasal Drop

9. Which component is often added to throat paints to ensure it adheres to the throat mucosa?

    A) Ethanol

    B) Glycerin

    C) Sodium chloride

    D) Cetylpyridinium chloride

10. What is the primary function of nasal drops?

    A) To treat ear infections

B) To moisturize and relieve nasal congestion

C) To soothe a sore throat

D) To alleviate muscle pain

11. Which of the following is an active ingredient commonly found in nasal drops for treating allergic rhinitis?

A) Oxymetazoline

B) Methyl salicylate

C) Menthol

D) Hydrocortisone

12. Enemas are typically administered:

A) Orally

B) Through the nasal passages

C) Rectally

D) Topically

13. Which of the following is a common active ingredient in laxative enemas?

A) Sodium phosphate

B) Glycerin

C) Cetylpyridinium chloride

D) Zinc sulfate

14. Syrups are typically characterized by:

A) A low concentration of sugars

B) A high concentration of alcohol

C) A viscous, sweet consistency

D) An oil-in-water emulsion

15. Which of the following is a sweetening agent commonly used in syrups?

A) Glycerin

B) Fructose

C) Mineral oil

D) Oxymetazoline

16.Elixirs are known to contain a significant amount of:

A) Water

B) Alcohol

C) Oil

D) Glycerin

17.Which ingredient is commonly found in liniments to provide analgesic effects?

A) Menthol

B) Oxymetazoline

C) Fluoride

D) Cetylpyridinium chloride

18.Lotions are primarily used for:

A) Oral hygiene

B) Nasal decongestion

C) Skin hydration and treatment

D) Rectal administration

19.Which type of preparation is typically used to treat muscle and joint pain?

A) Elixir

B) Suspension

C) Liniment

D) Enema

20.What is the role of emulsifiers in lotions?

A) To add color

B) To stabilize the mixture of water and oils

C) To provide fragrance

D) To act as a preservative

Short Answer Type Questions (Subjective)

1. What are monophasic liquids, and how do they differ from biphasic systems?

2. Describe the main types of monophasic liquids with examples.
3. Explain the advantages and disadvantages of using monophasic liquids in pharmaceuticals.
4. How are suspensions different from solutions in the context of monophasic liquids?
5. What considerations are important when formulating a monophasic liquid?
6. Define gargles and describe their primary use.
7. What are the common active ingredients found in gargles, and what is their purpose?
8. Explain the difference between gargles and mouthwashes.
9. Describe the process of preparing a mouthwash.
10. What are the quality control measures necessary for mouthwashes?
11. What is the purpose of throat paints, and how are they applied?
12. Describe the preparation method of eardrops and their primary uses.
13. What are nasal drops, and what conditions are they used to treat?
14. List the common active ingredients in nasal drops and their functions.
15. What are enemas, and how are they administered?
16. Describe the preparation method for medicinal syrups.
17. Explain the role of alcohol in elixirs.
18. What are liniments, and how are they used for pain relief?
19. Describe the key components of a lotion and their functions.
20. How do emulsifiers work in the formulation of lotions?

Long Answer Type Questions (Subjective)

1. Discuss the formulation considerations for monophasic liquids and their importance in pharmaceutical preparations.
2. Compare and contrast solutions, suspensions, and emulsions as types of monophasic liquids. Provide examples of each.
3. Explain the process of preparing gargles, including the types of active ingredients used and their therapeutic purposes.

4. Describe the various components of mouthwashes and their roles in oral hygiene.
5. Discuss the preparation, quality control, and usage of throat paints and eardrops.
6. Explain the formulation and application of nasal drops, including the types of conditions they treat.
7. Discuss the types of enemas, their formulation, and the therapeutic purposes they serve.
8. Provide a detailed explanation of syrups, including their formulation, types, and uses in medicine.
9. Discuss the role of alcohol in elixirs and how it affects the formulation and stability of these monophasic liquids.
10. Compare liniments and lotions in terms of their formulation, application, and therapeutic uses.

Answer Key for MCQs

1. C (Uniform composition throughout)
2. C (Solution)
3. D (Ointment)
4. B (For cleansing and soothing the throat)
5. C (Chlorhexidine)
6. B (Monophasic liquids)
7. B (Water)
8. B (Throat Paint)
9. B (Glycerin)
10. B (To moisturize and relieve nasal congestion)
11. A (Oxymetazoline)
12. C (Rectally)
13. A (Sodium phosphate)
14. C (A viscous, sweet consistency)

15.B (Fructose)

16.B (Alcohol)

17.A (Menthol)

18.C (Skin hydration and treatment)

19.C (Liniment)

20.B (To stabilize the mixture of water and oils)

CHAPTER – 9

SUSPENSIONS

INTRODUCTION:

Definition and Characteristics:

1. **Suspensions** are a type of heterogeneous mixture where solid particles are dispersed throughout a liquid medium but do not dissolve in it. These particles are typically larger than those in solutions, often ranging from 1 micron to several millimeters.
2. The particles in a suspension remain suspended due to the continuous agitation or shaking of the mixture. Without agitation, the solid particles will eventually settle at the bottom over time, forming a sediment.

Pharmaceutical Suspensions:

1. In the pharmaceutical industry, suspensions are used to deliver medications that are poorly soluble in liquids. These formulations allow for controlled dosing and improved patient compliance.
2. **Advantages:** They can mask the taste of unpleasant drugs, are often easier to administer, and can provide controlled release of the drug.
3. **Disadvantages:** They can be less stable compared to solutions, with the risk of particle settling and potential variability in dose if not properly shaken before use.

Components of Suspensions:

1. **Active Ingredient:** The drug or therapeutic agent that needs to be delivered.
2. **Dispersing Medium:** The liquid in which the solid particles are suspended. It can be water, oil, or a combination, depending on the nature of the drug and the intended use.

3. **Suspending Agents:** Polymers or other compounds used to increase the viscosity of the medium and prevent the settling of particles. Examples include xanthan gum, cellulose derivatives, and alginates.
4. **Stabilizers:** Additives that prevent the aggregation of particles and improve the stability of the suspension. Examples include surfactants and emulsifiers.
5. **Preservatives:** Added to prevent microbial growth and extend shelf life.

Types of Suspensions:

1. **Oral Suspensions:** Designed for oral administration, often used for drugs that are not available in liquid form or to make them easier to ingest.
2. **Topical Suspensions:** Applied to the skin for local effects, such as in the treatment of dermatological conditions.
3. **Injectable Suspensions:** For intramuscular or subcutaneous injections, these require careful formulation to ensure proper dispersion and dosage.

Preparation and Quality Control:

1. **Preparation:** Involves mixing the active ingredient with the dispersing medium and other excipients under controlled conditions. The mixing process must ensure that the particles are evenly distributed and that the suspension has the desired viscosity.
2. **Quality Control:** Includes testing for particle size distribution, sedimentation rate, viscosity, and stability over time. Ensuring the suspension remains homogenous and effective throughout its shelf life is crucial.

Examples of Suspensions:

1. **Oral Antibiotics:** Such as amoxicillin suspension, used for children or those who have difficulty swallowing tablets.
2. **Topical Corticosteroids:** For inflammatory skin conditions.
3. **Injectable Insulin Suspensions:** For controlled release of insulin in diabetes management.

DEFINITION OF SUSPENSIONS

A **suspension** is a type of heterogeneous mixture in which solid particles are dispersed throughout a liquid or gas medium but are not dissolved. Unlike solutions, where the solute is completely integrated into the solvent, suspensions involve particles that remain distinct and can eventually settle out if the mixture is allowed to stand undisturbed.

Key Characteristics:

1. **Particle Size:** The solid particles in a suspension are typically larger than those found in solutions, often ranging from 1 micrometer to several millimeters. These particles are large enough to be seen under a microscope or with the naked eye.
2. **Settling:** Over time, solid particles in a suspension tend to settle at the bottom due to gravity. The rate at which this settling occurs depends on factors such as particle size, density, and the viscosity of the medium.
3. **Agitation:** To maintain a uniform distribution of particles, suspensions often require constant agitation or shaking. Without such agitation, the particles will aggregate and settle, leading to an uneven mixture.
4. **Heterogeneity:** Suspensions are heterogeneous mixtures, meaning that their composition is not uniform throughout. The distribution of particles can vary depending on how well the suspension is mixed.

Types of Suspensions:

1. **Oral Suspensions:** Used for administering medications that are not soluble in liquids. These are commonly used in pediatric medicine or for patients who have difficulty swallowing tablets.
2. **Topical Suspensions:** Applied to the skin or mucous membranes to provide local therapeutic effects. These are used in dermatology and for treating localized infections or conditions.

3. **Injectable Suspensions:** Used for drug delivery via injections. These require precise formulation to ensure that the particles remain properly dispersed and do not cause blockages in needles.

Components of Suspensions:

1. **Dispersed Phase (Solid Particles):** The active ingredient or therapeutic agent that is not dissolved in the medium. The particles must be evenly distributed to ensure consistent dosing.
2. **Dispersion Medium:** The liquid or gas in which the solid particles are suspended. Common dispersion media include water, oils, or aqueous solutions.
3. **Suspending Agents:** Polymers or agents added to the dispersion medium to increase viscosity and prevent particle settling. Examples include xanthan gum, cellulose derivatives, and polyvinyl alcohol.
4. **Stabilizers:** Substances that prevent the aggregation of particles and maintain the stability of the suspension. Surfactants and emulsifiers are often used for this purpose.
5. **Preservatives:** Added to prevent microbial growth and ensure the suspension remains safe and effective over time.

Examples of Suspensions:

1. **Oral Antibiotic Suspensions:** Such as amoxicillin suspension, which is used to treat infections in patients who cannot take tablets.
2. **Topical Corticosteroid Suspensions:** Used to manage skin conditions like eczema or psoriasis.
3. **Injectable Insulin Suspensions:** Designed for controlled release and management of diabetes.

ADVANTAGES OF SUSPENSIONS

Suspensions offer several benefits in pharmaceutical and industrial applications. Here's a detailed look at the advantages:

1. **Enhanced Solubility for Poorly Soluble Drugs**
    a. **Improved Bioavailability:** Suspensions can be used to administer drugs that have poor solubility in aqueous solutions. By suspending the drug particles in a liquid, it is possible to create a formulation that is easier to swallow and better absorbed in the body.
    b. **Controlled Release:** Suspensions can be formulated to provide controlled or sustained release of the drug, which can be beneficial for managing chronic conditions or ensuring consistent drug levels in the bloodstream.
2. **Taste Masking**
    a. **Improved Patient Compliance:** For medications with an unpleasant taste, suspensions can mask the taste of the active ingredient. This is particularly useful in pediatric formulations, where taste can significantly impact a child's willingness to take the medication.
3. **Flexible Dosage Forms**
    a. **Adjustable Dosing:** Suspensions allow for flexible dosing, as the concentration of the drug can be adjusted easily by changing the amount of active ingredient in the formulation. This is useful for tailoring doses to individual patient needs, especially in pediatric or geriatric populations.
4. **Ease of Administration**
    a. **Suitable for Different Patient Populations:** Suspensions are particularly advantageous for patients who have difficulty swallowing tablets or capsules, such as young children, elderly individuals, or those with certain medical conditions affecting their ability to swallow.
5. **Extended Shelf Life**
    a. **Stability of Active Ingredients:** For some drugs, suspensions can offer better stability compared to solutions. The drug particles are less likely to

degrade in a suspension compared to being dissolved in a solution, which can extend the shelf life of the medication.

6. **Customization and Versatility**
   a. **Formulation Flexibility:** Suspensions can be tailored to meet specific needs, such as modifying the viscosity, particle size, and release characteristics. This versatility allows for the development of specialized formulations for various therapeutic applications.

7. **Controlled and Targeted Delivery**
   a. **Local Treatment:** In certain cases, suspensions can be used to deliver medications directly to the site of action, such as in topical suspensions for dermatological conditions. This localized delivery can enhance the therapeutic effect while minimizing systemic side effects.

8. **Reduced Irritation**
   a. **Gentler on the Gastrointestinal Tract:** For drugs that are irritating to the gastrointestinal tract, suspensions can sometimes provide a gentler alternative to tablets or capsules, as the drug is dispersed in a liquid medium which can be less harsh on the digestive system.

9. **Viscosity Adjustment**
   a. **Improved Suspension Characteristics:** The viscosity of suspensions can be adjusted using various thickening agents and polymers. This can help in controlling the flow and stability of the suspension, making it easier to administer and manage.

10. **Cost-Effective Production**
   a. **Simplified Manufacturing:** For some drugs, suspensions can be easier and more cost-effective to produce compared to complex formulations like controlled-release tablets or injectables, especially if the active ingredient is difficult to solubilize.

DISADVANTAGES OF SUSPENSIONS

Despite their advantages, suspensions also have several drawbacks that can impact their efficacy, stability, and ease of use. Here are the detailed disadvantages:

1. Particle Settling

a. **Sedimentation:** Over time, the solid particles in a suspension tend to settle at the bottom due to gravity. This sedimentation can lead to an uneven distribution of the drug, resulting in inaccurate dosing if not properly shaken before use.

b. **Re-Suspension Difficulty:** Re-suspending the particles to ensure a uniform mixture can be challenging, particularly if the particles are prone to aggregation or if the suspension has been allowed to settle for a long period.

2. Formulation Complexity

a. **Stability Issues:** Developing a stable suspension can be complex. Ensuring that the particles remain uniformly dispersed and do not aggregate or form clumps requires careful selection of suspending agents, stabilizers, and other excipients.

b. **Viscosity Control:** Adjusting the viscosity to ensure proper flow and stability while preventing excessive thickening can be difficult. Improper viscosity can affect the ease of administration and the uniformity of the dosage.

3. Storage and Handling

a. **Storage Requirements:** Suspensions may have specific storage requirements to maintain their stability. For example, they may need to be stored in controlled temperatures or protected from light.

b. **Handling Precautions:** They require careful handling and proper agitation before use. Failure to mix properly can lead to inconsistent dosing, with a higher concentration of the drug in the sediment and a lower concentration in the supernatant.

4. Patient Compliance

a. **Taste and Texture:** While suspensions can mask unpleasant tastes, they can sometimes have an unpalatable texture or appearance, which may still affect patient compliance.

b. **Preparation Requirements:** Some suspensions require specific preparation steps before use, such as shaking or stirring, which can be inconvenient for patients or caregivers.

5. Dose Variability

a. **Inconsistent Dosage:** If not shaken properly, suspensions can lead to dose variability. The amount of active ingredient in a dose can differ depending on the distribution of particles in the suspension.

b. **Measurement Challenges:** Accurate dosing may be challenging, especially if the suspension is not uniformly mixed or if the measuring device (like a dropper or spoon) is not calibrated properly.

6. Limited Shelf Life

a. **Stability Concerns:** Suspensions may have a shorter shelf life compared to solid dosage forms due to potential chemical instability of the drug or physical instability of the suspension. Sedimentation, particle aggregation, or microbial growth can affect the suspension over time.

7. Potential for Microbial Contamination

a. **Preservation Needs:** Suspensions, especially those intended for oral use, can be prone to microbial contamination. This necessitates the inclusion of preservatives, which may not always be well-tolerated by all patients.

8. Cost and Complexity of Production

a. **Manufacturing Costs:** The production of suspensions can be more complex and expensive than that of simple solutions or tablets. This complexity arises from the need for specialized equipment and processes to ensure proper dispersion and stability.

9. Appearance and Aesthetics

a. **Visual Appeal:** Suspensions can have an unappealing appearance due to the presence of suspended particles. This can be a drawback, particularly for products intended for patient populations sensitive to visual aspects, such as children.

CLASSIFICATIONS OF SUSPENSIONS

Suspensions can be classified based on various criteria, including their intended use, particle size, and physical characteristics. Here's a detailed look at the different classifications:

1. Based on Intended Use

a. **Oral Suspensions:**
   i. **Purpose:** Administered by mouth for systemic effects.
   ii. **Characteristics:** Typically formulated to improve taste and make medication easier to swallow. They can be used for pediatric or geriatric patients who have difficulty with solid dosage forms.
   iii. **Examples:** Amoxicillin suspension, antacid suspensions.

b. **Topical Suspensions:**
   i. **Purpose:** Applied to the skin or mucous membranes for local effects.
   ii. **Characteristics:** Designed to treat dermatological conditions or provide localized relief. They are generally formulated to minimize irritation and enhance skin compatibility.
   iii. **Examples:** Corticosteroid suspensions for eczema, anti-acne treatments.

c. **Injectable Suspensions:**
   i. **Purpose:** Administered via injection for systemic effects.

   ii. **Characteristics:** Requires careful formulation to ensure that the particles remain dispersed and do not clog needles or cause adverse reactions.
   iii. **Examples:** Injectable insulin suspensions, depot formulations of certain drugs.

d. **Ophthalmic Suspensions:**
   i. **Purpose:** Applied to the eyes for local treatment.
   ii. **Characteristics:** Must be sterile and formulated to be compatible with the delicate tissues of the eye. They often include preservatives to prevent microbial contamination.
   iii. **Examples:** Antibiotic or anti-inflammatory eye drops.

e. **Nasal Suspensions:**
   i. **Purpose:** Administered via the nasal route for local or systemic effects.
   ii. **Characteristics:** Designed to deliver medications directly to the nasal mucosa. These suspensions may have specific characteristics to ensure proper delivery and absorption.
   iii. **Examples:** Nasal corticosteroids for allergic rhinitis.

2. Based on Particle Size

a. **Coarse Suspensions:**
   i. **Particle Size:** Particles larger than 10 micrometers.
   ii. **Characteristics:** These suspensions are generally less stable and prone to rapid sedimentation. They often require frequent shaking to maintain uniformity.
   iii. **Examples:** Certain topical suspensions.

b. **Fine Suspensions:**
   i. **Particle Size:** Particles between 1 and 10 micrometers.

   ii. **Characteristics:** More stable than coarse suspensions, with slower sedimentation rates. They often have improved consistency and dosing accuracy.
   iii. **Examples:** Oral antibiotic suspensions.

c. **Colloidal Suspensions:**
   i. **Particle Size:** Particles between 1 nanometer and 1 micrometer.
   ii. **Characteristics:** These suspensions have very small particles that remain dispersed for longer periods. They often exhibit high stability and require less frequent agitation.
   iii. **Examples:** Some intravenous drug formulations and certain diagnostic agents.

3. Based on Physical Characteristics

a. **Flocculated Suspensions:**
   i. **Characteristics:** Particles form loosely bound clusters (flocs) that can easily be re-suspended. These suspensions tend to have better stability and less sedimentation.
   ii. **Examples:** Certain oral suspensions with added flocculating agents.

b. **Deflocculated Suspensions:**
   i. **Characteristics:** Particles remain separate and do not form clusters. These suspensions may have a higher tendency for sedimentation and require thorough agitation to ensure uniformity.
   ii. **Examples:** Suspensions of very fine particles.

c. **Structured Vehicle Suspensions:**
   i. **Characteristics:** The dispersion medium is thickened or gelled to maintain particle dispersion and reduce sedimentation. These suspensions have enhanced stability and consistency.
   ii. **Examples:** Many oral and topical suspensions use structured vehicles to improve performance.

4. Based on Stability and Behavior

a. **Sedimentation Suspensions:**

   i. **Characteristics:** Characterized by the tendency of particles to settle over time. Requires regular shaking to ensure uniform dispersion.

   ii. **Examples:** Many over-the-counter suspensions for oral use.

b. **Reconstituted Suspensions:**

   i. **Characteristics:** Prepared as a dry powder that must be mixed with a liquid before use. These suspensions are often more stable in powder form and need to be reconstituted just before administration.

   ii. **Examples:** Some antibiotics and vaccines come in powder form that needs to be mixed with a diluent.

c. **Controlled-Release Suspensions:**

   i. **Characteristics:** Designed to release the drug gradually over time. These suspensions aim to provide prolonged therapeutic effects and reduce dosing frequency.

   ii. **Examples:** Certain oral suspensions for chronic conditions.

PREPARATION OF SUSPENSIONS

The preparation of suspensions involves several key steps to ensure that the final product is stable, uniform, and effective. Here's a detailed guide to the process:

1. Selection of Ingredients

a. **Active Ingredient:**

   i. The drug or therapeutic agent that will be suspended. It should be chosen based on its solubility, particle size, and therapeutic properties.

b. **Dispersion Medium:**

i. The liquid in which the solid particles are suspended. It could be water, oil, or an aqueous solution, depending on the nature of the drug and intended use.

c. **Suspending Agents:**

i. Polymers or agents that increase the viscosity of the dispersion medium to prevent sedimentation of particles. Examples include xanthan gum, cellulose derivatives, and alginates.

d. **Stabilizers:**

i. Compounds that prevent the aggregation of particles and enhance the stability of the suspension. Common stabilizers include surfactants and emulsifiers.

e. **Preservatives:**

i. Additives that prevent microbial growth and extend the shelf life of the suspension. Examples include benzyl alcohol and parabens.

2. Preparation Steps

a. **Particle Size Reduction:**

i. **Milling or Grinding:** The active ingredient is often reduced to a fine particle size using milling or grinding techniques. This helps in achieving a uniform suspension and preventing the particles from settling quickly.

ii. **Micronization:** In some cases, particles are micronized to enhance their dispersion and stability in the medium.

b. **Mixing:**

i. **Dry Mixing:** The active ingredient and any dry excipients (e.g., suspending agents) are blended together to ensure even distribution before adding the dispersion medium.

ii. **Wet Mixing:** The dry mixture is then gradually added to the dispersion medium while continuously stirring. This helps in achieving a uniform suspension of particles.

c. **Formation of the Suspension:**

   i. **Dispersion:** The mixture is thoroughly stirred or agitated to disperse the particles evenly throughout the medium. Equipment such as homogenizers, stirrers, or high-shear mixers may be used.

   ii. **Adjustment of Viscosity:** Suspensions are adjusted to the desired viscosity using thickening agents or suspending agents. This ensures that the particles remain suspended and the suspension flows appropriately.

d. **Incorporation of Additives:**

   i. **Addition of Stabilizers:** Stabilizers and surfactants are added to prevent particle aggregation and improve the stability of the suspension.

   ii. **Inclusion of Preservatives:** Preservatives are added to inhibit microbial growth and extend the shelf life of the suspension.

e. **Homogenization:**

   i. **High Shear Mixing:** The suspension may be subjected to high shear mixing or homogenization to ensure that the particles are uniformly distributed and to break down any agglomerates.

   ii. **Filtration:** The suspension may be filtered to remove any large particles or impurities that could affect its stability or performance.

f. **Quality Control:**

   i. **Testing for Particle Size:** Ensuring that the particle size is within the desired range for effective suspension and to prevent rapid sedimentation.

   ii **Viscosity Measurement:** Checking that the viscosity of the suspension is appropriate for its intended use.

   iii. **Stability Testing:** Assessing the stability of the suspension over time, including sedimentation rate, re-suspendability, and any potential changes in appearance or consistency.

7. Packaging:

a. **Container Selection:**

i. **Choosing Containers:** Selecting appropriate containers that can prevent contamination and maintain the stability of the suspension. Options include bottles with screw caps, squeeze tubes, or specialized dispensers.

b. **Labeling:**

i. **Instructions for Use:** Clearly labeling the container with instructions for use, storage conditions, and any required agitation before use.

ii. **Expiration Date:** Including an expiration date based on stability testing to ensure the product is used within its effective period.

c. **Filling:**

i. **Filling the Containers:** The suspension is carefully filled into containers in a controlled environment to minimize contamination and ensure accurate volume.

8. Storage and Handling:

a. **Storage Conditions:** Storing the suspension under recommended conditions to maintain its stability and prevent degradation. This may involve controlling temperature, light, and humidity.

b. **Handling Instructions:** Providing guidelines for proper handling, including shaking or stirring before use to ensure uniform dispersion of particles.

FLOCCULATED SUSPENSION

A **flocculated suspension** is a type of suspension in which the solid particles form loose clusters or "flocs" rather than settling as individual particles. This type of suspension is characterized by improved stability and better re-suspendability compared to non-flocculated or deflocculated suspensions. Here's a detailed overview:

1. **Characteristics of Flocculated Suspensions**

   a. **Particle Aggregation:** In flocculated suspensions, particles aggregate into loosely bound clusters or flocs. These flocs are held together by weak forces, such as van der Waals forces or hydrogen bonds.

   b. **Improved Re-Suspendability:** The loosely bound nature of the flocs allows for easier re-suspension upon shaking or stirring. This helps maintain uniformity in the suspension and ensures accurate dosing.

   c. **Reduced Sedimentation Rate:** Flocculated suspensions tend to have a slower sedimentation rate compared to deflocculated suspensions. The flocs settle more slowly and form a more porous sediment, which can be easily re-dispersed.

2. **Formation of Flocculated Suspensions**

   a. **Use of Flocculating Agents:**

      i. **Electrolytes:** Certain electrolytes, such as sodium chloride or potassium chloride, can induce flocculation by neutralizing the electrostatic charges on the particle surfaces. This reduces the repulsive forces between particles, allowing them to aggregate.

      ii. **Polymers and Surfactants:** Flocculating agents such as specific polymers or surfactants can promote the formation of flocs by bridging particles and facilitating their aggregation.

   b. **Controlled Conditions:**

      i. **pH Adjustment:** Adjusting the pH of the dispersion medium can influence the flocculation process. Some drugs and excipients flocculate better at specific pH levels.

      ii. **Concentration:** The concentration of the suspending agents and other excipients can be optimized to achieve the desired flocculation effect.

3. **Advantages of Flocculated Suspensions**

   a. **Enhanced Stability:**

   i. **Reduced Sedimentation:** Flocculated suspensions generally exhibit improved stability compared to non-flocculated suspensions. The flocs settle more slowly and are less likely to form a dense sediment, which can be difficult to re-suspend.

b. **Improved Re-Suspendability:**
   i. **Ease of Mixing:** Flocculated suspensions can be easily re-suspended with shaking or stirring, ensuring that the drug is evenly distributed and the dose is consistent.

c. **Minimized Caking:**
   i. **Prevention of Cake Formation:** The formation of a cake at the bottom of the container is less likely in flocculated suspensions. This helps prevent the suspension from becoming difficult to use over time.

d. **Better Flow Properties:**
   i. **Viscosity Control:** The controlled aggregation of particles in flocculated suspensions can help in achieving desired flow properties, making the suspension easier to pour or administer.

4. Preparation and Control

a. **Formulation Considerations:**
   i. **Selecting Flocculating Agents:** Choosing the right flocculating agents and optimizing their concentration is crucial for achieving the desired flocculation effect without compromising the stability of the suspension.
   ii. **Balancing Viscosity:** Proper balance of viscosity and flocculation is essential to ensure that the suspension remains uniform and easy to handle.

b. **Quality Control:**

i. **Sedimentation Rate Testing:** Monitoring the rate of sedimentation and the appearance of the sediment helps in evaluating the effectiveness of flocculation.

ii. **Re-Suspendability Testing:** Testing how well the suspension re-suspends after standing is important for ensuring that it maintains uniformity upon shaking or stirring.

c. **Storage and Handling:**

i. **Storage Conditions:** Proper storage conditions should be maintained to prevent changes in the flocculation and ensure the suspension remains stable and effective.

ii. **Handling Instructions:** Providing clear instructions for shaking or stirring before use helps in maintaining the uniformity of the suspension.

5. Examples of Flocculated Suspensions

a. **Oral Antibiotics:** Many oral antibiotic suspensions are formulated as flocculated suspensions to improve stability and ensure that the medication is evenly distributed.

b. **Topical Suspensions:** Some topical treatments for dermatological conditions are also formulated as flocculated suspensions to enhance their performance and ease of use.

DEFLOCCULATED SUSPENSION

A **deflocculated suspension** is a type of suspension in which the solid particles do not aggregate into clusters or "flocs" but instead remain dispersed as individual particles. This type of suspension has different characteristics and implications compared to flocculated suspensions. Here's a detailed overview:

1. Characteristics of Deflocculated Suspensions

a. **Individual Particle Dispersion:** In deflocculated suspensions, the particles remain separate and do not form loose aggregates. This results in a more uniform distribution of particles throughout the dispersion medium.

b. **Higher Sedimentation Rate:** Deflocculated suspensions generally have a higher rate of sedimentation compared to flocculated suspensions. The individual particles tend to settle more quickly due to their lack of aggregation, forming a dense cake at the bottom.

c. **Difficulty in Re-Suspension:** The sediment formed in deflocculated suspensions can be more difficult to re-suspend. This is because the individual particles can form a dense, hard cake that is challenging to disperse back into the liquid.

2. Formation of Deflocculated Suspensions

a. **Use of Deflocculating Agents:**

i. **Electrolytes and Surfactants:** Certain deflocculating agents, such as surfactants or electrolytes, are used to prevent particle aggregation. These agents work by increasing the repulsive forces between particles, which helps keep them dispersed.

ii. **High-Viscosity Media:** Sometimes, a high-viscosity medium is used to keep particles from settling too quickly. However, this approach does not address the underlying tendency of particles to aggregate and settle.

b. **Controlled Dispersion:**

i. **High Shear Mixing:** Intensive mixing techniques, such as high shear mixing or homogenization, can help maintain particle dispersion. However, these methods often require precise control to prevent the formation of aggregates.

3. Advantages of Deflocculated Suspensions

a. **Uniformity of Distribution:**

i. **Consistent Dosing:** Since the particles are dispersed individually, the suspension can provide a consistent dose of the active ingredient, assuming proper mixing before use.

b. **Clear Appearance:**

i. **Visual Appeal:** Deflocculated suspensions tend to have a clearer appearance because the particles do not form visible aggregates or flocs.

c. **Improved Stability for Certain Formulations:**

i. **Stability for Specific Drugs:** For some drugs or formulations, deflocculated suspensions might offer better stability in terms of chemical degradation or interaction with other components.

4. Disadvantages of Deflocculated Suspensions

a. **Increased Sedimentation Rate:**

i. **Faster Settling:** Individual particles settle more quickly and form a dense sediment, which can be challenging to re-suspend and may result in inconsistent dosing if not mixed properly.

b. **Difficulty in Re-Suspension:**

i. **Hard Cake Formation:** The sediment can form a hard cake at the bottom of the container, making it difficult to re-suspend the particles and potentially leading to dosing inaccuracies.

c. **Handling Challenges:**

i. **Agitation Requirements:** Deflocculated suspensions often require thorough agitation before use to ensure uniformity, which can be inconvenient and affect patient compliance.

5. Preparation and Control

a. **Formulation Considerations:**

i. **Selection of Deflocculating Agents:** Choosing the right deflocculating agents and optimizing their concentration is crucial for maintaining particle dispersion and preventing aggregation.

ii. **Viscosity Adjustment:** The viscosity of the dispersion medium may need to be adjusted to balance the rate of sedimentation and ease of handling.

b. **Quality Control:**

i. **Sedimentation Rate Testing:** Monitoring the rate at which particles settle helps assess the effectiveness of the deflocculation and the stability of the suspension.

ii. **Re-Suspendability Testing:** Evaluating how well the suspension re-suspends after standing is important for ensuring that it remains uniform and effective.

c. **Storage and Handling:**

i. **Storage Conditions:** Proper storage conditions should be maintained to minimize changes in the suspension and ensure its stability.

ii. **Handling Instructions:** Providing clear instructions for mixing or shaking before use helps ensure that the suspension remains uniform and that accurate dosing is achieved.

6. Examples of Deflocculated Suspensions

a. **Certain Injectable Suspensions:** Some injectable suspensions are formulated as deflocculated to ensure precise dosing and stability during storage.

b. **Specific Oral Formulations:** Oral suspensions of drugs that are more stable in a deflocculated state may be formulated this way, depending on the drug's properties and the desired therapeutic effect.

DIFFERENCE BETWEEN OF FLOCCULATED AND DEFLOCCULATED SUSPENSION

Flocculated and deflocculated suspensions are two types of particle dispersions with distinct characteristics and behaviors. Here's a detailed comparison:

1. **Particle Behavior**

   a. **Flocculated Suspension:**

      i. **Particle Aggregation:** Particles form loose clusters or "flocs" held together by weak forces (e.g., van der Waals forces, hydrogen bonds). These flocs remain loosely aggregated and are more easily re-suspended.

      ii. **Sedimentation:** Flocculated suspensions tend to settle more slowly. The sediment formed is usually porous and less dense, making it easier to re-disperse.

   b. **Deflocculated Suspension:**

      i. **Individual Dispersion:** Particles remain separate and do not aggregate into clusters. They are individually dispersed throughout the medium.

      ii. **Sedimentation:** Deflocculated suspensions have a higher sedimentation rate. The sediment formed is denser and more compact, leading to a hard cake that is challenging to re-suspend.

2. **Stability and Sedimentation**

   a. **Flocculated Suspension:**

      i. **Stability:** Generally more stable over time due to slower sedimentation and a more manageable sediment structure. The flocs settle more slowly, reducing the risk of hard cake formation.

      ii. **Re-Suspendability:** Easier to re-suspend. The loosely bound flocs can be easily redistributed with shaking or stirring, ensuring uniformity.

   b. **Deflocculated Suspension:**

      i. **Stability:** Can be less stable due to rapid sedimentation. The dense cake that forms can be difficult to re-disperse and may affect the uniformity of the suspension.

ii. **Re-Suspendability:** More challenging to re-suspend. The hard cake formed at the bottom of the container is often difficult to break up, leading to potential dosing inconsistencies.

3. Formulation and Preparation

a. **Flocculated Suspension:**

i. **Formulation:** Achieved by using flocculating agents such as electrolytes, polymers, or surfactants that induce particle aggregation. The formulation needs to be carefully balanced to ensure proper flocculation without compromising stability.

ii. **Preparation:** Often involves careful control of the concentration and type of flocculating agents, pH adjustments, and mixing conditions to achieve the desired flocculation.

b. **Deflocculated Suspension:**

i. **Formulation:** Achieved by using deflocculating agents or high-viscosity media that prevent particle aggregation. The formulation aims to keep particles individually dispersed.

ii. **Preparation:** Requires the use of deflocculating agents and potentially high-shear mixing to maintain dispersion. Care must be taken to prevent the formation of aggregates.

4. Advantages and Disadvantages

a. **Flocculated Suspension:**

i. **Advantages:**

1. **Improved Re-Suspendability:** Easier to re-disperse the particles, ensuring uniformity and accurate dosing.
2. **Reduced Caking:** Less likely to form a hard cake at the bottom of the container.
3. **Enhanced Stability:** Slower sedimentation and manageable sediment structure contribute to overall stability.

ii. **Disadvantages:**

1. **Possible Visual Appearance:** Flocculated suspensions may appear cloudy due to the presence of flocs.
2. **Complexity in Formulation:** Requires careful selection and optimization of flocculating agents.

b. **Deflocculated Suspension:**

i. **Advantages:**

1. **Clear Appearance:** Generally has a clearer appearance due to the absence of visible aggregates.
2. **Consistent Dosage:** Individual dispersion of particles can ensure uniform dosing, assuming proper mixing.

ii. **Disadvantages:**

1. **Increased Sedimentation Rate:** Particles settle more quickly, forming a dense sediment that is hard to re-suspend.
2. **Handling Challenges:** Requires thorough agitation before use to ensure uniformity and effective dosing.

5. Applications

a. **Flocculated Suspension:**

i. **Applications:** Often used in oral suspensions for antibiotics, topical suspensions, and some injectable formulations where re-suspendability and stability are critical.

b. **Deflocculated Suspension:**

i. **Applications:** Used in cases where a clear appearance is desired, or where specific drug properties necessitate individual particle dispersion. Examples include certain injectable formulations and oral suspensions

STABILITY PROBLEMS AND METHODS TO OVERCOME IN SUSPENSIONS

Suspensions, like any pharmaceutical dosage form, can face various stability issues that impact their effectiveness, safety, and quality. Addressing these problems is crucial for ensuring that suspensions maintain their intended therapeutic properties throughout their shelf life. Here's a detailed overview of common stability problems and methods to overcome them:

1. Sedimentation

Problem:

a. **Sedimentation Rate:** The rate at which particles settle out of the suspension can lead to uneven distribution of the active ingredient. In deflocculated suspensions, this problem is more pronounced due to rapid sedimentation.

Methods to Overcome:

a. **Flocculation:** Use flocculating agents to promote the formation of loose particle clusters (flocs) that settle more slowly and form a more easily re-suspendable sediment.

b. **Suspending Agents:** Incorporate suspending agents or thickeners to increase the viscosity of the dispersion medium, which helps to reduce the sedimentation rate.

c. **Optimized Formulation:** Adjust the concentration of active ingredients and excipients to achieve a balance that minimizes sedimentation while maintaining desired properties.

2. Caking

Problem:

a. **Cake Formation:** Over time, the sediment in the suspension may form a dense, hard cake at the bottom of the container, which is difficult to re-suspend and can lead to dosing inconsistencies.

Methods to Overcome:

a. **Flocculation:** Using flocculating agents can help prevent the formation of a hard cake by promoting the formation of loose aggregates.

b. **Re-suspendability Testing:** Formulate the suspension to ensure that it can be easily re-suspended with shaking or stirring, even after prolonged storage.

c. **Proper Container Design:** Use containers that facilitate easy agitation and prevent the formation of a dense cake.

3. Aggregation and Coalescence

Problem:

a. **Particle Aggregation:** Particles in the suspension may aggregate or clump together, which can lead to instability and reduced efficacy of the suspension.

Methods to Overcome:

a. **Deflocculating Agents:** Employ deflocculating agents to keep particles dispersed individually and prevent aggregation.

b. **Surfactants:** Use surfactants to stabilize the dispersion and reduce the tendency of particles to aggregate.

c. **Adjusting pH and Ionic Strength:** Optimize the pH and ionic strength of the medium to minimize particle interactions and aggregation.

4. Microbial Contamination

Problem:

a. **Microbial Growth:** Suspensions are prone to microbial contamination, which can affect their safety and efficacy.

Methods to Overcome:

a. **Preservatives:** Add preservatives, such as benzyl alcohol or parabens, to inhibit microbial growth and extend shelf life.

b. **Sterilization:** Employ sterilization methods, such as autoclaving or filtration, to ensure the suspension is free of microorganisms before packaging.

c. **Proper Packaging:** Use containers that minimize the risk of contamination and maintain the integrity of the product.

5. Chemical Degradation

Problem:

a. **Degradation of Active Ingredients:** The active ingredient in the suspension may degrade over time due to factors such as oxidation, hydrolysis, or light exposure.

Methods to Overcome:

a. **Stabilizers:** Incorporate stabilizers or antioxidants to protect the active ingredient from degradation.

b. **Light-Resistant Packaging:** Use opaque or light-resistant containers to protect the suspension from light-induced degradation.

c. **Optimal Storage Conditions:** Store the suspension under recommended conditions, such as controlled temperature and humidity, to minimize degradation.

6. Viscosity Changes

Problem:

a. **Inconsistent Viscosity:** Changes in viscosity over time can affect the flow properties and ease of use of the suspension.

Methods to Overcome:

a. **Thickeners and Gelling Agents:** Use thickeners or gelling agents to maintain consistent viscosity and prevent changes over time.

b. **Regular Quality Control:** Monitor the viscosity of the suspension during stability studies to ensure it remains within the desired range.

7. Appearance and Physical Changes

Problem:

a. **Changes in Appearance:** Suspensions may undergo physical changes such as color alteration, phase separation, or precipitation, which can affect their quality and acceptability.

Methods to Overcome:

a. **Formulation Adjustments:** Optimize the formulation to prevent unwanted physical changes, such as precipitation or phase separation.
b. **Quality Control Testing:** Conduct regular visual inspections and physical tests to monitor any changes in appearance and address them promptly.

8. Agitation and Mixing Issues

Problem:

a. **Inadequate Mixing:** Insufficient mixing or agitation before use can result in uneven distribution of the active ingredient, leading to inaccurate dosing.

Methods to Overcome:

a. **Container Design:** Use containers that facilitate effective agitation and mixing.
b. **Instructions for Use:** Provide clear instructions to users on how to properly shake or stir the suspension before use to ensure uniformity.

Multiple Choice Questions (Objective)

1. Which of the following best describes a suspension?
   A) A homogeneous mixture of two or more substances
   B) A heterogeneous mixture where solid particles are dispersed in a liquid or gas
   C) A solution where the solute is completely dissolved in the solvent
   D) A mixture where gases are dissolved in liquids
2. What is the typical size range of particles in a suspension?
   A) 0.1 nm to 1 nm
   B) 1 nm to 100 nm
   C) 1 micron to several millimeters
   D) Larger than several millimeters
3. What is the main disadvantage of suspensions compared to solutions?

A) They are easier to formulate

B) They have a longer shelf life

C) Particles can settle over time

D) They are always more stable

4. Which of the following is a common suspending agent used in suspensions?

A) Water

B) Alcohol

C) Xanthan gum

D) Sodium chloride

5. In a pharmaceutical suspension, what role do preservatives play?

A) They prevent the active ingredient from degrading

B) They increase the viscosity of the suspension

C) They prevent microbial growth

D) They help in dispersing the particles

6. What is a key characteristic of a flocculated suspension?

A) Particles remain separate and do not form aggregates

B) Particles form loose clusters that are easily re-suspended

C) The suspension is more stable due to faster sedimentation

D) The suspension has a clearer appearance

7. Which of the following is an example of an oral suspension?

A) Amoxicillin suspension

B) Injectable insulin suspension

C) Topical corticosteroid suspension

D) Ophthalmic suspension

8. What is a common method to reduce particle size in the preparation of suspensions?

A) Filtration

B) Centrifugation

C) Milling or grinding

D) Evaporation

9. Which factor is primarily responsible for the sedimentation of particles in a suspension?

    A) Viscosity of the medium

    B) Particle size and density

    C) The color of the suspension

    D) The taste of the active ingredient

10. Which of the following is a disadvantage of deflocculated suspensions?

    A) They are easier to re-suspend

    B) They have a slower sedimentation rate

    C) They form a dense cake that is hard to re-suspend

    D) They are less likely to cause irritation

11. What is the main advantage of using flocculating agents in suspensions?

    A) They prevent microbial growth

    B) They enhance the taste of the suspension

    C) They promote the formation of loose aggregates

    D) They decrease the viscosity of the suspension

12. Which type of suspension is likely to require sterilization during preparation?

    A) Oral suspension

    B) Topical suspension

    C) Injectable suspension

    D) Nasal suspension

13. What is the purpose of stabilizers in a suspension?

    A) To increase the viscosity

    B) To prevent particle aggregation

    C) To enhance the taste

    D) To reduce the particle size

14. Which method is commonly used to achieve a controlled-release suspension?

A) Use of thickening agents

B) Inclusion of preservatives

C) High shear mixing

D) Addition of polymers

15. Which of the following problems can be addressed by using suspending agents?

A) Caking

B) Microbial contamination

C) Chemical degradation

D) Particle settling

16. Why might a suspension be preferred over a solution for certain drugs?

A) Suspensions are always easier to manufacture

B) Suspensions provide a clearer appearance

C) Suspensions can mask the taste of unpleasant drugs

D) Suspensions are less prone to microbial contamination

17. What is the main difference between flocculated and deflocculated suspensions?

A) Flocculated suspensions have larger particles

B) Deflocculated suspensions are easier to re-suspend

C) Flocculated suspensions form loose clusters of particles

D) Deflocculated suspensions settle more slowly

18. Which of the following is NOT a type of suspension based on intended use?

A) Oral suspension

B) Colloidal suspension

C) Topical suspension

D) Injectable suspension

19. What does "controlled conditions" in the preparation of suspensions typically involve?

A) Adjusting particle size only

B) Balancing pH, viscosity, and temperature

C) Using preservatives exclusively

D) Avoiding the use of flocculating agents

20. What is the role of homogenization in suspension preparation?

A) To decrease the viscosity of the suspension

B) To filter out impurities

C) To ensure uniform distribution of particles

D) To reduce the size of the container

Short Answer Type Questions (Subjective)

1. Define a suspension and describe its key characteristics.
2. Explain why suspensions are often preferred for administering poorly soluble drugs.
3. What are the common components of a pharmaceutical suspension?
4. Discuss the role of suspending agents in the stability of suspensions.
5. How does particle size affect the stability of a suspension?
6. Describe the difference between flocculated and deflocculated suspensions.
7. What are the main advantages of using a flocculated suspension?
8. Why is sedimentation a concern in suspensions, and how can it be minimized?
9. Explain the importance of preservatives in the formulation of suspensions.
10. How is particle size reduction achieved in the preparation of suspensions?
11. Discuss the role of viscosity in the stability and administration of suspensions.
12. What are the potential disadvantages of using a deflocculated suspension?
13. How can caking be prevented in pharmaceutical suspensions?

14. Describe the process of homogenization and its importance in suspension preparation.
15. What are the key quality control tests for ensuring the stability of a suspension?
16. Explain the significance of re-suspendability in suspensions.
17. What are the considerations for choosing the appropriate container for a suspension?
18. Discuss the stability problems associated with microbial contamination in suspensions.
19. How can chemical degradation be minimized in suspensions?
20. What factors should be considered when designing a suspension for controlled release?

Long Answer Type Questions (Subjective)

1. Describe the classification of suspensions based on particle size and physical characteristics. Provide examples for each type.
2. Explain the preparation process of a pharmaceutical suspension, including the selection of ingredients, mixing, and quality control measures.
3. Discuss the stability problems commonly encountered in suspensions and the methods used to overcome them.
4. Compare and contrast flocculated and deflocculated suspensions in terms of their characteristics, advantages, disadvantages, and applications.
5. What are the critical factors that affect the re-suspendability of a suspension? How can these be optimized during formulation?
6. Discuss the role of flocculating and deflocculating agents in suspension formulation, including examples and their mechanisms of action.
7. Explain the significance of viscosity control in suspensions and the methods used to adjust viscosity during formulation.

8. Describe the impact of particle aggregation and coalescence on the stability of suspensions and the strategies used to prevent these issues.
9. What are the specific challenges associated with the storage and handling of suspensions, and how can these be addressed in pharmaceutical practice?
10. Analyze the importance of controlled release in suspension formulations and the methods used to achieve this therapeutic goal.

Answer Key for MCQs

1. B)
2. C)
3. C)
4. C)
5. C)
6. B)
7. A)
8. C)
9. B)
10. C)
11. C)
12. C)
13. B)
14. D)
15. D)
16. C)
17. C)
18. B)
19. B)
20. C)

CHAPTER – 10

EMULSIONS

INTRODUCTION:

Emulsions are a type of colloidal system where two immiscible liquids are mixed together with the help of an emulsifying agent. In an emulsion, one liquid is dispersed as small droplets throughout the other. Emulsions are commonly encountered in various fields, including pharmaceuticals, cosmetics, and food industries.

Types of Emulsions:

1. **Oil-in-Water (O/W) Emulsion:**
    a. **Description**: Oil droplets are dispersed in water.
    b. **Examples**: Milk, some topical medications, and certain cosmetic creams.
2. **Water-in-Oil (W/O) Emulsion:**
    a. **Description**: Water droplets are dispersed in oil.
    b. **Examples**: Butter, some ointments, and certain types of sunscreen.

Components of Emulsions:

1. **Dispersed Phase**: The liquid that is distributed in the form of droplets (either oil or water).
2. **Continuous Phase**: The liquid in which the dispersed phase is distributed.
3. **Emulsifier (or Stabilizer)**: A substance that helps to stabilize the emulsion by reducing the surface tension between the two immiscible liquids. Emulsifiers have both hydrophilic (water-attracting) and lipophilic (oil-attracting) properties.

Formation of Emulsions:

Emulsions are created through the process of mixing the two immiscible liquids together with mechanical agitation, such as stirring or shaking. The emulsifier plays a crucial role by lowering the interfacial tension between the liquids, allowing for the formation of smaller droplets and enhancing the stability of the mixture.

Types of Emulsifiers:

1. **Surfactants**: Compounds with both hydrophilic and lipophilic groups, such as lecithin, polysorbates, and sodium lauryl sulfate.
2. **Hydrocolloids**: Polysaccharides like xanthan gum and guar gum, which help in stabilizing the emulsion by increasing the viscosity of the continuous phase.
3. **Proteins:** Such as casein in milk or gelatin, which can act as emulsifying agents.

Properties of Emulsions:

1. **Stability**: The ability of the emulsion to maintain its uniform dispersion of droplets over time. Stability can be influenced by factors like the type and concentration of emulsifier, temperature, and the ratio of the dispersed to continuous phase.
2. **Viscosity**: The thickness or flow resistance of the emulsion, which can affect its application and performance.
3. **Appearance**: The visual characteristics, including color and opacity, which can be influenced by the size and distribution of droplets.

Applications of Emulsions:

1. **Pharmaceuticals:** Emulsions are used to deliver drugs in a more palatable or effective form, such as in topical creams, oral suspensions, and intravenous emulsions.
2. **Cosmetics**: Emulsions are common in lotions, creams, and makeup products, providing desired textures and moisturizing effects.

3. **Food Industry**: Emulsions are used in products like mayonnaise, salad dressings, and sauces, where they contribute to texture, stability, and flavor.

Challenges in Emulsion Formulation:

1. **Instability**: Emulsions can be prone to breaking down over time, leading to phase separation or droplet coalescence.
2. **Preservation**: Emulsions may be susceptible to microbial contamination, requiring appropriate preservatives.
3. **Manufacturing**: Achieving a consistent emulsion can be challenging and requires precise control of the formulation and processing conditions.

DEFINITION OF EMULSIONS

An emulsion is a type of colloidal system in which two immiscible liquids are combined to form a stable mixture. In an emulsion, one liquid (known as the dispersed phase) is dispersed in the form of tiny droplets throughout another liquid (known as the continuous phase). The stability of this dispersion is achieved with the help of an emulsifying agent, which lowers the interfacial tension between the two liquids and helps to prevent the droplets from coalescing or separating out.

Key Points:

1. **Colloidal System:** Emulsions are a subclass of colloidal systems, meaning the dispersed droplets are typically in the range of 1 nanometer to 1 micrometer in size, which makes them visible under a microscope but not to the naked eye.
2. **Immiscibility:** The two liquids in an emulsion are immiscible, meaning they do not naturally mix together. Common examples include oil and water.
3. **Dispersed and Continuous Phases:**
    a. **Dispersed Phase:** The liquid that is distributed throughout the continuous phase in the form of droplets. In an oil-in-water

emulsion, the dispersed phase is oil; in a water-in-oil emulsion, the dispersed phase is water.

   b. **Continuous Phase:** The liquid in which the dispersed phase is suspended. In an oil-in-water emulsion, the continuous phase is water; in a water-in-oil emulsion, the continuous phase is oil.

4. **Emulsifying Agent (Emulsifier):** A substance added to stabilize the emulsion by reducing the surface tension between the two immiscible liquids. Emulsifiers typically have both hydrophilic (water-attracting) and lipophilic (oil-attracting) properties. Examples include surfactants, proteins, and polymers.
5. **Stability:** For an emulsion to remain stable, the emulsifying agent must effectively keep the droplets dispersed and prevent them from coalescing. The stability of an emulsion is influenced by the choice and concentration of the emulsifier, the ratio of the dispersed to continuous phase, and external factors such as temperature and agitation.

CLASSIFICATION OF EMULSIONS

Emulsions can be classified based on the nature of their dispersed and continuous phases. This classification helps in understanding their behavior, stability, and applications. Here's a detailed classification:

1. Based on the Dispersed and Continuous Phases:

1. **Oil-in-Water (O/W) Emulsions:**
   a. **Description:** In these emulsions, oil droplets are dispersed in water. The continuous phase is water.
   b. **Characteristics:** These emulsions generally have a watery feel and are often used in products where a lighter texture is desirable.
   c. **Examples:** Milk, some topical creams, and oral drug formulations.
2. **Water-in-Oil (W/O) Emulsions:**
   a. **Description:** In these emulsions, water droplets are dispersed in oil. The continuous phase is oil.

b. **Characteristics:** These emulsions tend to be greasier and more occlusive, making them suitable for products requiring moisturizing properties.
c. **Examples:** Butter, certain ointments, and some types of sunscreens.

3. **Multiple Emulsions (Complex Emulsions):**
    a. **Description:** These are emulsions within emulsions, where one type of emulsion is dispersed within another. They can be classified further into:
        i. **Oil-in-Water-in-Oil (O/W/O) Emulsions:** An oil-in-water emulsion dispersed in a continuous oil phase.
        ii. **Water-in-Oil-in-Water (W/O/W) Emulsions:** A water-in-oil emulsion dispersed in a continuous water phase.
    b. **Characteristics:** Multiple emulsions are used to achieve specific release profiles or to incorporate multiple active ingredients.
    c. **Examples:** Certain advanced drug delivery systems and complex cosmetic formulations.

2. Based on the Type of Emulsifier Used:

1. **Surface Active Agents (Surfactants):**
    a. **Description:** These emulsifiers have both hydrophilic and lipophilic properties, which help stabilize the emulsion by reducing interfacial tension.
    b. **Examples:** Lecithin, polysorbates (e.g., Tween), and sodium lauryl sulfate.
2. **Hydrocolloids:**
    a. **Description:** Polysaccharides or polymers that increase the viscosity of the continuous phase, helping to stabilize the emulsion through thickening.
    b. **Examples:** Xanthan gum, guar gum, and alginates.

3. **Proteins:**
    a. **Description:** Proteins can act as emulsifiers due to their ability to interact with both aqueous and oily phases.
    b. **Examples:** Casein (in milk) and gelatin.
4. **Particulate Emulsifiers:**
    a. **Description:** Solid particles that stabilize emulsions by forming a film around droplets.
    b. **Examples:** Silica particles and clay.

3. Based on the Droplet Size:

1. **Macroemulsions:**
    a. **Description:** These emulsions have relatively large droplets (typically 1 micrometer or more) and are commonly used in everyday products.
    b. **Examples:** Most food emulsions and topical creams.
2. **Microemulsions:**
    a. **Description:** These emulsions have very small droplets (typically 10-100 nanometers), resulting in a clear or translucent appearance.
    b. **Examples:** Certain pharmaceuticals and enhanced drug delivery systems.
3. **Nanoscale Emulsions:**
    a. **Description:** These have droplets in the nanometer range (less than 100 nanometers), offering unique properties and stability.
    b. **Examples:** Advanced drug delivery systems and high-tech cosmetic formulations.

4. Based on Physical Appearance:

1. **Creams:**
    a. **Description:** Semi-solid emulsions used in cosmetics and pharmaceuticals.
    b. **Examples:** Facial creams and topical ointments.

2. **Lotions:**
    a. **Description:** Thin, fluid emulsions often used for moisturization or medicinal purposes.
    b. **Examples:** Body lotions and topical solutions.
3. **Gels:**
    a. **Description:** Emulsions with a gel-like consistency, often used for controlled release of active ingredients.
    b. **Examples:** Gel-based sunscreens and topical medications.

5. Based on Stability:

1. **Stable Emulsions:**
    a. **Description:** Emulsions that maintain their dispersion of droplets over time without significant phase separation or coalescence.
2. **Unstable Emulsions:**
    a. **Description:** Emulsions prone to breaking down over time, leading to phase separation or droplet aggregation.

EMULSIFYING AGENT

Emulsifying agents, also known as emulsifiers, are substances that help stabilize emulsions by reducing the surface tension between the immiscible liquids (e.g., oil and water) and preventing the droplets from coalescing. They play a crucial role in forming and maintaining the stability of emulsions. Here's a detailed look at emulsifying agents:

1. Types of Emulsifying Agents:

a. **Surfactants (Surface-Active Agents):**
    i. **Description:** Surfactants have both hydrophilic (water-attracting) and lipophilic (oil-attracting) groups, which help to reduce the interfacial tension between the oil and water phases.
    ii. **Examples:**

1. **Nonionic Surfactants:** Such as polysorbates (e.g., Tween 80), which are used in a variety of applications due to their stability across different pH levels and temperatures.
2. **Anionic Surfactants:** Such as sodium lauryl sulfate, which are commonly used in detergents and shampoos.
3. **Cationic Surfactants:** Such as cetyltrimethylammonium bromide, which are used in hair conditioners and fabric softeners.
4. **Amphoteric Surfactants:** Such as lecithin, which has both positive and negative charges, making it useful in various formulations.

b. **Hydrocolloids:**

i. **Description:** Hydrocolloids are polysaccharides or polymers that increase the viscosity of the continuous phase and can help stabilize emulsions by thickening the solution and reducing droplet movement.

ii. **Examples:**

1. **Gums:** Such as xanthan gum, guar gum, and agar.
2. **Pectins:** Derived from fruits and used in jams and jellies.
3. **Alginate:** Derived from seaweed and used in various food and pharmaceutical products.

c. **Proteins:**

i. **Description:** Proteins can act as emulsifiers due to their ability to interact with both aqueous and oily phases, forming a protective layer around droplets

ii. **Examples:**

1. **Casein:** Found in milk, used in dairy products.
2. **Gelatin:** Used in confections and pharmaceuticals.

3. **Whey Protein:** Used in various food and beverage applications.

d. **Particulate Emulsifiers:**

i. **Description:** Solid particles that stabilize emulsions by forming a physical barrier around droplets or through interactions with the liquid phases.

ii. **Examples:**

1. **Silica Particles:** Used in some cosmetics and pharmaceuticals.
2. **Clay:** Such as bentonite, used in certain industrial and cosmetic products.

e. **Polymers:**

i. **Description:** Large molecules that can stabilize emulsions by increasing the viscosity of the continuous phase and forming a protective layer around droplets.

ii. **Examples:**

1. **Polyethylene Glycol (PEG):** Used in pharmaceuticals and cosmetics.
2. **Polyvinyl Alcohol (PVA):** Used in various industrial and consumer products.

2. Mechanism of Action:

a. **Reduction of Interfacial Tension:**

i. Emulsifiers reduce the surface tension at the interface between the oil and water phases, allowing for the formation of smaller droplets and a more stable dispersion.

b. **Formation of a Stabilizing Film:**

i. Emulsifiers form a film around the droplets, preventing them from coalescing and separating out. This film can be hydrophilic, lipophilic, or both, depending on the nature of the emulsifier.

c. **Increasing Viscosity:**

   i. By increasing the viscosity of the continuous phase, emulsifiers reduce the mobility of droplets, which helps prevent them from merging.

3. Selection Criteria:

a. **Compatibility:**

   i. The emulsifier must be compatible with the other components in the formulation, including the oil and water phases, as well as any active ingredients.

b. **Stability:**

   i. The emulsifier should provide long-term stability to the emulsion, preventing phase separation or droplet aggregation over time.

c. **Regulatory Approval:**

   i. For pharmaceuticals and food products, the emulsifier must be approved by regulatory agencies for safety and efficacy.

d. **Functionality:**

   i. The choice of emulsifier depends on the desired properties of the final product, such as texture, appearance, and ease of application.

4. Applications:

a. **Pharmaceuticals:**

   i. Emulsifiers are used in topical creams, oral suspensions, and intravenous emulsions to improve drug delivery and patient compliance.

b. **Cosmetics:**

   i. Emulsifiers are essential in lotions, creams, and makeup products to achieve desired textures and stability.

c. **Food Industry:**

   i. Emulsifiers are used in products like mayonnaise, salad dressings, and sauces to maintain texture and prevent separation.

d. **Industrial Applications:**

   i. Emulsifiers are used in paints, coatings, and lubricants to enhance performance and stability.

TEST FOR THE IDENTIFICATION OF TYPE OF EMULSION

Identifying the type of emulsion (oil-in-water [O/W] or water-in-oil [W/O]) is crucial for determining its application and stability. Several tests and methods can be used to identify the type of emulsion. Here's a detailed overview of these tests:

1. Dilution Test:

a. **Oil-in-Water (O/W) Emulsion:**

   i. **Procedure:** Add a few drops of the emulsion to water. If the emulsion is O/W, it will readily mix with water, forming a uniform solution.

   ii. **Observation:** The emulsion will disperse in water, indicating that it is an O/W emulsion.

b. **Water-in-Oil (W/O) Emulsion:**

   i. **Procedure:** Add a few drops of the emulsion to oil. If the emulsion is W/O, it will mix with oil, forming a uniform mixture.

   ii. **Observation:** The emulsion will disperse in oil, indicating that it is a W/O emulsion.

2. Conductivity Test:

a. **Oil-in-Water (O/W) Emulsion:**

   i. **Procedure:** Measure the electrical conductivity of the emulsion using a conductivity meter. O/W emulsions typically conduct electricity because water, the continuous phase, is a good conductor.

   ii. **Observation:** A high conductivity reading indicates an O/W emulsion.

b. **Water-in-Oil (W/O) Emulsion:**

i. **Procedure:** Measure the electrical conductivity of the emulsion. W/O emulsions generally have low conductivity because the water is dispersed as droplets in the oil, which is a poor conductor.

ii. **Observation:** A low conductivity reading indicates a W/O emulsion.

3. Dye Test:

a. **Oil-in-Water (O/W) Emulsion:**

i. **Procedure:** Add a water-soluble dye to the emulsion. If it is an O/W emulsion, the dye will evenly distribute throughout the emulsion.

ii. **Observation:** A uniform color throughout the emulsion indicates an O/W type.

b. **Water-in-Oil (W/O) Emulsion:**

i. **Procedure:** Add an oil-soluble dye to the emulsion. If it is a W/O emulsion, the dye will color the oil phase and not mix well with water.

ii. **Observation:** A distinct coloration in the oil phase indicates a W/O type.

4. Microscopic Examination:

a. **Oil-in-Water (O/W) Emulsion:**

i. **Procedure:** Use a microscope to examine the emulsion. O/W emulsions will show small oil droplets dispersed in a continuous aqueous phase.

ii. **Observation:** Small, well-dispersed droplets in a clear aqueous medium indicate an O/W emulsion.

b. **Water-in-Oil (W/O) Emulsion:**

i. **Procedure:** Use a microscope to examine the emulsion. W/O emulsions will show small water droplets dispersed in a continuous oil phase.

ii. **Observation:** Small water droplets in an oily medium indicate a W/O emulsion.

5. Spreadability Test:

a. **Oil-in-Water (O/W) Emulsion:**

i. **Procedure:** Place a small amount of the emulsion on a flat surface and spread it with a spatula. O/W emulsions tend to spread easily due to their water content.

ii. **Observation:** If the emulsion spreads easily and forms a thin layer, it is likely an O/W emulsion.

b. **Water-in-Oil (W/O) Emulsion:**

i. **Procedure:** Perform the same spreading test as above. W/O emulsions are typically thicker and more resistant to spreading.

ii. **Observation:** If the emulsion resists spreading and feels greasy, it is likely a W/O emulsion.

6. Smell and Feel Test:

a. **Oil-in-Water (O/W) Emulsion:**

i. **Procedure:** Observe the texture and smell of the emulsion. O/W emulsions often have a lighter, more watery feel and may not have a strong oily smell.

ii. **Observation:** A light, less greasy feel suggests an O/W emulsion.

b. **Water-in-Oil (W/O) Emulsion:**

i. **Procedure:** Observe the texture and smell. W/O emulsions usually have a thicker, greasier feel and a more pronounced oily smell.

ii. **Observation:** A thick, greasy texture indicates a W/O emulsion.

METHODS OF PREPARATION OF EMULSIONS

The preparation of emulsions involves combining two immiscible liquids (such as oil and water) with the aid of emulsifying agents to create a stable mixture. The choice of preparation method depends on the desired characteristics of the emulsion, including its stability, droplet size, and intended application. Here's a detailed overview of various methods for preparing emulsions:

1. Mechanical Methods:

a. **High-Shear Mixing:**

i. **Description:** This method uses high-shear mixers or homogenizers to apply intense mechanical force to the mixture, breaking the dispersed phase into fine droplets.

ii. **Equipment:** High-shear mixers, rotor-stator homogenizers, and colloid mills.

iii. **Procedure:** The oil and water phases, along with the emulsifier, are mixed under high shear conditions to form a uniform emulsion.

iv. **Advantages:** Produces emulsions with small droplet sizes and high stability.

b. **Homogenization:**

i. **Description:** A specific type of high-shear mixing that involves forcing the mixture through a narrow gap to achieve intense turbulence and droplet breakup.

ii. **Equipment:** Homogenizers (e.g., high-pressure homogenizers).

iii. **Procedure:** The emulsion is forced through a homogenization valve, resulting in reduced droplet size and improved stability.

iv. **Advantages:** Provides precise control over droplet size and consistency.

c. **Stirring or Agitation:**

i. **Description:** Mechanical stirring or agitation is used to mix the phases and emulsify the liquids.

ii. **Equipment:** Magnetic stirrers, overhead stirrers

iii. **Procedure:** The oil and water phases, along with emulsifiers, are stirred vigorously until a stable emulsion is formed.

iv. **Advantages:** Simple and cost-effective, suitable for low-viscosity emulsions.

2. Physical Methods:

a. **Ultrasonication:**

i. **Description:** Uses ultrasonic waves to create high shear forces and cavitation, which help break up the dispersed phase into smaller droplets.

ii. **Equipment:** Ultrasonicators.

iii. **Procedure:** The emulsion is exposed to ultrasonic waves, resulting in droplet size reduction and improved stability.

iv. **Advantages:** Effective for creating nano-sized droplets and stable emulsions.

b. **Microwaving:**

i. **Description:** Uses microwave energy to heat and mix the phases, facilitating emulsification.

ii. **Equipment:** Microwave reactors.

iii. **Procedure:** The emulsion components are exposed to microwave radiation, which helps disperse the droplets.

iv. **Advantages:** Fast and efficient, can enhance emulsifier performance.

3. Chemical Methods:

a. **Phase Inversion:**

i. **Description:** Involves changing the emulsion type by altering the phase volume ratio or the temperature, which can lead to inversion from O/W to W/O or vice versa.

ii. **Procedure:** The emulsion is prepared under conditions that gradually invert the phase ratio or temperature, resulting in a different emulsion type.

iii. **Advantages:** Allows for the creation of multiple emulsion types.

b. **Solvent Evaporation:**
    i. **Description:** Emulsifiers are dissolved in a solvent that is then evaporated to leave behind a stable emulsion.
    ii. **Procedure:** The emulsifier solution is mixed with the oil and water phases, and the solvent is evaporated, forming the emulsion.
    iii. **Advantages:** Useful for encapsulating sensitive ingredients.

4. Phase Separation Methods:

a. **Adding Emulsifiers Directly:**
    i. **Description:** Emulsifiers are added directly to the mixture of oil and water, facilitating the formation of the emulsion.
    ii. **Procedure:** The emulsifier is added to either the oil or water phase, then mixed to form the emulsion.
    iii. **Advantages:** Straightforward and suitable for many types of emulsions.

b. **Inversion Point Method:**
    i. **Description:** Involves preparing an emulsion by first forming a specific type of emulsion (O/W or W/O) and then inverting it to the other type.
    ii. **Procedure:** Start with an emulsion type and gradually add components or adjust conditions to achieve the desired emulsion type.
    iii. **Advantages:** Useful for creating specific emulsion characteristics.

5. Industrial Methods:

a. **Static Mixers:**
    i. **Description:** Uses static elements to mix the phases and emulsifiers without moving parts.
    ii. **Equipment:** Static mixer units.
    iii. **Procedure:** The oil and water phases, along with emulsifiers, flow through a static mixer, which induces mixing and emulsification.

iv. **Advantages:** Continuous process, suitable for large-scale production.

b. **High-Speed Dispersers:**

i. **Description:** Uses high-speed rotating blades to disperse one phase into another.

ii. **Equipment:** High-speed dispersers.

iii. **Procedure:** The dispersed phase is introduced into the continuous phase under high-speed conditions.

iv. **Advantages:** Effective for creating emulsions with controlled droplet sizes.

STABILITY PROBLEMS AND METHODS TO OVERCOME IN EMULSIONS

Emulsions are prone to various stability issues due to the nature of their components and the interactions between them. Addressing these stability problems is crucial for ensuring that emulsions maintain their desired properties over time. Here's a detailed look at common stability problems and methods to overcome them:

Phase Separation:

Phase separation is a common stability problem in emulsions, where the dispersed phase (e.g., oil droplets) either rises to the top (creaming) or settles to the bottom (sedimentation). This separation can compromise the uniformity and effectiveness of the emulsion. Here's a detailed look at phase separation and methods to overcome it:

1. Creaming:

Definition: Creaming is the phenomenon where the dispersed phase (e.g., oil droplets) rises to the top of the emulsion, forming a layer of concentrated droplets.

Causes:

a. **Density Difference:** A significant difference in density between the dispersed phase and the continuous phase.
b. **Droplet Size:** Larger droplets are more likely to cream because they are less stable and more affected by buoyancy forces.

Methods to Overcome Creaming:

a. **Increase Viscosity of Continuous Phase:**
   i. **Description:** Adding thickening agents or hydrocolloids to increase the viscosity of the continuous phase (e.g., water).
   ii. **Examples:** Xanthan gum, guar gum, pectin, and alginate.
   iii. **Effect:** Higher viscosity reduces the mobility of droplets, decreasing the tendency for them to rise.
b. **Use of Stabilizers:**
   i. **Description:** Adding stabilizers to prevent droplet aggregation and creaming.
   ii. **Examples:** Emulsifying agents such as polysorbates or lecithin.
   iii. **Effect:** Stabilizers create a protective barrier around droplets, reducing their tendency to coalesce and cream.
c. **Optimize Emulsifier Concentration:**
   i. **Description:** Ensuring an appropriate concentration of emulsifiers to stabilize the droplets.
   ii. **Examples:** Emulsifiers like Tween 80 or Span 60.
   iii. **Effect:** Proper emulsifier concentration enhances droplet stability and reduces creaming.
d. **Reduce Droplet Size:**
   i. **Description:** Using high-shear mixers or homogenizers to create smaller droplets.
   ii. **Examples:** High-pressure homogenizers or rotor-stator mixers.
   iii. **Effect:** Smaller droplets rise more slowly, reducing creaming.
e. **Control Storage Conditions:**

i. **Description:** Storing emulsions under controlled temperature and conditions to prevent creaming.
ii. **Examples:** Store at a consistent temperature and avoid extreme conditions.
iii. **Effect:** Stable storage conditions minimize changes in emulsion stability.

2. Sedimentation:

Definition: Sedimentation is the process where the dispersed phase settles at the bottom of the emulsion container.

Causes:

a. **Density Difference:** A significant density difference between the dispersed phase and the continuous phase.
b. **Droplet Size:** Larger droplets are more likely to sediment due to gravity.

Methods to Overcome Sedimentation:

a. **Increase Viscosity of Continuous Phase:**
   i. **Description:** Similar to preventing creaming, increasing the viscosity of the continuous phase helps suspend droplets.
   ii. **Examples:** Use thickening agents or hydrocolloids.
   iii. **Effect:** Higher viscosity reduces the rate at which droplets settle.
b. **Optimize Emulsifier Concentration:**
   i. **Description:** Ensuring adequate emulsifier concentration to keep droplets suspended.
   ii. **Examples:** Emulsifiers that provide effective stabilization.
   iii. **Effect:** Proper emulsifier levels help maintain droplet dispersion and prevent settling.
c. **Reduce Droplet Size:**
   i. **Description:** Using techniques to create smaller droplets that are less affected by gravity.

ii. **Examples:** Homogenization or high-shear mixing.

iii. **Effect:** Smaller droplets settle more slowly, reducing sedimentation.

d. **Use of Stabilizers:**

i. **Description:** Adding stabilizers to improve the stability of the dispersed phase.

ii. **Examples:** Gums, proteins, or polymeric stabilizers.

iii. **Effect:** Stabilizers help maintain droplet dispersion and prevent settling.

e. **Increase Density of Continuous Phase:**

i. **Description:** Adjusting the density of the continuous phase to be closer to that of the dispersed phase.

ii. **Examples:** Adding density-modifying agents.

iii. **Effect:** Reducing the density difference decreases the tendency for sedimentation.

3. General Strategies to Improve Emulsion Stability:

a. **Proper Emulsifier Selection:**

i. **Description:** Choose emulsifiers that match the desired type of emulsion (O/W or W/O) and provide adequate stabilization.

ii. **Examples:** Nonionic surfactants, ionic surfactants, or proteins.

iii. **Effect:** Effective emulsifiers enhance overall stability and reduce phase separation.

b. **Control Formulation Parameters:**

i. **Description:** Optimize the formulation by adjusting the ratio of oil to water and the concentration of emulsifiers and stabilizers.

ii. **Examples:** Formulation adjustments based on desired emulsion properties.

iii. **Effect:** Proper formulation ensures a balanced emulsion and reduces phase separation.

c. **Minimize Air Entrapment:**
    i. **Description:** Avoid introducing air during preparation, as it can affect stability.
    ii. **Examples:** Use proper mixing techniques to avoid air bubbles.
    iii. **Effect:** Reducing air entrapment improves the stability of the emulsion.

d. **Temperature Control:**
    i. **Description:** Maintain consistent temperature during preparation and storage.
    ii. **Examples:** Use temperature-controlled equipment and storage conditions.
    iii. **Effect:** Stable temperature helps prevent changes in emulsion stability.

Physical Stability Issues:

Physical stability issues in emulsions relate to changes in the physical properties of the emulsion, such as droplet size, dispersion, and phase behavior. These issues can affect the appearance, texture, and effectiveness of the emulsion. Here's a detailed look at common physical stability issues and methods to overcome them:

1. Ostwald Ripening:

Definition: Ostwald ripening is a process where larger droplets in an emulsion grow at the expense of smaller ones due to differences in solubility. The smaller droplets dissolve into the continuous phase and redeposit onto larger droplets, leading to an increase in droplet size.

Causes:

a. Differences in the solubility of droplets.
b. High temperatures that accelerate the diffusion of molecules.

Methods to Overcome Ostwald Ripening:

a. **Use of Emulsifiers with Good Stabilization:**

    i. **Description:** Choose emulsifiers that provide strong steric or electrostatic stabilization to reduce droplet coalescence.
    ii. **Examples:** High molecular weight polymers or surfactants with long hydrophilic chains.
    iii. **Effect:** Stronger emulsifier layers prevent the migration of molecules and stabilize droplet size.

b. **Control Storage Temperature:**
    i. **Description:** Store emulsions at lower temperatures to slow down the diffusion rates and minimize ripening.
    ii. **Examples:** Refrigerated or controlled temperature storage.
    iii. **Effect:** Reduced temperature slows the ripening process and helps maintain droplet size.

c. **Optimize Droplet Size:**
    i. **Description:** Use homogenization or high-shear mixing to create smaller droplets that are less susceptible to ripening.
    ii. **Examples:** High-pressure homogenizers or microfluidizers.
    iii. **Effect:** Smaller droplets are less likely to dissolve and redeposit, reducing ripening.

2. Phase Inversion:

Definition: Phase inversion occurs when an emulsion changes from one type (e.g., oil-in-water [O/W]) to another type (e.g., water-in-oil [W/O]) due to changes in formulation conditions or environmental factors.

Causes:

a. Changes in the ratio of oil to water.
b. Temperature fluctuations.
c. Variations in emulsifier concentration.

Methods to Overcome Phase Inversion:

a. **Optimize Emulsifier Concentration:**

i. **Description:** Ensure that the concentration of emulsifiers is appropriate for the type of emulsion and its intended use.
ii. **Examples:** Adjusting the amount of emulsifier based on the oil-to-water ratio.
iii. **Effect:** Proper emulsifier concentration helps maintain the emulsion type and prevents inversion.

b. **Maintain Stable Formulation Conditions:**
i. **Description:** Keep the oil-to-water ratio and other formulation parameters constant.
ii. **Examples:** Precise formulation and mixing processes.
iii. **Effect:** Consistent conditions prevent changes in emulsion type.

c. **Control Temperature:**
i. **Description:** Avoid temperature fluctuations that can lead to phase inversion.
ii. **Examples:** Use temperature-controlled equipment and storage conditions.
iii. **Effect:** Stable temperature conditions help maintain the emulsion type.

3. Droplet Aggregation (Flocculation):

Definition: Flocculation is the process where dispersed droplets cluster together to form aggregates, leading to instability.

Causes:

a. Weak emulsifier layers.
b. High concentrations of electrolytes or salts.
c. Poor emulsifier compatibility.

Methods to Overcome Droplet Aggregation:

a. **Improve Emulsifier Compatibility:**
i. **Description:** Use emulsifiers that provide strong steric or electrostatic repulsion between droplets.

ii. **Examples:** Surfactants with appropriate hydrophilic-lipophilic balance (HLB) values.

iii. **Effect:** Enhanced repulsion reduces aggregation and improves stability.

b. **Control Electrolyte Concentration:**

i. **Description:** Reduce the concentration of electrolytes that can disrupt the emulsifier layers and cause aggregation.

ii. **Examples:** Use low-salt or salt-free formulations.

iii. **Effect:** Lower electrolyte concentration prevents destabilization and flocculation.

c. **Use of Stabilizers:**

i. **Description:** Add stabilizers to prevent droplet aggregation and improve stability.

ii. **Examples:** Gums, proteins, or polymers that provide additional steric stabilization.

iii. **Effect:** Stabilizers help maintain droplet dispersion and prevent aggregation.

4. Creaming and Sedimentation:

Definition: Creaming and sedimentation are processes where the dispersed phase rises to the top (creaming) or settles at the bottom (sedimentation) of the emulsion container.

Causes:

a. Density differences between the dispersed and continuous phases.

b. Large droplet sizes.

Methods to Overcome Creaming and Sedimentation:

a. **Increase Viscosity of Continuous Phase:**

i. **Description:** Add thickening agents or hydrocolloids to increase the viscosity of the continuous phase.

ii. **Examples:** Xanthan gum, guar gum, or pectin.

iii. **Effect:** Higher viscosity reduces the rate of creaming and sedimentation by hindering droplet movement.

b. **Reduce Droplet Size:**

i. **Description:** Use high-shear mixing or homogenization to create smaller droplets.

ii. **Examples:** High-pressure homogenizers or rotor-stator mixers.

iii. **Effect:** Smaller droplets rise or settle more slowly, improving stability.

c. **Optimize Emulsifier Concentration:**

i. **Description:** Ensure appropriate emulsifier levels to maintain droplet dispersion.

ii. **Examples:** Use emulsifiers that stabilize the dispersion effectively.

iii. **Effect:** Proper emulsifier concentration helps prevent creaming and sedimentation.

5. Microbial Contamination:

Definition: Microbial contamination occurs when microorganisms grow in the emulsion, leading to instability and potential spoilage.

Causes:

a. Presence of water, nutrients, and inadequate preservation.

Methods to Overcome Microbial Contamination:

a. **Add Preservatives:**

i. **Description:** Incorporate antimicrobial agents to inhibit microbial growth.

ii. **Examples:** Parabens, phenoxyethanol, or natural preservatives.

iii. **Effect:** Preservatives help maintain emulsion stability and prevent spoilage.

b. **Maintain Good Hygiene:**

i. **Description:** Ensure clean and sterile conditions during preparation and storage.

ii. **Examples:** Use sterilized equipment and clean production environments.

iii. **Effect:** Reduces the risk of microbial contamination and maintains stability.

Chemical Stability Issues:

Chemical stability issues in emulsions involve reactions and degradations that affect the quality and efficacy of the product over time. These issues can lead to changes in the composition, color, odor, or functionality of the emulsion. Here's a detailed look at common chemical stability problems and methods to overcome them:

1. Oxidation:

Definition: Oxidation is a chemical reaction where the dispersed phase (especially oils) reacts with oxygen, leading to degradation and formation of undesirable by-products.

Causes:

a. Exposure to air and light.
b. Presence of metals or catalysts.
c. High temperatures.

Methods to Overcome Oxidation:

a. **Incorporate Antioxidants:**

i. **Description:** Add antioxidants to the emulsion to inhibit oxidative reactions.

ii. **Examples:** Vitamin E (tocopherol), ascorbic acid, BHT (butylated hydroxytoluene), BHA (butylated hydroxyanisole).

iii. **Effect:** Antioxidants scavenge free radicals and slow down oxidation.

b. **Use of Oxygen Scavengers:**

i. **Description:** Include substances that remove oxygen from the emulsion or packaging.

ii. **Examples:** Oxygen absorbers or scavengers.

iii. **Effect:** Reduces the amount of dissolved oxygen and minimizes oxidation.

c. **Store in Opaque Containers:**

i. **Description:** Use containers that block light to prevent photoxidation.

ii. **Examples:** Amber or dark-colored bottles.

iii. **Effect:** Protects the emulsion from light-induced oxidation.

d. **Control Storage Conditions:**

i. **Description:** Store the emulsion at lower temperatures to slow down oxidative reactions.

ii. **Examples:** Refrigeration or cool storage.

iii. **Effect:** Reduces the rate of oxidation.

e. **Use of Metal Chelators:**

i. **Description:** Add chelating agents to bind and remove metal ions that can catalyze oxidation.

ii. **Examples:** EDTA (ethylenediaminetetraacetic acid).

iii. **Effect:** Prevents metal-catalyzed oxidation reactions.

2. Hydrolysis:

Definition: Hydrolysis is a chemical reaction where components of the emulsion (such as emulsifiers or active ingredients) react with water, leading to degradation or breakdown.

Causes:

a. High water content.

b. Exposure to moisture.

c. Hydrolytic instability of ingredients.

Methods to Overcome Hydrolysis:

a. **Choose Stable Emulsifiers:**

i. **Description:** Use emulsifiers that are resistant to hydrolysis.

ii. **Examples:** Polysorbates, nonionic surfactants.

iii. **Effect:** Reduces the risk of hydrolysis and maintains emulsion stability.

b. **Control Water Content:**

i. **Description:** Minimize the water content in the formulation to reduce the potential for hydrolysis.

ii. **Examples:** Use anhydrous or low-water formulations.

iii. **Effect:** Decreases the likelihood of hydrolytic reactions.

c. **Incorporate Stabilizers:**

i. **Description:** Add stabilizers that protect against hydrolysis.

ii. **Examples:** Hydrocolloids, thickeners.

iii. **Effect:** Helps to maintain the integrity of the emulsion.

d. **Use of Desiccants:**

i. **Description:** Include desiccants in the packaging to absorb moisture.

ii. **Examples:** Silica gel packets.

iii. **Effect:** Prevents moisture-induced hydrolysis.

3. Degradation of Active Ingredients:

Definition: Active ingredients in the emulsion can degrade over time due to chemical reactions, reducing their efficacy.

Causes:

a. Sensitivity to light, heat, or oxygen.

b. Chemical instability of active ingredients.

Methods to Overcome Degradation of Active Ingredients:

a. **Protect from Light:**

i. **Description:** Use opaque or UV-protective packaging to shield active ingredients from light.

ii. **Examples:** Amber bottles or UV-blocking materials.

iii. **Effect:** Prevents light-induced degradation of active ingredients.

b. **Control Temperature:**
    i. **Description:** Store the emulsion at optimal temperatures to prevent thermal degradation.
    ii. **Examples:** Refrigeration or controlled room temperature.
    iii. **Effect:** Maintains the stability of active ingredients.

c. **Optimize pH:**
    i. **Description:** Adjust the pH of the emulsion to match the stability profile of active ingredients.
    ii. **Examples:** Use pH buffers or adjust formulation.
    iii. **Effect:** Prevents pH-induced degradation.

d. **Use Stabilizers:**
    i. **Description:** Add stabilizers or preservatives that protect active ingredients from degradation.
    ii. **Examples:** Chelating agents, antioxidants.
    iii. **Effect:** Enhances the stability of active ingredients.

4. Color Changes:

Definition: Color changes can occur in emulsions due to chemical reactions, leading to undesired alterations in appearance.

Causes:

a. Oxidation of colorants or active ingredients.
b. Chemical reactions with packaging materials.

Methods to Overcome Color Changes:

a. **Use Stable Colorants:**
    i. **Description:** Choose colorants that are resistant to oxidation and degradation.
    ii. **Examples:** Use dyes or pigments known for stability.
    iii. **Effect:** Maintains the desired color of the emulsion.

b. **Protect from Light and Oxygen:**

i. **Description:** Use packaging that protects against light and air exposure.
ii. **Examples:** Opaque or vacuum-sealed containers.
iii. **Effect:** Prevents color changes due to oxidation or photodegradation.

c. **Optimize Formulation:**
    i. **Description:** Adjust the formulation to minimize factors that lead to color changes.
    ii. **Examples:** Use buffering agents or stabilizers.
    iii. **Effect:** Helps maintain the color stability of the emulsion.

5. Odor Changes:

Definition: Odor changes can occur due to the degradation of ingredients or chemical reactions, leading to off-putting smells.

Causes:

a. Oxidation of oils or other volatile components.
b. Degradation of fragrance components.

Methods to Overcome Odor Changes:

a. **Incorporate Odor Neutralizers:**
    i. **Description:** Add substances that neutralize or mask unwanted odors.
    ii. **Examples:** Odor-neutralizing agents or fragrances.
    iii. **Effect:** Maintains a pleasant smell and masks undesirable odors.

b. **Control Exposure to Air:**
    i. **Description:** Minimize exposure to air to prevent oxidation and odor formation
    ii. **Examples:** Use airtight packaging.
    iii. **Effect:** Reduces the risk of odor changes due to oxidation.

c. **Use of Fresh Ingredients:**

i. **Description:** Ensure the use of fresh, high-quality ingredients to minimize the risk of odor changes.

ii. **Examples:** Use recently manufactured oils and fragrances.

iii. **Effect:** Maintains a stable and pleasant odor.

Method-Specific Issues:

Method-specific issues refer to problems that arise due to the specific techniques or processes used in the preparation and handling of emulsions. These issues can impact the stability, quality, and performance of the emulsion. Here's a detailed look at common method-specific issues and how to address them:

1. Issues Related to High-Shear Mixing:

Definition: High-shear mixing involves using mechanical forces to disperse and stabilize the emulsion. While effective, it can introduce specific stability problems.

Common Issues:

a. **Heat Generation:** High shear can generate heat, potentially causing thermal degradation of components.

b. **Oxidation:** Increased exposure to air during high shear can lead to oxidation of sensitive ingredients.

c. **Phase Inversion:** High shear may alter the ratio of components, leading to phase inversion.

Methods to Overcome Issues:

a. **Control Temperature:**

i. **Description:** Monitor and manage the temperature during mixing to prevent overheating.

ii. **Examples:** Use cooling jackets or temperature-controlled mixing vessels.

iii. **Effect:** Prevents thermal degradation of sensitive ingredients.

b. **Minimize Air Exposure:**

i. **Description:** Use mixing equipment designed to reduce air incorporation.
ii. **Examples:** Use vacuum mixing systems or deaeration techniques.
iii. **Effect:** Reduces oxidation and maintains emulsion stability.

c. **Optimize Shear Conditions:**
i. **Description:** Adjust shear rates and mixing times to avoid excessive force that could cause phase inversion.
ii. **Examples:** Conduct trial runs to determine optimal conditions.
iii. **Effect:** Ensures proper dispersion without destabilizing the emulsion.

2. Issues Related to Homogenization:

Definition: Homogenization involves using high pressure to reduce droplet size and achieve a uniform emulsion. Specific issues can arise during this process.

Common Issues:

a. **Inconsistent Droplet Size:** Variability in droplet size can occur if the homogenization process is not well-controlled.
b. **Equipment Wear:** Wear and tear on homogenization equipment can lead to reduced performance and stability issues.
c. **Phase Separation:** Inadequate homogenization may lead to incomplete dispersion and phase separation.

Methods to Overcome Issues:

a. **Regular Equipment Maintenance:**
i. **Description:** Perform routine checks and maintenance on homogenization equipment to ensure optimal performance.
ii. **Examples:** Calibrate equipment, replace worn parts, and clean regularly
iii. **Effect:** Maintains consistent performance and emulsion stability.

b. **Optimize Homogenization Parameters:**

i. **Description:** Adjust pressure, flow rates, and number of passes to achieve desired droplet size and uniformity.
ii. **Examples:** Conduct experiments to determine the optimal settings.
iii. **Effect:** Ensures uniform droplet size and prevents phase separation.

c. **Use of Stabilizers:**

i. **Description:** Incorporate stabilizers to support the emulsion during and after homogenization.
ii. **Examples:** Use polysaccharides or proteins that enhance stability.
iii. **Effect:** Supports the emulsion structure and reduces phase separation.

3. Issues Related to Emulsion Storage:

Definition: Storage conditions can impact the stability and quality of the emulsion over time.

Common Issues:

a. **Temperature Fluctuations:** Variations in storage temperature can lead to instability.
b. **Exposure to Light:** Light can cause degradation of sensitive components.
c. **Contamination:** Improper sealing or handling can introduce contaminants.

Methods to Overcome Issues:

a. **Controlled Storage Conditions:**

i. **Description:** Store emulsions under stable temperature and humidity conditions.
ii. **Examples:** Use temperature-controlled storage rooms or refrigeration.
iii. **Effect:** Minimizes the risk of instability due to environmental factors.

b. **Use of Light-Blocking Packaging:**
    i. **Description:** Choose packaging materials that protect against light exposure.
    ii. **Examples:** Use opaque or amber-colored bottles.
    iii. **Effect:** Prevents photodegradation of sensitive ingredients.

c. **Ensure Proper Sealing:**
    i. **Description:** Use airtight packaging to prevent contamination and maintain freshness.
    ii. **Examples:** Employ vacuum sealing or use tamper-evident closures.
    iii. **Effect:** Reduces the risk of microbial contamination and spoilage.

4. Issues Related to Ingredient Compatibility:

Definition: The interaction between ingredients can impact the stability and effectiveness of the emulsion.

Common Issues:

a. **Chemical Reactions:** Incompatibilities can lead to chemical reactions that destabilize the emulsion.
b. **Phase Separation:** Incompatible ingredients may cause phase separation or instability.
c. **Degradation of Active Ingredients:** Certain ingredients may degrade or react with others.

Methods to Overcome Issues:

a. **Conduct Compatibility Studies:**
    i. **Description:** Test the compatibility of ingredients before formulation.
    ii. **Examples:** Perform stability studies and compatibility tests.
    iii. **Effect:** Identifies potential issues and ensures ingredient compatibility.

b. **Optimize Formulation:**

i. **Description:** Adjust the formulation to avoid incompatibilities and stabilize the emulsion.
ii. **Examples:** Modify concentrations or use alternative ingredients.
iii. **Effect:** Achieves a stable and effective emulsion.

c. **Use Stabilizers and Buffers:**
   i. **Description:** Incorporate stabilizers and pH buffers to maintain ingredient stability.
   ii. **Examples:** Use buffers to maintain optimal pH, and stabilizers to prevent reactions.
   iii. **Effect:** Enhances the stability of active ingredients and prevents destabilization.

5. Issues Related to Emulsion Processing:

Definition: The processing methods used to create and handle the emulsion can impact its stability.

Common Issues:

a. **Inconsistent Mixing:** Uneven mixing can lead to instability and poor quality.
b. **Improper Handling:** Handling errors can cause damage to the emulsion structure.

Methods to Overcome Issues:

a. **Ensure Consistent Mixing:**
   i. **Description:** Use well-calibrated mixing equipment and techniques to achieve consistent results.
   ii. **Examples:** Implement standardized procedures and training for operators.
   iii. **Effect:** Ensures uniform emulsion quality and stability.
b. **Implement Quality Control Measures:**
   i. **Description:** Establish rigorous quality control procedures to monitor and adjust processing methods.

ii. **Examples:** Conduct regular inspections and tests during production.

iii. **Effect:** Maintains product consistency and prevents processing-related issues.

Multiple Choice Questions (Objective)

1. What is the dispersed phase in an oil-in-water (O/W) emulsion?
   A) Water droplets dispersed in oil
   B) Oil droplets dispersed in water
   C) Both oil and water dispersed in each other
   D) Solid particles dispersed in water
2. Which of the following is a characteristic of a water-in-oil (W/O) emulsion?
   A) Watery feel and lighter texture
   B) Oil droplets dispersed in water
   C) Greasy and occlusive texture
   D) High electrical conductivity
3. What role does an emulsifier play in an emulsion?
   A) Increases the viscosity of the dispersed phase
   B) Dissolves the continuous phase
   C) Stabilizes the emulsion by reducing interfacial tension
   D) Separates the two immiscible liquids
4. Which type of emulsion is most likely used in a facial cream?
   A) Oil-in-water (O/W) emulsion
   B) Water-in-oil (W/O) emulsion
   C) Multiple emulsion
   D) Microemulsion
5. What is a common method used to identify the type of emulsion?
   A) Sedimentation test

B) Filtration test

C) Dilution test

D) Viscosity test

6. Which emulsifier type is typically used in milk?

A) Anionic surfactants

B) Proteins like casein

C) Hydrocolloids like xanthan gum

D) Silica particles

7. What is the main cause of creaming in an emulsion?

A) Increased viscosity of the continuous phase

B) Large droplet size and density difference

C) High temperature during storage

D) Use of non-ionic surfactants

8. How can phase inversion in an emulsion be prevented?

A) By increasing the oil-to-water ratio

B) By reducing the emulsifier concentration

C) By maintaining stable formulation conditions

D) By using low-shear mixing

9. Which test can be used to determine if an emulsion is oil-in-water (O/W)?

A) Conductivity test

B) Spreadability test

C) Smell and feel test

D) None of the above

10. What is Ostwald ripening in emulsions?

A) Phase inversion due to temperature change

B) Growth of larger droplets at the expense of smaller ones

C) Sedimentation of dispersed particles

D) Increase in emulsion viscosity over time

11. Which method is commonly used for the industrial production of emulsions?

A) Ultrasonication

B) Homogenization

C) Microwaving

D) Centrifugation

12. Which of the following is NOT a type of emulsifying agent?

A) Surfactants

B) Hydrocolloids

C) Proteins

D) Glycerol

13. What is the primary function of preservatives in emulsions?

A) To reduce viscosity

B) To enhance the taste

C) To prevent microbial contamination

D) To increase droplet size

14. How does increasing the viscosity of the continuous phase help stabilize an emulsion?

A) It increases the droplet size

B) It reduces the mobility of droplets

C) It increases the interfacial tension

D) It decreases the shelf life

15. What is the role of antioxidants in emulsions?

A) To reduce the viscosity of the emulsion

B) To prevent oxidation of the oil phase

C) To increase the droplet size

D) To enhance the emulsification process

16. Which of the following can lead to the hydrolysis of emulsifiers in emulsions?

A) High water content

B) Low temperature

C) Use of stabilizers

D) Low emulsifier concentration

17. What is the effect of using light-blocking packaging for emulsions?

    A) It reduces the viscosity of the emulsion

    B) It prevents photodegradation of sensitive ingredients

    C) It increases the droplet size

    D) It enhances the emulsifying process

18. Which of the following is a method to prevent microbial contamination in emulsions?

    A) Use of antioxidants

    B) Increase in water content

    C) Incorporation of preservatives

    D) Use of non-ionic surfactants

19. What is phase separation in emulsions?

    A) The increase in viscosity over time

    B) The change in color of the emulsion

    C) The separation of the dispersed phase from the continuous phase

    D) The reduction in droplet size

20. How can sedimentation in an emulsion be minimized?

    A) By reducing droplet size

    B) By increasing the oil-to-water ratio

    C) By decreasing the viscosity of the continuous phase

    D) By adding more water to the emulsion

Short Answer Type Questions (Subjective)

1. Define an emulsion and describe its key components.
2. Explain the difference between oil-in-water (O/W) and water-in-oil (W/O) emulsions.
3. What role do emulsifying agents play in the stability of emulsions?

4. Describe the dilution test for identifying the type of emulsion.
5. How does the conductivity test help in determining the type of emulsion?
6. What are the common causes of phase separation in emulsions?
7. Discuss the significance of droplet size in the stability of emulsions.
8. What is the impact of viscosity on the stability of an emulsion?
9. Explain the phenomenon of Ostwald ripening and its effect on emulsions.
10. How can microbial contamination in emulsions be prevented?
11. Describe the role of antioxidants in the stabilization of emulsions.
12. What are the challenges associated with the storage of emulsions?
13. How can creaming in an emulsion be reduced or prevented?
14. What is the purpose of using preservatives in emulsions?
15. Discuss the importance of maintaining consistent temperature conditions during the preparation and storage of emulsions.
16. How does phase inversion occur in emulsions, and how can it be controlled?
17. What are the different types of emulsifying agents used in emulsions?
18. How does the method of homogenization affect the droplet size in an emulsion?
19. What is the role of hydrocolloids in emulsion stabilization?
20. Explain how light-blocking packaging helps in maintaining the stability of emulsions.

Long Answer Type Questions (Subjective)

1. Discuss the various methods used for the preparation of emulsions, highlighting the advantages and disadvantages of each method.
2. Explain in detail the factors that affect the stability of emulsions and the methods used to overcome common stability issues
3. Describe the classification of emulsions based on their dispersed and continuous phases, including examples and applications of each type.

4. Analyze the role of emulsifying agents in the formation and stabilization of emulsions, including a discussion of different types of emulsifiers.
5. Explain the common tests used to identify the type of emulsion and their significance in emulsion formulation and stability.
6. Discuss the phenomenon of phase separation in emulsions, including the causes, effects, and methods to prevent or minimize this issue.
7. Describe the impact of storage conditions on the stability of emulsions and the best practices for maintaining emulsion stability over time.
8. Explain the challenges and methods of ensuring the chemical stability of active ingredients in emulsions, including the role of antioxidants and preservatives.
9. Discuss the physical and chemical stability issues associated with emulsions, including Ostwald ripening, phase inversion, and hydrolysis.
10. Analyze the importance of method-specific considerations in emulsion preparation, including high-shear mixing, homogenization, and ingredient compatibility.

Answer Key for MCQs

1. B)
2. C)
3. C)
4. B)
5. C)
6. B)
7. B)
8. C)
9. A)
10. B)
11. B)

12.D)

13.C)

14.B)

15.B)

16.A)

17.B)

18.C)

19.C)

20.A)

CHAPTER – 11

SUPPOSITORIES

INTRODUCTION:

1. Definition and Purpose: Suppositories are solid dosage forms designed to be inserted into body cavities, where they melt, dissolve, or disintegrate to release their active ingredients. They are commonly used for local or systemic effects and can be administered via the rectum, vagina, or urethra.

2. Types of Suppositories:

a. **Rectal Suppositories:** Used for systemic effects (e.g., pain relief, fever reduction) or local effects (e.g., treatment of hemorrhoids). They are often used when oral administration is not feasible.

b. **Vaginal Suppositories:** Primarily used for local effects such as treatment of infections or hormone delivery (e.g., estrogen therapy).

c. **Urethral Suppositories:** Less common, used for local effects in the urethra, such as treating erectile dysfunction with medications like alprostadil.

3. Composition:

a. **Active Ingredients:** The drug substances intended to exert therapeutic effects.

b. **Base (Vehicle):** The substance that facilitates the release and absorption of the active ingredient. Common bases include cocoa butter, glycerin, and polyethylene glycol (PEG). Bases are chosen based on their ability to melt or dissolve at body temperature.

4. Mechanism of Action:

a. **Rectal Suppositories:** Upon insertion, the suppository melts or dissolves in the rectal cavity. The drug is then absorbed through the rectal mucosa into the systemic circulation or acts locally.

b. **Vaginal Suppositories:** Melts or dissolves in the vaginal cavity, where it releases the drug for local or systemic absorption.

c. **Urethral Suppositories:** Dissolve or melt in the urethra, allowing the drug to act locally or be absorbed into the systemic circulation.

5. Advantages:

a. **Bypass of Digestive Enzymes:** Useful for drugs that are poorly absorbed or degraded in the gastrointestinal tract.

b. **Alternative to Oral Administration:** Beneficial for patients who are vomiting, unconscious, or unable to swallow.

c. **Local Effect:** Direct application to the site of action, minimizing systemic side effects.

6. Disadvantages:

a. **Inconvenience:** Some patients may find suppositories uncomfortable or difficult to use.

b. **Variable Absorption:** Factors like rectal or vaginal condition, and the presence of fecal matter or vaginal secretions, can affect drug absorption.

7. Preparation and Quality Control:

a. **Manufacturing:** Suppositories are prepared using methods like molding or extrusion. The active ingredients and base are mixed, molded into the desired shape, and cooled or solidified.

b. **Quality Control:** Ensures that suppositories meet specifications for drug content, consistency, and dissolution characteristics. Tests may include visual inspection, melting point determination, and dissolution testing.

8. Clinical Considerations:

a. **Patient Education:** Patients should be informed about proper insertion techniques and storage conditions.

b. **Storage:** Suppositories should be stored in a cool place to prevent premature melting.

DEFINITION OF SUPPOSITORIES

Suppositories are solid or semi-solid dosage forms designed for insertion into body cavities, where they dissolve, melt, or disintegrate to release their active pharmaceutical ingredients. These dosage forms are specifically formulated to provide therapeutic effects either locally at the site of insertion or systemically through absorption into the bloodstream. They are used in various medical treatments to address issues when oral or other forms of drug administration are unsuitable or less effective.

Key Points:

1. **Form and Structure:**
    a. Suppositories typically have a cylindrical or torpedo shape and are designed to fit into the body cavity for which they are intended. They are composed of a base (also called a vehicle) and an active ingredient.
2. **Administration Routes:**
    a. **Rectal Suppositories:** Inserted into the rectum; used for both local (e.g., hemorrhoids) and systemic effects (e.g., fever reduction).
    b. **Vaginal Suppositories:** Inserted into the vagina; used for local treatments such as infections or hormone delivery.
    c. **Urethral Suppositories:** Inserted into the urethra; used for localized treatments, such as erectile dysfunction.
3. **Function:**
    a. Upon insertion, the suppository melts or dissolves due to the body temperature and releases the active ingredient. This release can provide a local effect at the site of insertion or systemic absorption through the mucous membranes of the cavity.
4. **Formulation:**
    a. The active pharmaceutical ingredient is combined with a base that facilitates the release and absorption of the drug. Common bases

include fats (e.g., cocoa butter), waxes, and hydrophilic polymers (e.g., polyethylene glycol).

5. **Advantages:**
    a. **Avoidance of Gastrointestinal Issues:** Useful for drugs that are degraded by the digestive system or when oral administration is not feasible.
    b. **Local Effect:** Can provide targeted treatment with minimal systemic side effects.
6. **Disadvantages:**
    a. **Patient Acceptance:** Some patients find suppositories uncomfortable or inconvenient.
    b. **Absorption Variability:** Factors such as the condition of the body cavity and the presence of fecal matter or vaginal secretions can influence absorption.

TYPES OF SUPPOSITORIES

Suppositories are categorized based on their intended use and the body cavity they are designed for. Each type has specific applications, characteristics, and considerations. Here's a detailed look at the main types of suppositories:

1. Rectal Suppositories:

a. **Purpose:**
    i. **Systemic Effect:** Used to deliver medications that are absorbed through the rectal mucosa into the systemic circulation. Examples include pain relievers, anti-nausea drugs, and fever reducers.
    ii. **Local Effect:** Applied to treat conditions affecting the rectum or lower gastrointestinal tract, such as hemorrhoids, anal fissures, or inflammatory bowel disease.

b. **Examples:**
    i. **Acetaminophen Suppositories:** Used for fever and pain relief.
    ii. **Glycerin Suppositories:** Used as a laxative to relieve constipation.

c. **Characteristics:**

   i. Designed to dissolve or melt at body temperature, releasing the drug for absorption or local action.

   ii. Typically have a cylindrical or torpedo shape for easy insertion.

2. Vaginal Suppositories:

a. **Purpose:**

   i. **Local Effect:** Often used to treat vaginal infections (e.g., yeast infections) or to deliver hormones locally (e.g., estrogen therapy).

   ii. **Systemic Effect:** Can also be used for systemic absorption of certain medications, though this is less common.

b. **Examples:**

   i. **Clotrimazole Suppositories:** Used to treat vaginal yeast infections.

   ii. **Progesterone Suppositories:** Used for hormone replacement therapy or to support early pregnancy.

c. **Characteristics:**

   i. Typically designed to dissolve or disperse in the vaginal environment, allowing for local or systemic absorption.

   ii. Often have a bullet or oval shape for easy insertion and effective release of the drug.

3. Urethral Suppositories:

a. **Purpose:**

   i. **Local Effect:** Used for conditions affecting the urethra, such as erectile dysfunction.

b. **Examples:**

   i. **Alprostadil Suppositories:** Used to treat erectile dysfunction by dilating blood vessels in the urethra and increasing blood flow to the penis.

c. **Characteristics:**

i. Designed to dissolve or melt upon insertion, allowing the drug to act locally or be absorbed into the systemic circulation.

ii. Usually slender and streamlined for insertion into the urethra.

4. Nasal Suppositories (less common):

a. **Purpose:**

i. Intended for drug delivery directly into the nasal cavity. This type is less common but can be used for localized or systemic effects.

b. **Examples:**

i. **Nasal corticosteroids:** Used for treating nasal congestion and allergies.

c. **Characteristics:**

i. Designed to dissolve or disintegrate in the nasal cavity, allowing for absorption through the nasal mucosa.

General Characteristics of Suppositories:

a. **Base Composition:** Suppositories are formulated with a base that melts or dissolves at body temperature. Common bases include:

i. **Cocoa Butter:** A fatty substance that melts at body temperature.

ii. **Polyethylene Glycol (PEG):** A hydrophilic base that dissolves in body fluids.

iii. **Glycerin:** A water-soluble base often used in rectal suppositories.

b. **Manufacturing Methods:** Suppositories can be made using various methods, including molding, extrusion, or compression. The choice of method depends on the type of base and the desired properties of the final product.

c. **Quality Control:** Ensuring consistency in drug content, dissolution rate, and physical characteristics is crucial for effective and reliable therapeutic outcomes. Quality control tests may include visual inspection, melting point determination, and dissolution testing.

ADVANTAGES OF SUPPOSITORIES

Suppositories offer several distinct advantages in medication delivery, making them a valuable option in various clinical scenarios. Here's a detailed look at the benefits:

1. Bypassing the Gastrointestinal Tract:

a. **Avoids Degradation:** Suppositories help avoid the gastrointestinal tract, where some drugs may be degraded by stomach acid or digestive enzymes. This is particularly useful for drugs that have poor oral bioavailability or are unstable in the digestive system.

b. **Alternative to Oral Administration:** Useful for patients who cannot take medications orally due to nausea, vomiting, or difficulty swallowing.

2. Local Treatment:

a. **Targeted Action:** Suppositories can deliver medication directly to the site of action, providing targeted relief for local conditions. For example:

i. **Rectal Suppositories:** Treat hemorrhoids, anal fissures, or inflammatory bowel disease directly at the affected site.

ii. **Vaginal Suppositories:** Treat infections or deliver hormones directly where they are needed.

3. Systemic Absorption:

a. **Effective for Systemic Drug Delivery:** Suppositories can be used for systemic drug absorption through the mucosal lining of the rectum or vagina. This can be advantageous when other routes are impractical. For example:

i. **Rectal Suppositories:** Used for systemic delivery of drugs like acetaminophen for pain and fever relief.

ii. **Vaginal Suppositories:** Used for hormone therapy or systemic absorption of certain medications.

4. Non-Oral Route:

a. **Ideal for Certain Conditions:** Suppositories are beneficial when oral administration is not feasible due to conditions such as:

    i. **Unconsciousness or Coma:** In situations where a patient cannot swallow, suppositories provide a viable alternative.

    ii. **Severe Nausea or Vomiting:** Suppositories can be used when oral medications would induce or exacerbate nausea.

5. Reduced First-Pass Metabolism:

a. **Direct Absorption:** Rectal suppositories can bypass the liver's first-pass metabolism to some extent, allowing for higher bioavailability of certain drugs. This can result in more effective systemic concentrations and potentially lower doses required.

6. Convenience and Ease of Use:

a. **Ease of Administration:** Suppositories can be administered without the need for special equipment. They are generally straightforward to use once proper instructions are followed.

b. **Patient Compliance:** For patients who have difficulty with oral medications, suppositories offer an alternative that may improve adherence to treatment.

7. Customizable Release Profiles:

a. **Controlled Release:** Suppositories can be formulated to provide controlled or sustained release of medication. This allows for extended therapeutic effects and reduces the frequency of dosing.

b. **Variable Absorption Rates:** The formulation can be adjusted to achieve the desired release and absorption characteristics based on the therapeutic need.

8. Minimal Systemic Side Effects:

a. **Localized Treatment:** By delivering medication directly to the site of action, suppositories can minimize systemic side effects that might occur with oral or systemic routes of administration.

9. Suitable for Pediatric and Geriatric Patients:

a. **Alternative for Children and Elderly:** Suppositories are often used in pediatric and geriatric populations who may have difficulty swallowing pills or capsules, making them a practical option for these groups.

DISADVANTAGES OF SUPPOSITORIES

While suppositories offer various advantages, they also come with certain limitations and challenges. Here's a detailed look at the disadvantages of using suppositories:

1. Patient Discomfort and Acceptance:

a. **Discomfort:** Some patients find the insertion of suppositories uncomfortable or unpleasant, which can impact adherence to treatment.

b. **Stigma and Embarrassment:** The nature of suppositories can cause embarrassment or reluctance in some patients, potentially affecting their willingness to use them.

2. Variable Absorption:

a. **Inconsistent Absorption:** Absorption of the drug from suppositories can be affected by various factors, including the presence of fecal matter, the condition of the rectal or vaginal mucosa, and individual differences in anatomy.

b. **Local Conditions:** Conditions such as rectal inflammation or excessive vaginal secretions can impact the dissolution or absorption of the suppository.

3. Limited Drug Types:

a. **Not Suitable for All Drugs:** Not all medications can be effectively formulated into suppositories. The choice of drug and base must be compatible, and some drugs may not be stable or effective in this form.

b. **Restricted Use:** Certain medications or treatments are not available in suppository form, limiting options for patients who might benefit from this delivery method.

4. **Storage and Stability:**
   a. **Temperature Sensitivity:** Suppositories may be sensitive to temperature changes and can melt or degrade if not stored properly. This requires careful handling and storage, often in a cool place.
   b. **Shelf Life:** The stability of the active ingredient and the base can affect the shelf life and effectiveness of suppositories over time.
5. **Variable Dissolution Rates:**
   a. **Inconsistent Release:** The rate at which a suppository dissolves or melts can vary based on the formulation and the patient's body temperature. This can lead to inconsistent drug release and absorption.
   b. **Formulation Issues:** Poorly designed or manufactured suppositories may have issues with uniform dissolution or drug distribution.
6. **Limited Therapeutic Indications:**
   a. **Specific Applications:** Suppositories are often used for specific conditions or types of drugs. For some therapeutic needs, other forms of medication (e.g., oral, injectable) might be more appropriate or effective.
7. **Potential for Irritation:**
   a. **Local Irritation:** Some suppositories can cause irritation or discomfort at the site of insertion, leading to potential side effects or discontinuation of use.
   b. **Allergic Reactions:** In rare cases, patients may experience allergic reactions to the base or other components of the suppository.
8. **Complexity of Use:**
   a. **Insertion Technique:** Proper insertion technique is necessary to ensure effective use of suppositories. Incorrect insertion can lead to ineffective treatment or discomfort.
   b. **Patient Education:** Patients need to be educated on how to use suppositories correctly, which can be a barrier for some individuals, particularly if they have limited health literacy.

9. Social and Psychological Factors:

a. **Psychological Barriers:** The perception of using suppositories can be psychologically challenging for some patients, which may affect their willingness to use them despite their therapeutic benefits.

TYPES OF BASES OF SUPPOSITORIES

The base (or vehicle) in a suppository plays a crucial role in its function. It provides the structural framework for the suppository and affects how the active ingredient is released and absorbed. Here's a detailed look at the different types of bases used in suppositories:

1. Fatty Bases:

a. **Cocoa Butter (Theobroma Oil):**

i. **Description:** Cocoa butter is a natural fat derived from cocoa beans. It is commonly used due to its excellent compatibility with many drugs and its ability to melt at body temperature.

ii. **Properties:** It solidifies at room temperature but melts at body temperature, releasing the active ingredient.

iii. **Advantages:** Good release profile and stability, with a smooth texture that helps in easy insertion.

iv. **Considerations:** May be affected by temperature variations, which can lead to melting or hardening.

b. **Hydrogenated Vegetable Oils:**

i. **Description:** These are synthetic fats derived from vegetable oils through hydrogenation processes. Examples include hydrogenated palm oil and soy oil.

ii. **Properties:** They are solid at room temperature and have a melting point close to body temperature.

iii. **Advantages:** Provides a stable base with good drug-release properties.

iv. **Considerations:** Can be more consistent than cocoa butter in terms of melting characteristics.

2. **Water-Soluble or Hydrophilic Bases:**

a. **Polyethylene Glycol (PEG):**

i. **Description:** PEG is a polymer that is hydrophilic (water-attracting) and used in various molecular weights to create different melting points.

ii. **Properties:** PEG bases dissolve in body fluids rather than melting. They can be tailored to provide a range of melting points and dissolution rates.

iii. **Advantages:** Stable, non-greasy, and can be formulated to dissolve slowly, providing controlled drug release.

iv. **Considerations:** May not be suitable for all drugs and can sometimes cause irritation.

b. **Glycerin:**

i. **Description:** Glycerin is a simple polyol compound that is hygroscopic (absorbs water) and used in combination with other bases.

ii. **Properties:** It dissolves slowly in body fluids and has a mild laxative effect.

iii. **Advantages:** Good for rectal suppositories, particularly for those with constipation.

iv. **Considerations:** Can be too hygroscopic in some cases, potentially leading to excessive moisture absorption.

3. **Miscellaneous Bases:**

a. **Gelatin Bases:**

i. **Description:** Gelatin is used in some suppository formulations, often combined with other bases.

ii. **Properties:** Gelatin bases can provide a clear, flexible structure that dissolves or melts at body temperature.
iii. **Advantages:** Flexible and often used in combination with other bases to enhance properties.
iv. **Considerations:** May not be suitable for all types of drugs and can be less stable than other bases.

b. **Waxes (e.g., Beeswax):**
   i. **Description:** Waxes can be used in combination with other bases to adjust the melting point and consistency of the suppository.
   ii. **Properties:** Waxes are solid at room temperature and provide a firm texture.
   iii. **Advantages:** Provides structural integrity and modifies the melting profile of the suppository.
   iv. **Considerations:** Can be less commonly used and may require careful formulation to avoid undesirable characteristics.

Selection of Base:

Choosing the appropriate base for a suppository depends on several factors, including:

a. **Drug Compatibility:** The base must be compatible with the active ingredient to ensure stability and efficacy.
b. **Melting Point:** The melting point of the base should be close to body temperature to facilitate proper release of the drug.
c. **Release Profile:** The base affects how quickly the drug is released and absorbed, which must be tailored to the therapeutic need.
d. **Patient Comfort:** The base should provide a smooth texture to ensure ease of insertion and minimize irritation.

METHODS OF PREPARATIONS OF SUPPOSITORIES

The preparation of suppositories involves creating a uniform mixture of the active ingredient with a suitable base, then molding or shaping this mixture into the desired form. Several methods can be used depending on the type of base, the properties of the active ingredient, and the desired characteristics of the final product. Here's a detailed look at the common methods of preparing suppositories:

1. Molding Method:

a. **Description:** This is the most common method for preparing suppositories, especially when using fatty bases like cocoa butter or hydrogenated vegetable oils.

b. **Procedure:**

   i. **Melting:** The base (e.g., cocoa butter) is melted in a controlled environment, typically using a water bath to ensure even heating.

   ii. **Mixing:** The active ingredient is then incorporated into the melted base. This can be done by stirring or blending to ensure a homogeneous mixture.

   iii. **Pouring:** The mixture is poured into molds that are shaped according to the desired suppository form (e.g., cylindrical or torpedo-shaped).

   iv. **Cooling:** The molds are allowed to cool and solidify. The cooling process must be controlled to ensure that the suppositories solidify uniformly without defects.

   v. **Demolding:** Once solidified, the suppositories are removed from the molds. They are then inspected and packaged.

c. **Advantages:**

   i. Suitable for both large and small-scale production.

   ii. Allows for precise control over the size and shape of the suppositories.

d. **Considerations:**

   i. Requires careful temperature control to prevent overheating and degradation of sensitive active ingredients.

2. Hand Rolling Method:

a. **Description:** This method is less commonly used but can be suitable for small-scale or custom preparations.

b. **Procedure:**

   i. **Preparation:** The base and active ingredient are mixed together to form a homogeneous paste or dough.

   ii. **Shaping:** Small amounts of the mixture are manually rolled into cylindrical shapes or other desired forms.

   iii. **Cooling:** The shaped suppositories are allowed to cool and solidify.

c. **Advantages:**

   i. Simple and suitable for small batches or compounding pharmacies.

   ii. Flexible for custom formulations.

d. **Considerations:**

   i. Less precise and more labor-intensive compared to molding methods.

   ii. Requires skill to ensure uniformity and consistency.

3. Fusion Method:

a. **Description:** This method is similar to the molding method but specifically involves the fusion of different types of bases or active ingredients.

b. **Procedure:**

   i. **Melting:** Different components of the base are melted together. For example, a blend of cocoa butter and PEG may be used.

   ii. **Incorporation:** The active ingredient is added to the melted mixture, ensuring even distribution.

   iii. **Pouring and Cooling:** The mixture is poured into molds and allowed to cool and solidify.

c. **Advantages:**

   i. Allows for the use of combined bases to achieve desired melting and release characteristics.

   ii. Suitable for complex formulations.

d. **Considerations:**

   i. Requires careful control of melting points and blending to ensure compatibility and stability.

4. Extrusion Method:

a. **Description:** This method is used for bases that are more viscous or for creating suppositories with specific shapes.

b. **Procedure:**

   i. **Mixing:** The base and active ingredient are mixed to form a homogeneous, semi-solid paste.

   ii. **Extruding:** The mixture is forced through an extruder to form long, continuous shapes.

   iii. **Cutting and Shaping:** The extruded material is cut into individual suppositories and allowed to cool and solidify.

c. **Advantages:**

   i. Efficient for large-scale production and provides consistent shapes.

   ii. Can be used to produce suppositories with specialized shapes or designs.

d. **Considerations:**

   i. Requires specialized equipment and careful control of extrusion conditions.

5. Compression Method:

a. **Description:** This method involves compressing a powder or paste into suppository molds.

b. **Procedure:**

i. **Mixing:** The active ingredient and base are combined to form a uniform powder or paste.

ii. **Compression:** The mixture is placed into molds and compressed using a tablet press or similar equipment.

iii. **Cooling and Removal:** The compressed suppositories are allowed to cool and solidify before being removed from the molds.

c. **Advantages:**

i. Useful for bases that are not easily melted or when a more solid form is desired.

ii. Allows for precise control over the dosage and shape.

d. **Considerations:**

i. Requires specific equipment for compression and careful handling to ensure uniformity.

6. Manual Mixing and Molding (Compounding):

a. **Description:** Used primarily in compounding pharmacies for custom prescriptions.

b. **Procedure:**

i. **Manual Mixing:** The base and active ingredient are manually mixed to ensure uniformity.

ii. **Hand-Molding:** The mixture is manually placed into molds to form suppositories.

iii. **Cooling and Finalizing:** The suppositories are cooled and solidified before packaging.

c. **Advantages:**

i. Provides flexibility for custom formulations.

ii. Useful for personalized medicine and small-scale preparations.

d. **Considerations:**

i. Less precise than industrial methods and requires careful handling to ensure quality.

Quality Control:

Regardless of the preparation method, quality control is essential to ensure that suppositories meet the required standards. Key quality control aspects include:

a. **Uniformity of Drug Content:** Ensuring that each suppository contains the correct amount of active ingredient.

b. **Dissolution Testing:** Confirming that the suppository dissolves or melts at the appropriate rate.

c. **Appearance and Consistency:** Checking for visual defects and ensuring consistent texture and shape.

DISPLACEMENT VALUE & ITS CALCULATIONS OF SUPPOSITORIES

Displacement Value is a crucial concept in the formulation of suppositories. It refers to the volume of a base that is displaced by a given amount of the active ingredient when incorporated into the suppository mixture. Understanding displacement value helps ensure that suppositories have the correct size and weight to deliver the appropriate dose of medication.

1. Definition of Displacement Value:

a. **Displacement Value:** The amount of base displaced by a specified quantity of active ingredient in the formulation of a suppository. It is typically expressed in milliliters (mL) or grams (g) per gram of the active ingredient.

2. Importance of Displacement Value:

a. **Accuracy in Dosage:** Ensures that the final suppository contains the correct amount of active ingredient and maintains the proper size and weight.

b. **Uniformity:** Helps in achieving consistent suppository sizes and weights during manufacturing, which is essential for both efficacy and safety.

c. **Base Adjustment:** Allows for precise adjustments in the amount of base needed when the quantity of active ingredient varies.

3. Calculations of Displacement Value:

Step-by-Step Calculation:

a. **Determine the Displacement Value of the Active Ingredient:**

   i. This is usually provided in the form of a standard or can be determined experimentally. For example, the displacement value might be provided as 0.8 mL per gram of active ingredient.

b. **Calculate the Amount of Base Required:**

   i. **Formula:**

$$\text{Amount of Base} = \text{Total Volume of Base} - (\text{Displacement Value} \times \text{Amo}$$

   ii. **Example Calculation:**

      1. Suppose you need to prepare 100 grams of suppositories, and you have an active ingredient with a displacement value of 0.8 mL/gram. If you need 10 grams of the active ingredient:

$$\text{Displaced Volume} = 0.8\,\text{mL}/\text{gram} \times 10\,\text{grams} = 8\,\text{mL}$$

      2. If the total volume of the suppository mixture is 100 mL, then:

$$\text{Amount of Base} = 100\,\text{mL} - 8\,\text{mL} = 92\,\text{mL}$$

c. **Preparation of the Suppositories:**

   i. **Mixing:** Combine the active ingredient with the required amount of base, ensuring thorough mixing.

   ii. **Molding:** Pour the mixture into molds and allow it to solidify.

4. Experimental Determination of Displacement Value:

If the displacement value is not provided, it can be determined experimentally by:

a. **Measuring the Volume Displacement:**

   i. Weigh a known quantity of the active ingredient.

ii. Mix it with the base and measure the final volume of the mixture.

iii. Calculate the displacement value using the difference in volume before and after adding the active ingredient.

b. **Example:**

i. Measure 10 mL of the base.

ii. Add 1 gram of the active ingredient and mix.

iii. Measure the final volume of the mixture, which is 10.8 mL.

iv. The displacement value is calculated as:

$$\text{Displacement Value} = \frac{\text{Final Volume} - \text{Initial Volume}}{\text{Amount of Active Ingredient}}$$

$$\text{Displacement Value} = \frac{10.8\,\text{mL} - 10\,\text{mL}}{1\,\text{gram}} = 0.8\,\text{mL/gram}$$

5. Factors Affecting Displacement Value:

a. **Type of Active Ingredient:** Different active ingredients have different displacement values based on their density and physical properties.

b. **Base Composition:** The type of base and its properties can affect how much volume is displaced by the active ingredient.

6. Practical Considerations:

a. **Accuracy:** Ensure accurate measurements and mixing to maintain consistency in suppository preparation.

b. **Quality Control:** Regularly check and validate the displacement values and calculations to ensure the efficacy and safety of the suppositories.

EVALUATION OF SUPPOSITORIES

valuating suppositories is crucial to ensure their quality, effectiveness, and safety. This process involves various tests to assess the physical characteristics, drug release, and stability of the suppositories. Here's a detailed overview of the evaluation procedures:

1. **Visual Inspection:**

a. **Appearance:** Examine the suppositories for any visible defects such as cracks, chips, or discoloration.
b. **Shape and Size:** Ensure that the suppositories are uniform in size and shape according to the specifications.
c. **Consistency:** Check for consistency in texture and smoothness. There should be no irregularities or lumps.

2. **Weight Uniformity:**
    a. **Purpose:** To ensure each suppository contains the correct amount of active ingredient and base.
    b. **Procedure:** Weigh a sample of suppositories individually and compare the weights to ensure they are within the acceptable range.
    c. **Acceptance Criteria:** Typically, the weight variation should be within ±5% of the labeled weight.

3. **Content Uniformity:**
    a. **Purpose:** To verify that the active ingredient is evenly distributed throughout each suppository.
    b. **Procedure:** Analyze a sample of suppositories to determine the amount of active ingredient using appropriate analytical methods such as high-performance liquid chromatography (HPLC) or spectrophotometry.
    c. **Acceptance Criteria:** The content of the active ingredient should be within ±10% of the labeled amount.

4. **Melting Point:**
    a. **Purpose:** To ensure that the suppository melts at the correct temperature for effective release and absorption.
    b. **Procedure:** Use a melting point apparatus to determine the temperature at which the suppository base melts.
    c. **Acceptance Criteria:** The melting point should be close to the body temperature, typically between 30°C and 37°C, depending on the base used.

5. **Dissolution Test:**
    a. **Purpose:** To evaluate how well the suppository releases its active ingredient in a simulated physiological environment.
    b. **Procedure:** Dissolve the suppository in a dissolution apparatus or a simulated body fluid and measure the rate and extent of drug release over time.
    c. **Acceptance Criteria:** The drug should release a specified percentage of the active ingredient within a set period, as defined in pharmacopeial standards.
6. **Disintegration Test:**
    a. **Purpose:** To determine how quickly the suppository breaks down in a physiological environment.
    b. **Procedure:** Place the suppository in a disintegration apparatus and monitor the time it takes for the suppository to disintegrate into smaller particles or completely dissolve.
    c. **Acceptance Criteria:** Suppositories should disintegrate within a specified time frame, often within 30 minutes to 1 hour.
7. **Stability Testing:**
    a. **Purpose:** To assess the stability of the suppository over time under various conditions.
    b. **Procedure:** Store the suppositories under different environmental conditions (e.g., temperature, humidity) and periodically test them for changes in physical characteristics, drug content, and release properties.
    c. **Acceptance Criteria:** Suppositories should maintain their quality and efficacy throughout their shelf life.
8. **pH Testing (for Vaginal Suppositories):**
    a. **Purpose:** To ensure that the pH of the suppository is compatible with the vaginal environment.

b. **Procedure:** Measure the pH of the suppository using a pH meter or test strips.

c. **Acceptance Criteria:** The pH should be within the acceptable range for vaginal use, typically around 4.0 to 4.5.

9. **Compatibility Testing:**

   a. **Purpose:** To verify that the active ingredient does not interact adversely with the base or other excipients.

   b. **Procedure:** Conduct compatibility studies by mixing the active ingredient with the base and observing any changes in physical properties, stability, or drug release.

   c. **Acceptance Criteria:** There should be no adverse interactions or changes in the formulation.

10. **Microbial Testing:**

    a. **Purpose:** To ensure that the suppositories are free from harmful microorganisms.

    b. **Procedure:** Test for microbial contamination using standard microbiological methods.

    c. **Acceptance Criteria:** Suppositories should be free from pathogenic bacteria, yeast, and molds.

11. **Consistency and Texture:**

    a. **Purpose:** To assess the uniformity and smoothness of the suppository.

    b. **Procedure:** Test the consistency and texture by breaking or cutting a suppository and evaluating the smoothness of the surface.

    c. **Acceptance Criteria:** The suppository should have a smooth texture and uniform consistency.

12. **Release Kinetics:**

    a. **Purpose:** To study the release profile of the active ingredient from the suppository over time.

b. **Procedure:** Perform kinetic studies to determine how the drug is released from the suppository in a simulated physiological environment.

c. **Acceptance Criteria:** The release profile should match the intended therapeutic action and dosage regimen.

Multiple Choice Questions (MCQs)

1. What is a suppository primarily designed to do upon insertion?

    A) Dissolve in the stomach

    B) Release active ingredients through chewing

    C) Melt, dissolve, or disintegrate in a body cavity

    D) Provide a crunchy texture for ease of consumption

2. Which type of suppository is most commonly used to treat hemorrhoids?

    A) Vaginal suppository

    B) Rectal suppository

    C) Urethral suppository

    D) Nasal suppository

3. What is a common base used in fatty suppository formulations?

    A) Polyethylene glycol (PEG)

    B) Cocoa butter

    C) Glycerin

    D) Gelatin

4. What is a primary advantage of using rectal suppositories for drug delivery?

    A) Faster onset of action than injections

    B) Avoidance of first-pass metabolism in the liver

    C) Immediate dissolution in the bloodstream

    D) Complete replacement for oral medications

5. Which method is the most common for preparing suppositories?

    A) Hand rolling

    B) Compression method

C) Molding method

D) Extrusion method

6. What is the primary function of the base in a suppository?

A) Provide flavor to the drug

B) Facilitate the release and absorption of the active ingredient

C) Increase the shelf life of the medication

D) Enhance the color and appearance of the suppository

7. Which of the following is a disadvantage of using suppositories?

A) Consistent absorption

B) Easy administration

C) Inconsistent absorption due to local conditions

D) Rapid systemic effects

8. What is the typical shape of rectal suppositories?

A) Round

B) Cylindrical or torpedo-shaped

C) Flat disc

D) Square

9. How are displacement values used in suppository formulation?

A) To determine the taste of the suppository

B) To calculate the amount of base displaced by the active ingredient

C) To enhance the color of the suppository

D) To increase the active ingredient concentration

10. Which base is known for being hydrophilic and dissolving in body fluids rather than melting?

A) Cocoa butter

B) Polyethylene glycol (PEG)

C) Glycerin

D) Beeswax

11. What factor can affect the dissolution rate of a suppository?

A) The color of the suppository

B) The shape of the suppository

C) The body temperature and base composition

D) The fragrance used in the suppository

12. Which of the following is a key consideration in the stability testing of suppositories?

A) The pH level

B) The presence of active ingredient

C) The environmental storage conditions like temperature and humidity

D) The color of the base used

13. Which suppository type is primarily used to treat vaginal infections?

A) Rectal suppository

B) Vaginal suppository

C) Urethral suppository

D) Nasal suppository

14. What is the purpose of the visual inspection during suppository evaluation?

A) To check the fragrance

B) To assess the appearance, shape, and size

C) To measure the melting point

D) To determine the pH level

15. Which method is least commonly used for preparing suppositories but is suitable for custom formulations?

A) Hand rolling

B) Molding method

C) Compression method

D) Extrusion method

16. What is the importance of content uniformity in suppository evaluation?

A) To ensure the flavor is consistent

B) To verify that the active ingredient is evenly distributed

C) To check the color distribution

D) To measure the size uniformity

17. What is the primary disadvantage of storing suppositories at room temperature?

A) They may lose color

B) They can melt or degrade

C) They become too hard

D) They lose their fragrance

18. Which of the following describes the process of hand rolling in suppository preparation?

A) Using molds to shape the suppositories

B) Manually rolling a mixture into cylindrical shapes

C) Compressing the mixture into solid forms

D) Extruding the mixture into long shapes

19. Which base is often used in glycerin suppositories?

A) Cocoa butter

B) Polyethylene glycol (PEG)

C) Beeswax

D) Glycerin

20. Which type of suppository base melts at body temperature and is commonly used in rectal formulations?

A) Glycerin

B) Polyethylene glycol (PEG)

C) Cocoa butter

D) Gelatin

Short Answer Type Questions (Subjective)

1. Define suppositories and their primary purpose.
2. List the three main types of suppositories and their uses.

3. Explain the role of the base in a suppository formulation.
4. What are the advantages of using rectal suppositories for drug delivery?
5. Describe the molding method of suppository preparation.
6. Discuss the factors that can affect the absorption of drugs from suppositories.
7. Explain the concept of displacement value in suppository formulation.
8. What are the disadvantages of using suppositories?
9. How does the base type influence the melting point of a suppository?
10. Describe the importance of stability testing in suppository formulation.
11. Explain the difference between fatty bases and water-soluble bases used in suppositories.
12. What are the key steps involved in the quality control of suppositories?
13. How does the compression method differ from the extrusion method in suppository preparation?
14. Why is patient education important when using suppositories?
15. What are the challenges associated with storing suppositories?
16. Describe the process and purpose of dissolution testing in suppository evaluation.
17. How can improper insertion technique affect the effectiveness of suppositories?
18. What factors should be considered when selecting a base for suppository formulation?
19. Explain the use of glycerin in suppositories and its effects.
20. What is the importance of weight uniformity in suppository quality control?

Long Answer Type Questions (Subjective)

1. Discuss the different types of suppositories, their formulations, and their specific uses in clinical practice.
2. Explain the methods of preparing suppositories, including their advantages and limitations.

3. Describe the role of bases in suppository formulation, including the differences between fatty and water-soluble bases.
4. Discuss the concept of displacement value and its importance in the accurate formulation of suppositories.
5. Explain the quality control processes involved in the evaluation of suppositories, including key tests and their significance.
6. Discuss the advantages and disadvantages of using suppositories as a drug delivery system.
7. Explain the factors affecting drug absorption from suppositories and how these can be controlled during formulation.
8. Describe the challenges associated with the storage and stability of suppositories and how they can be addressed.
9. Discuss the role of patient education in ensuring the effective use of suppositories and addressing common barriers.
10. Explain the significance of content uniformity, weight uniformity, and dissolution testing in the quality control of suppositories.

Answer Key for MCQs

1. C) Melt, dissolve, or disintegrate in a body cavity
2. B) Rectal suppository
3. B) Cocoa butter
4. B) Avoidance of first-pass metabolism in the liver
5. C) Molding method
6. B) Facilitate the release and absorption of the active ingredient
7. C) Inconsistent absorption due to local conditions
8. B) Cylindrical or torpedo-shaped
9. B) To calculate the amount of base displaced by the active ingredient
10. B) Polyethylene glycol (PEG)
11. C) The body temperature and base composition

12.C) The environmental storage conditions like temperature and humidity

13.B) Vaginal suppository

14.B) To assess the appearance, shape, and size

15.A) Hand rolling

16.B) To verify that the active ingredient is evenly distributed

17.B) They can melt or degrade

18.B) Manually rolling a mixture into cylindrical shapes

19.D) Glycerin

20.C) Cocoa butter

CHAPTER – 12

PHARMACEUTICAL INCOMPATIBILITIES

INTRODUCTION:

Pharmaceutical incompatibilities refer to situations where two or more substances, when mixed together, interact in a way that affects their intended therapeutic effect, alters their stability, or creates harmful effects. These incompatibilities can be classified into different types:

1. Physical Incompatibilities

a. **Precipitation:** Occurs when two solutions mixed together cause a substance to come out of solution, forming a solid. For example, mixing calcium chloride with sodium carbonate can result in a precipitate of calcium carbonate.

b. **Cloudiness:** Some solutions may become cloudy when mixed, indicating the formation of insoluble particles.

c. **Phase Separation:** When two liquids are mixed, they might separate into distinct phases, like oil and water.

2. Chemical Incompatibilities

a. **Degradation:** The chemical reaction between drugs can lead to the breakdown of one or both substances. For example, mixing certain antibiotics with other drugs can lead to their degradation.

b. **Neutralization:** When an acidic and a basic drug are mixed, they may neutralize each other, resulting in reduced efficacy.

3. Pharmaceutical Incompatibilities

a. **pH Changes:** Altering the pH of a solution can affect the solubility and stability of drugs. For example, some drugs are only stable within a specific pH range.

b. **Oxidation-Reduction Reactions:** Some drugs can react with each other in oxidation-reduction reactions, leading to the formation of new, potentially harmful compounds.

4. Biological Incompatibilities

a. **Toxicity:** The combination of certain drugs can produce toxic effects, either through the formation of toxic metabolites or through interactions that increase the toxicity of one or both substances.

b. **Synergistic or Antagonistic Effects:** Sometimes, drugs can enhance or inhibit each other's effects, leading to unintended therapeutic outcomes.

Prevention and Management

a. **Compatibility Testing:** Before mixing drugs, it's crucial to test their compatibility. This can involve checking solubility, stability, and the potential for reactions.

b. **Proper Formulation:** Ensuring that drugs are formulated in a way that minimizes the risk of incompatibilities, such as using appropriate solvents and stabilizers.

c. **Professional Guidance:** Consulting with pharmacists or other healthcare professionals to ensure that drug combinations are safe and effective.

DEFINITION OF PHARMACEUTICAL INCOMPATIBILITIES

Pharmaceutical incompatibilities refer to the undesirable interactions between pharmaceutical substances that occur when they are combined, either in a formulation or during administration. These interactions can lead to various issues, including:

1. **Altered Drug Efficacy:** The therapeutic effect of one or more drugs may be diminished or enhanced unintentionally due to the interaction.
2. **Formation of Harmful Products:** Incompatibilities can lead to the formation of harmful by-products or degradation products that could be toxic.

3. **Physical Changes:** The mixture of drugs may cause physical changes such as precipitation, cloudiness, or phase separation, which can affect the drug's performance and safety.
4. **Stability Issues:** Drugs may become unstable when combined, leading to a reduced shelf life and potentially rendering them ineffective or dangerous.
5. **Reduced Solubility:** Changes in solubility due to drug interactions can result in poor absorption and therapeutic failure.

Types of Pharmaceutical Incompatibilities:

1. **Physical Incompatibilities:** These occur when the physical properties of the drugs are altered. Examples include precipitation, cloudiness, and phase separation.
2. **Chemical Incompatibilities:** These involve chemical reactions between drugs, such as hydrolysis, oxidation-reduction reactions, and neutralization, which can lead to the degradation of one or more components.
3. **Pharmaceutical Incompatibilities:** These are related to changes in the formulation or formulation conditions, such as pH changes, which can affect drug stability and efficacy.
4. **Biological Incompatibilities:** These occur when the interaction between drugs results in adverse biological effects, such as toxicity or unexpected side effects.

Importance of Understanding Pharmaceutical Incompatibilities:

1. **Safety:** Preventing adverse reactions and toxicity by avoiding incompatible drug combinations.
2. **Efficacy:** Ensuring that drugs maintain their intended therapeutic effects when administered together.
3. **Stability:** Maintaining the stability and shelf life of drug formulations.

4. **Patient Outcomes:** Improving overall patient outcomes by preventing complications arising from drug interactions.

CLASSIFICATION OF PHARMACEUTICAL INCOMPATIBILITIES

Pharmaceutical incompatibilities can be classified into several categories based on the nature of their interactions and effects. Here's a detailed classification:

1. Physical Incompatibilities

These occur when drugs or substances interact in a way that causes a physical change in the formulation.

a. **Precipitation:** When two or more drugs are mixed, they may form a solid precipitate. This can occur due to changes in solubility, such as mixing solutions of calcium chloride and sodium carbonate, which leads to the formation of calcium carbonate precipitate.

b. **Cloudiness or Turbidity:** Some drug mixtures may become cloudy or turbid due to the formation of fine particles or emulsions. For example, an aqueous solution of a drug might become cloudy when mixed with another drug.

c. **Phase Separation:** This involves the separation of a mixture into different phases, such as an oil-water separation, which can affect the uniformity and effectiveness of the drug.

d. **Viscosity Changes:** Mixing drugs can alter the viscosity of the solution, affecting the drug's administration and absorption.

2. Chemical Incompatibilities

These involve chemical reactions between drugs or between drugs and excipients that alter the drug's properties.

a. **Degradation Reactions:** Chemical reactions that result in the breakdown of one or more drugs. For example, some drugs may degrade in the presence of light or oxygen, leading to reduced efficacy and potential formation of harmful products.

b. **Neutralization Reactions:** When acidic and basic drugs are mixed, they may neutralize each other, potentially reducing their therapeutic effects. For instance, mixing hydrochloric acid with sodium hydroxide will result in the formation of water and sodium chloride.
c. **Oxidation-Reduction Reactions:** Reactions where one drug is oxidized while another is reduced, potentially leading to the formation of toxic by-products or the degradation of the drugs.
d. **Complex Formation:** Formation of insoluble complexes that can affect the solubility and availability of the drugs. For example, certain metal ions can form complexes with antibiotics, reducing their effectiveness.

3. Pharmaceutical Incompatibilities

These occur due to changes in the drug formulation or the conditions under which the drugs are combined.

a. **pH Changes:** Altering the pH of a solution can affect the solubility and stability of drugs. For instance, the solubility of certain drugs is pH-dependent, and changes in pH can lead to precipitation or degradation.
b. **Temperature Effects:** Temperature changes can impact drug stability. For example, some drugs may degrade at higher temperatures or may precipitate out of solution if cooled.
c. **Light Sensitivity:** Some drugs are sensitive to light and can degrade when exposed to light, affecting their stability and efficacy.

4. Biological Incompatibilities

These involve interactions that can have biological effects on the patient.

a. **Toxicity:** The interaction of drugs may produce toxic effects due to the formation of harmful by-products or increased toxicity of one or both drugs. For example, certain drug combinations can enhance the risk of adverse effects like nephrotoxicity or hepatotoxicity.
b. **Synergistic or Antagonistic Effects:** Drug interactions can lead to enhanced (synergistic) or reduced (antagonistic) therapeutic effects. For

instance, combining two drugs that both depress the central nervous system can lead to excessive sedation.

c. **Pharmacokinetic Interactions:** These involve changes in the absorption, distribution, metabolism, or excretion of drugs due to their interaction. For example, one drug may inhibit the metabolism of another, leading to increased drug levels and potential toxicity.

PHYSICAL PHARMACEUTICAL INCOMPATIBILITIES WITH EXAMPLES

Physical pharmaceutical incompatibilities refer to undesirable physical changes that occur when two or more substances are combined, affecting their stability, appearance, or efficacy. These incompatibilities can lead to problems in drug formulation and administration. Here are detailed examples of each type:

1. Precipitation

Definition: The formation of a solid from a solution when two or more substances are mixed.

Examples:

a. **Calcium Chloride and Sodium Carbonate:** When solutions of calcium chloride and sodium carbonate are mixed, calcium carbonate precipitates out of the solution. This is a classic example of precipitation due to the formation of an insoluble compound.

b. **Tetracycline and Calcium:** Tetracycline antibiotics can form a precipitate when mixed with calcium salts (e.g., calcium gluconate), which reduces the effectiveness of the antibiotic due to decreased solubility and absorption.

2. Cloudiness or Turbidity

Definition: The formation of a cloudy or turbid appearance in a solution, usually due to the presence of fine particles or the formation of an emulsion.

Examples:

a. **Mixing Injectable Solutions:** Certain injectable solutions can become cloudy or turbid when mixed. For example, mixing a solution containing propofol (an oil-in-water emulsion) with another drug can cause cloudiness, potentially leading to instability and reduced efficacy.
b. **Antibiotics in Suspension:** When certain antibiotics are reconstituted in suspension, they can appear cloudy. For instance, amoxicillin suspensions can become cloudy if not properly mixed or if they are past their expiration date.

3. Phase Separation

Definition: The separation of a mixture into different distinct phases, such as an oil layer and a water layer.

Examples:

a. **Oil-Water Separation:** Some drug formulations, especially those that are emulsions, can exhibit phase separation if not properly stabilized. For example, emulsified drug formulations like certain topical creams can separate into an oil phase and a water phase if they are not adequately mixed.
b. **Incompatible Injectable Formulations:** Mixing certain injectable drugs can lead to phase separation. For example, combining lipid-based formulations with aqueous solutions may result in separation of the lipid phase from the aqueous phase.

4. Viscosity Changes

Definition: Alteration in the thickness or fluidity of a solution due to the interaction of drugs.

Examples:

a. **Mixing Drug Solutions:** The addition of certain drugs to a solution can increase its viscosity. For instance, adding a high concentration of a viscosifying agent to a solution of another drug can make the solution too thick to be administered properly.

b. **Oral Suspensions:** Combining drugs in oral suspensions may alter their viscosity. For example, the addition of certain excipients or thickeners to a suspension can change its consistency, potentially affecting its administration and effectiveness.

5. Color Changes

Definition: The change in color of a drug solution due to interactions or chemical reactions.

Examples:

a. **Oxidation Reactions:** Some drugs, like epinephrine, can change color due to oxidation reactions. For example, epinephrine solutions can turn brown upon oxidation, indicating a degradation reaction that can affect the drug's potency.

b. **Formation of Complexes:** Certain drug combinations can result in color changes due to complex formation. For example, mixing iron salts with other drugs can cause a color change that might indicate a chemical interaction or instability.

Managing Physical Incompatibilities:

1. **Compatibility Testing:** Conduct tests to check for potential physical incompatibilities before combining drugs or formulations.
2. **Proper Storage:** Store drugs under recommended conditions to minimize physical changes such as precipitation or separation.
3. **Use of Stabilizers:** Incorporate stabilizers or appropriate excipients to maintain the stability and appearance of drug formulations.
4. **Professional Consultation:** Consult with pharmacists or formulators to ensure that drug combinations are safe and effective, taking into account potential physical incompatibilities.

CHEMICAL PHARMACEUTICAL INCOMPATIBILITIES WITH EXAMPLES

Chemical pharmaceutical incompatibilities occur when drugs or substances interact chemically, leading to undesirable changes in their properties. These interactions can result in the degradation of the drugs, formation of harmful products, or loss of therapeutic efficacy. Here's a detailed look at various types of chemical incompatibilities with examples:

1. Degradation Reactions

Definition: Chemical reactions that lead to the breakdown of one or more drugs, resulting in reduced efficacy or formation of harmful products.

Examples:

a. **Hydrolysis:** Certain drugs are susceptible to hydrolysis in the presence of water. For instance, **penicillin** can undergo hydrolysis to form inactive penicilloic acid, especially in aqueous solutions with a high pH.

b. **Oxidation:** Drugs like **epinephrine** are prone to oxidation, which leads to the formation of inactive by-products. Oxidized epinephrine may appear brown and lose its therapeutic effectiveness.

2. Neutralization Reactions

Definition: Reactions between acidic and basic substances that result in the neutralization of one or both components.

Examples:

a. **Acid-Base Interactions:** When **proton pump inhibitors** (such as omeprazole) are mixed with **antacids** (such as magnesium hydroxide), the acidic and basic components can neutralize each other, reducing the effectiveness of the proton pump inhibitor.

b. **Insulin and Glucose Solutions:** Insulin solutions mixed with glucose solutions can result in a neutralization reaction, potentially altering the insulin's effectiveness.

3. Oxidation-Reduction Reactions

Definition: Reactions where one substance is oxidized and another is reduced, which can lead to the formation of new, potentially harmful compounds.

Examples:

a. **Reduction of Nitroglycerin:** Nitroglycerin, used for angina, can be reduced by substances like sodium nitrite, forming potentially harmful nitrites.

b. **Oxidation of Doxorubicin: Doxorubicin**, an anticancer agent, can undergo oxidation, leading to the formation of quinone metabolites that may be less effective or more toxic.

4. Complex Formation

Definition: Formation of insoluble or inactive complexes between drugs or between drugs and excipients.

Examples:

a. **Antibiotic-Cation Complexes: Tetracycline** antibiotics can form complexes with metal ions like calcium, magnesium, and iron, resulting in reduced absorption and efficacy. For example, tetracycline combined with calcium supplements can form an insoluble complex.

b. **Formation of Drug-Drug Complexes: Warfarin**, an anticoagulant, can interact with drugs like **phenylbutazone**, forming a complex that alters warfarin's anticoagulant activity.

5. Precipitation Reactions

Definition: The formation of a solid precipitate from a solution due to a chemical reaction.

Examples:

a. **Calcium and Phosphate:** Mixing solutions containing **calcium salts** with **phosphate salts** can result in the precipitation of calcium phosphate. This is particularly important in intravenous solutions where such reactions can lead to blockages in infusion lines.

b. **Penicillin and Procaine:** When **penicillin** is mixed with **procaine**, a precipitate can form due to the interaction between the drugs, potentially leading to a loss of therapeutic efficacy.

6. pH-Induced Reactions

Definition: Changes in pH that affect the stability and activity of drugs.

Examples:

a. **Vitamin C and Aspirin:** Vitamin C (ascorbic acid) can react with **aspirin** (acetylsalicylic acid) in an acidic environment, leading to degradation of both substances.

b. **Diazepam in Acidic Solutions: Diazepam** can be unstable in highly acidic solutions, leading to hydrolysis and reduced therapeutic effectiveness.

Managing Chemical Incompatibilities:

1. **Compatibility Testing:** Conduct chemical stability tests to ensure that drug combinations do not lead to unwanted chemical reactions.
2. **Proper Formulation:** Use appropriate formulations and stabilizers to prevent chemical interactions.
3. **pH Adjustment:** Adjust the pH of solutions to match the stability requirements of the drugs.
4. **Consultation with Professionals:** Work with pharmacists and other healthcare professionals to understand and manage potential chemical incompatibilities.

THERAPEUTIC INCOMPATIBILITIES WITH EXAMPLES

Therapeutic incompatibilities refer to interactions between drugs that lead to unexpected or undesirable therapeutic outcomes. These interactions can affect the efficacy of treatment, cause adverse effects, or alter the intended therapeutic response. Here's a detailed look at different types of therapeutic incompatibilities with examples:

Synergistic Effects:

Synergistic effects in therapeutic incompatibilities refer to situations where the combined effect of two or more drugs is greater than the sum of their individual effects. While synergistic interactions can sometimes enhance therapeutic outcomes, they can also lead to excessive or harmful effects. Here's a detailed look at synergistic effects with examples:

1. Central Nervous System Depressants

Definition: Drugs that depress the central nervous system (CNS) can have an additive effect when used together, leading to enhanced sedation or respiratory depression.

Examples:

a. **Benzodiazepines and Opioids:** Combining **benzodiazepines** (e.g., diazepam) with **opioids** (e.g., morphine) can produce a synergistic sedative effect. This combination significantly increases the risk of severe drowsiness, respiratory depression, and even coma. The enhanced depressant effects on the CNS can lead to life-threatening conditions.

b. **Alcohol and Sedatives:** Consuming alcohol with sedative-hypnotics like **barbiturates** (e.g., phenobarbital) or benzodiazepines can result in a synergistic effect, exacerbating sedation and impairing cognitive and motor functions. This can increase the risk of accidents and overdose.

2. Antihypertensives

Definition: Combining multiple antihypertensive agents can produce a greater reduction in blood pressure than expected, leading to potentially excessive hypotension.

Examples:

a. **ACE Inhibitors and Calcium Channel Blockers:** Using **ACE inhibitors** (e.g., lisinopril) together with **calcium channel blockers** (e.g., amlodipine) can lead to a synergistic effect on blood pressure reduction. This can be beneficial for controlling hypertension but may also result in excessive hypotension, dizziness, and fainting

b. **Diuretics and Beta-Blockers:** Combining **thiazide diuretics** (e.g., hydrochlorothiazide) with **beta-blockers** (e.g., atenolol) can enhance blood pressure-lowering effects. While this combination can be effective in treating hypertension, it may also lead to an increased risk of electrolyte imbalances and dehydration.

3. Anticoagulants

Definition: Combining anticoagulants or antiplatelet drugs can produce a synergistic effect on blood clotting, increasing the risk of bleeding.

Examples:

a. **Warfarin and Aspirin:** Using **warfarin** (an oral anticoagulant) with **aspirin** (an antiplatelet agent) can lead to a synergistic increase in the risk of bleeding complications. Both drugs affect different aspects of the coagulation process, leading to an elevated risk of gastrointestinal bleeding, hemorrhagic stroke, and other bleeding disorders.

b. **Heparin and Clopidogrel: Heparin** (an injectable anticoagulant) and **clopidogrel** (an antiplatelet medication) can also have synergistic effects on bleeding risk. This combination is used in certain clinical settings, such as during coronary interventions, but requires careful monitoring to manage bleeding risks.

4. Antidiabetic Agents

Definition: Combining different types of antidiabetic agents can have a synergistic effect on lowering blood glucose levels, which can be beneficial but also increases the risk of hypoglycemia.

Examples:

a. **Sulfonylureas and Insulin: Sulfonylureas** (e.g., glipizide) combined with **insulin** can produce a synergistic effect on glucose lowering. While this can improve glycemic control in diabetic patients, it also raises the risk of hypoglycemia, requiring careful monitoring and dose adjustment.

b. **Metformin and Thiazolidinediones:** Combining **metformin** with **thiazolidinediones** (e.g., pioglitazone) can have a synergistic effect on controlling blood sugar levels in type 2 diabetes. However, this combination may also increase the risk of side effects such as fluid retention and weight gain.

5. Antibiotics

Definition: Some antibiotic combinations can have synergistic effects, enhancing antibacterial activity.

Examples:

a. **Penicillin and Gentamicin:** The combination of **penicillin** (a beta-lactam antibiotic) and **gentamicin** (an aminoglycoside) can exhibit a synergistic effect against certain bacterial infections. Penicillin disrupts bacterial cell wall synthesis, while gentamicin inhibits protein synthesis, leading to a more effective bacterial kill.

b. **Trimethoprim and Sulfamethoxazole: Trimethoprim-sulfamethoxazole** (a combination antibiotic) works synergistically to inhibit bacterial folate synthesis. This combination is effective against a range of bacterial infections, including urinary tract infections and respiratory infections.

Managing Synergistic Effects:

1. **Dosage Adjustment:** Monitor and adjust dosages to avoid excessive therapeutic effects or adverse reactions.
2. **Close Monitoring:** Regularly check patients for signs of enhanced effects or side effects, particularly with drugs that have a high risk of synergistic interactions.
3. **Patient Education:** Inform patients about potential risks and signs of adverse effects related to their medication regimen.
4. **Consultation with Healthcare Providers:** Work with healthcare professionals to optimize drug therapy and manage potential synergistic effects effectively.

Antagonistic Effects:

Antagonistic effects in therapeutic incompatibilities occur when the combined use of two drugs leads to a reduced therapeutic effect or counteracts the intended outcomes of one or both drugs. This can result in therapeutic failure, suboptimal treatment, or adverse reactions. Here's a detailed look at antagonistic effects with examples:

1. Antacids and Antibiotics

Definition: Antacids can interfere with the absorption of certain antibiotics, reducing their effectiveness.

Examples:

a. **Tetracyclines and Antacids: Tetracycline antibiotics** (e.g., doxycycline) can form insoluble complexes with metal ions found in antacids (such as calcium, magnesium, or aluminum). This interaction decreases the absorption of tetracyclines from the gastrointestinal tract, leading to reduced therapeutic efficacy.

b. **Fluoroquinolones and Antacids: Fluoroquinolone antibiotics** (e.g., ciprofloxacin) can also interact with antacids, leading to reduced absorption and effectiveness. The metal ions in antacids bind to the antibiotic, preventing its proper absorption.

2. Diuretics and Antihypertensives

Definition: Combining diuretics with certain antihypertensives can result in antagonistic effects, affecting blood pressure control.

Examples:

a. **Potassium-Sparing Diuretics and ACE Inhibitors: Potassium-sparing diuretics** (e.g., spironolactone) and **ACE inhibitors** (e.g., enalapril) can have opposing effects on potassium levels. While ACE inhibitors can increase potassium levels, potassium-sparing diuretics may also contribute to hyperkalemia, complicating the management of potassium levels and potentially counteracting the antihypertensive effects.

b. **Thiazide Diuretics and Beta-Blockers: Thiazide diuretics** (e.g., hydrochlorothiazide) combined with **beta-blockers** (e.g., atenolol) can result in antagonistic effects on blood pressure control. Thiazides can cause potassium loss, while beta-blockers can affect the response to other antihypertensives, potentially leading to less effective blood pressure management.

3. Anticoagulants and Antiplatelet Agents

Definition: Using anticoagulants and antiplatelet agents together can sometimes lead to reduced effectiveness or increased risk of bleeding complications.

Examples:

a. **Warfarin and Aspirin:** Combining **warfarin** (an oral anticoagulant) with **aspirin** (an antiplatelet agent) can enhance bleeding risk. While both drugs prevent clot formation, their combined effect can lead to excessive bleeding and reduced therapeutic efficacy of warfarin in maintaining proper anticoagulation levels.

b. **Heparin and Clopidogrel: Heparin** (an injectable anticoagulant) and **clopidogrel** (an antiplatelet medication) can have an antagonistic effect on platelet function. Clopidogrel may counteract some of the effects of heparin, affecting the overall anticoagulation therapy and increasing bleeding risk.

4. Beta-Blockers and Beta-Adrenergic Agonists

Definition: Combining beta-blockers with beta-adrenergic agonists can result in antagonistic effects on cardiovascular and respiratory functions.

Examples:

a. **Propranolol and Albuterol: Propranolol** (a non-selective beta-blocker) can antagonize the effects of **albuterol** (a beta-2 adrenergic agonist) used for asthma. Propranolol can reduce the bronchodilatory effect of albuterol, leading to less effective asthma control.

b. **Metoprolol and Isoproterenol: Metoprolol** (a selective beta-1 blocker) can interfere with the effects of **isoproterenol** (a non-selective beta-agonist). This interaction can reduce the efficacy of isoproterenol in treating conditions like bradycardia or asthma.

5. Opioids and Antagonists

Definition: Combining opioids with opioid antagonists can reduce the effectiveness of opioid analgesia.

Examples:

a. **Morphine and Naloxone: Naloxone** is an opioid antagonist that can counteract the effects of opioids like **morphine**. When used together, naloxone can reverse the analgesic effects of morphine, leading to reduced pain relief and potential withdrawal symptoms in opioid-dependent patients.

b. **Buprenorphine and Naltrexone: Buprenorphine** (a partial opioid agonist) and **naltrexone** (an opioid antagonist) can have antagonistic effects. Naltrexone can block the effects of buprenorphine, reducing its efficacy in managing opioid dependence or pain.

Managing Antagonistic Effects:

1. **Careful Drug Selection:** Choose drugs with complementary mechanisms to avoid antagonistic interactions.
2. **Monitor Therapeutic Response:** Regularly assess the effectiveness of therapy and adjust doses as needed to manage antagonistic effects.
3. **Patient Education:** Inform patients about potential interactions and the importance of adhering to prescribed therapies.
4. **Consult Healthcare Providers:** Work with healthcare professionals to optimize drug therapy and manage potential antagonistic effects.

Additive Effects:

Additive effects in therapeutic incompatibilities occur when the combined effect of two drugs equals the sum of their individual effects. This can either enhance the therapeutic outcome or lead to increased risks of adverse effects, depending on the context. Here's a detailed look at additive effects with examples:

1. Anticoagulants and Antiplatelet Agents

Definition: When used together, anticoagulants and antiplatelet agents can have an additive effect on blood thinning, which may be beneficial or increase the risk of bleeding.

Examples:

a. **Warfarin and Aspirin:** Combining **warfarin** (an oral anticoagulant) with **aspirin** (an antiplatelet agent) can produce an additive effect on preventing blood clot formation. This combination is used in certain conditions, such as atrial fibrillation or after coronary artery stenting, to reduce the risk of thromboembolic events. However, the additive effect also increases the risk of bleeding complications.

b. **Heparin and Clopidogrel: Heparin** (an injectable anticoagulant) combined with **clopidogrel** (an antiplatelet medication) can enhance the overall effect of anticoagulation. This combination is often used in acute coronary syndrome to prevent clots but requires careful monitoring for bleeding risks.

2. Antihypertensive Agents

Definition: Combining different antihypertensive agents can result in an additive effect on lowering blood pressure, which can be beneficial or cause excessive hypotension.

Examples:

a. **ACE Inhibitors and Diuretics:** Using **ACE inhibitors** (e.g., lisinopril) with **thiazide diuretics** (e.g., hydrochlorothiazide) can have an additive effect on reducing blood pressure. This combination is commonly used in managing hypertension and heart failure, providing enhanced blood pressure control.

b. **Calcium Channel Blockers and Beta-Blockers:** Combining **calcium channel blockers** (e.g., amlodipine) with **beta-blockers** (e.g., metoprolol) can provide an additive effect in managing hypertension and angina. The combination helps to control heart rate and blood pressure more effectively but requires careful monitoring to avoid excessive hypotension or bradycardia.

3. Analgesics

Definition: Using multiple analgesics with different mechanisms can have an additive effect on pain relief, providing enhanced analgesia.

Examples:

a. **Acetaminophen and Ibuprofen:** Combining **acetaminophen** (e.g., Tylenol) with **ibuprofen** (e.g., Advil) can result in an additive effect on pain relief. This combination is often used for managing moderate pain, such as in postoperative settings, and can provide more effective pain control than either drug alone.

b. **Opioids and Non-Opioid Analgesics:** Using **opioids** (e.g., morphine) in combination with **non-opioid analgesics** (e.g., naproxen) can enhance pain relief through different mechanisms. This approach is useful in managing severe pain, such as in cancer patients, while reducing the opioid dose needed.

4. Antidiabetic Agents

Definition: Combining different antidiabetic agents can produce an additive effect on lowering blood glucose levels, which can help achieve better glycemic control.

Examples:

a. **Metformin and Sulfonylureas:** Combining **metformin** (e.g., glucophage) with **sulfonylureas** (e.g., glipizide) can provide an additive effect on glucose control in type 2 diabetes. Metformin reduces insulin resistance, while sulfonylureas increase insulin secretion, leading to better overall blood glucose management.

b. **Insulin and GLP-1 Agonists:** Combining **insulin** (e.g., insulin glargine) with **GLP-1 receptor agonists** (e.g., liraglutide) can result in an additive effect on controlling blood glucose levels. Insulin provides direct glucose lowering, while GLP-1 agonists enhance insulin secretion and reduce appetite.

5. Antihistamines

Definition: Combining antihistamines can produce an additive effect on alleviating allergic symptoms, although this practice is less common due to the risk of excessive sedation.

Examples:

a. **First-Generation Antihistamines:** Combining two **first-generation antihistamines** (e.g., diphenhydramine and chlorpheniramine) can provide enhanced relief from allergic symptoms. However, this combination is rarely recommended due to the risk of increased sedation and anticholinergic side effects.

b. **Antihistamines and Decongestants:** Combining **antihistamines** (e.g., cetirizine) with **decongestants** (e.g., pseudoephedrine) can offer an additive effect in treating allergic rhinitis. The antihistamine relieves allergic symptoms, while the decongestant alleviates nasal congestion.

Managing Additive Effects:

1. **Monitor for Adverse Effects:** Regularly assess patients for potential side effects or therapeutic excesses when using drug combinations with additive effects.
2. **Adjust Doses:** Carefully adjust dosages to achieve the desired therapeutic effect while minimizing the risk of adverse reactions.
3. **Patient Education:** Inform patients about the potential for enhanced effects and the importance of adhering to prescribed regimens.

4. **Consult Healthcare Providers:** Work with healthcare professionals to optimize drug combinations and manage additive effects effectively.

Pharmacokinetic Interactions:

Pharmacokinetic interactions in therapeutic incompatibilities occur when one drug affects the absorption, distribution, metabolism, or excretion of another drug, leading to altered therapeutic effects or adverse reactions. Here's a detailed look at pharmacokinetic interactions with examples:

1. Absorption Interactions

Definition: These interactions occur when one drug affects the absorption of another drug from the gastrointestinal tract, altering its bioavailability.

Examples:

a. **Antacids and Tetracyclines: Antacids** (containing calcium, magnesium, or aluminum) can bind with **tetracycline antibiotics** (e.g., doxycycline), forming insoluble complexes that reduce the absorption of the antibiotic. This decreases the effectiveness of the tetracycline.

b. **Grapefruit Juice and Statins: Grapefruit juice** contains compounds that inhibit the **CYP3A4 enzyme** in the liver and intestines. This enzyme is responsible for metabolizing many **statins** (e.g., atorvastatin). Inhibition of CYP3A4 leads to increased plasma levels of statins, enhancing their therapeutic effects but also increasing the risk of adverse effects like muscle toxicity.

2. Distribution Interactions

Definition: These interactions occur when one drug affects the distribution of another drug within the body, potentially altering its therapeutic effect.

Examples:

a. **Warfarin and NSAIDs: Warfarin** (an anticoagulant) and **NSAIDs** (e.g., ibuprofen) can compete for binding to plasma proteins. Since warfarin is highly protein-bound, competition with NSAIDs can increase the free (active) concentration of warfarin, heightening the risk of bleeding.

b. **Diuretics and Lithium: Diuretics** (e.g., hydrochlorothiazide) can alter the renal clearance of **lithium**, affecting its distribution. Diuretics can lead to decreased lithium clearance, increasing the risk of lithium toxicity.

3. Metabolism Interactions

Definition: These interactions occur when one drug alters the metabolism of another drug, often through induction or inhibition of metabolic enzymes.

Examples:

a. **CYP450 Enzyme Induction: Rifampin** (an antibiotic) is a potent inducer of **CYP450 enzymes**, particularly CYP3A4. This induction accelerates the metabolism of drugs metabolized by CYP3A4, such as **oral contraceptives** (e.g., ethinyl estradiol), potentially reducing their efficacy and increasing the risk of unintended pregnancies.

b. **CYP450 Enzyme Inhibition: Ketoconazole** (an antifungal) is a strong inhibitor of CYP3A4. When taken with drugs like **midazolam** (a benzodiazepine), ketoconazole can significantly increase midazolam levels, enhancing sedation and increasing the risk of adverse effects.

4. Excretion Interactions

Definition: These interactions occur when one drug affects the excretion of another drug, usually by influencing renal or hepatic elimination.

Examples:

a. **Probenecid and Penicillin: Probenecid** can inhibit the renal tubular secretion of **penicillin**, leading to increased plasma levels of penicillin. This interaction is sometimes used therapeutically to extend the duration of action of penicillin in infections.

b. **ACE Inhibitors and Diuretics: ACE inhibitors** (e.g., lisinopril) and **diuretics** (e.g., furosemide) can interact to alter renal function. Diuretics can lead to decreased renal blood flow, which might affect the excretion of ACE inhibitors and other drugs, potentially leading to increased drug levels and enhanced effects.

5. Food and Drug Interactions

Definition: The intake of certain foods can affect the pharmacokinetics of medications, altering their absorption, metabolism, or excretion.

Examples:

a. **Vitamin K-Rich Foods and Warfarin:** Foods high in **vitamin K** (e.g., spinach, kale) can counteract the effects of **warfarin** (an anticoagulant) by promoting clotting factor synthesis. Patients on warfarin are advised to maintain a consistent intake of vitamin K-rich foods to avoid fluctuations in anticoagulation levels.

b. **High-Fiber Foods and Digoxin: High-fiber diets** can reduce the absorption of **digoxin** (a heart medication) from the gastrointestinal tract. This can lead to reduced therapeutic effects of digoxin and may require dose adjustments.

Managing Pharmacokinetic Interactions:

1. **Drug Interaction Screening:** Regularly review and screen for potential drug interactions, especially when starting new medications or changing doses.
2. **Dose Adjustments:** Adjust drug doses based on the interaction effects to achieve the desired therapeutic outcomes while minimizing adverse effects.
3. **Patient Education:** Inform patients about the potential effects of food and drug interactions and the importance of adhering to prescribed therapies.
4. **Monitoring:** Regularly monitor patients for signs of altered drug efficacy or adverse reactions, particularly when drugs with known pharmacokinetic interactions are used.
5. **Consult Healthcare Providers:** Work with healthcare professionals to optimize drug therapy and manage pharmacokinetic interactions effectively.

Pharmacodynamic Interactions:

Pharmacodynamic interactions in therapeutic incompatibilities occur when one drug affects the pharmacological effect of another drug at the site of action. These interactions can either enhance or diminish the therapeutic effect of the drugs involved or lead to adverse effects. Here's a detailed look at pharmacodynamic interactions with examples:

1. Additive Effects

Definition: Additive effects occur when the combined effect of two drugs is equal to the sum of their individual effects. This can be beneficial or harmful depending on the context.

Examples:

a. **Pain Management:** Combining **acetaminophen** (e.g., Tylenol) with **ibuprofen** (e.g., Advil) can produce an additive effect on pain relief. Both drugs have different mechanisms of action, with acetaminophen mainly acting centrally and ibuprofen having anti-inflammatory properties. Together, they provide enhanced pain relief.

b. **Antihypertensives:** Using **ACE inhibitors** (e.g., lisinopril) with **calcium channel blockers** (e.g., amlodipine) can provide an additive effect in lowering blood pressure. The ACE inhibitor reduces blood pressure by inhibiting the renin-angiotensin system, while the calcium channel blocker relaxes blood vessels.

2. Synergistic Effects

Definition: Synergistic effects occur when the combined effect of two drugs is greater than the sum of their individual effects. This can enhance therapeutic outcomes but also increase the risk of adverse effects.

Examples:

a. **Antibiotic Therapy:** Combining **penicillin** (a beta-lactam antibiotic) with **gentamicin** (an aminoglycoside) can produce a synergistic effect against certain bacteria. Penicillin disrupts bacterial cell wall synthesis, while gentamicin inhibits protein synthesis, leading to more effective bacterial killing.

b. **Sedation:** Combining **benzodiazepines** (e.g., diazepam) with **opioids** (e.g., morphine) can have a synergistic effect on sedation and respiratory depression. This combination should be used cautiously due to the increased risk of severe sedation and respiratory complications.

3. Antagonistic Effects

Definition: Antagonistic effects occur when one drug reduces or counteracts the effect of another drug. This can lead to reduced therapeutic efficacy or increased risk of adverse effects.

Examples:

a. **Opioids and Naloxone: Naloxone** (an opioid antagonist) can reverse the effects of opioids such as **morphine**. While this is beneficial in cases of opioid overdose, it can also counteract the analgesic effects of opioids in patients who require pain management.

b. **Beta-Blockers and Beta-Adrenergic Agonists:** Combining **beta-blockers** (e.g., propranolol) with **beta-adrenergic agonists** (e.g., albuterol) can have antagonistic effects. The beta-blocker can reduce the efficacy of the beta-agonist in managing asthma symptoms.

4. Additive Toxicity

Definition: Additive toxicity occurs when the combined use of two drugs increases the risk of adverse effects due to their similar toxic profiles.

Examples:

a. **NSAIDs and Anticoagulants:** Combining **NSAIDs** (e.g., ibuprofen) with **anticoagulants** (e.g., warfarin) can lead to additive toxicity, specifically gastrointestinal bleeding. Both drugs increase bleeding risk, and their combined use enhances this risk.

b. **Aminoglycosides and Other Nephrotoxic Drugs: Aminoglycoside antibiotics** (e.g., gentamicin) combined with other nephrotoxic drugs (e.g., vancomycin) can result in additive nephrotoxicity. This combination increases the risk of kidney damage.

5. Pharmacological Interactions

Definition: Pharmacological interactions occur when one drug alters the effect of another by interacting at the same receptor site or influencing the same physiological pathway.

Examples:

a. **ACE Inhibitors and Potassium-Sparing Diuretics:** Combining **ACE inhibitors** (e.g., lisinopril) with **potassium-sparing diuretics** (e.g., spironolactone) can lead to hyperkalemia. Both drugs can increase potassium levels, and their combined effect can be harmful.

b. **Antihistamines and CNS Depressants:** Using **first-generation antihistamines** (e.g., diphenhydramine) with **CNS depressants** (e.g., benzodiazepines) can enhance sedation and impair cognitive function due to their cumulative depressant effects on the central nervous system.

Managing Pharmacodynamic Interactions:

1. **Careful Drug Selection:** Choose drugs with complementary effects to avoid antagonistic interactions and minimize the risk of additive toxicity.
2. **Monitor Therapeutic Responses:** Regularly assess patients for effectiveness and adverse effects of drug combinations.
3. **Adjust Doses:** Modify drug dosages as needed to achieve desired effects while minimizing risks.
4. **Educate Patients:** Inform patients about potential interactions and the importance of adhering to prescribed regimens.
5. **Consult Healthcare Providers:** Collaborate with healthcare professionals to optimize drug therapy and manage pharmacodynamic interactions effectively.

Therapeutic Duplication:

Therapeutic duplication in therapeutic incompatibilities occurs when two or more drugs with similar therapeutic effects are used simultaneously, leading to excessive or redundant treatment. This can result in increased risk of adverse effects, drug interactions, or diminished therapeutic efficacy. Here's a detailed look at therapeutic duplication with examples:

1. Antihypertensives

Definition: Therapeutic duplication occurs when multiple antihypertensive drugs with similar mechanisms of action are used together, potentially leading to excessive blood pressure reduction and increased risk of adverse effects.

Examples:

a. **ACE Inhibitors and ARBs:** Using **ACE inhibitors** (e.g., lisinopril) with **Angiotensin II Receptor Blockers (ARBs)** (e.g., losartan) can lead to therapeutic duplication. Both classes of drugs work on the renin-angiotensin system to lower blood pressure. Their combined use increases the risk of hypotension, hyperkalemia, and renal impairment without providing additional benefits over using either class alone.

b. **Beta-Blockers and Non-Selective Beta-Blockers:** Combining **beta-blockers** (e.g., metoprolol) with other **non-selective beta-blockers** (e.g., propranolol) can cause therapeutic duplication. Both drugs reduce heart rate and blood pressure through similar mechanisms, potentially leading to excessive bradycardia and hypotension.

2. Pain Management

Definition: Therapeutic duplication occurs when multiple analgesics with similar mechanisms are used, leading to increased risk of side effects and no added benefit.

Examples:

a. **Acetaminophen and Other Acetaminophen-Containing Products:** Using **acetaminophen** (e.g., Tylenol) with other products containing acetaminophen (e.g., some combination cold or flu medications) can lead to therapeutic duplication. Excessive acetaminophen intake increases the risk of liver toxicity.

b. **NSAIDs and Other NSAIDs:** Combining **NSAIDs** (e.g., ibuprofen) with other NSAIDs (e.g., naproxen) can cause therapeutic duplication. Both drugs have similar anti-inflammatory and analgesic effects, and their combined use can increase the risk of gastrointestinal bleeding, ulceration, and renal impairment.

3. Antibiotics

Definition: Therapeutic duplication occurs when multiple antibiotics with similar mechanisms of action are used together, potentially leading to unnecessary exposure and resistance.

Examples:

a. **Penicillins and Cephalosporins:** Using **penicillins** (e.g., amoxicillin) with **cephalosporins** (e.g., cefalexin) can result in therapeutic duplication if both are used to treat similar infections. Both classes of antibiotics target bacterial cell wall synthesis, and their combined use may increase the risk of adverse effects like allergic reactions and contribute to resistance.

b. **Macrolides and Other Macrolides:** Combining **macrolides** (e.g., azithromycin) with other macrolides (e.g., clarithromycin) can lead to therapeutic duplication. Both drugs have similar mechanisms of action against bacteria, and their use together can increase the risk of gastrointestinal disturbances and potential drug interactions.

4. Diuretics

Definition: Therapeutic duplication occurs when multiple diuretics with similar effects are used, which can lead to excessive fluid and electrolyte imbalances.

Examples:

a. **Thiazide Diuretics and Loop Diuretics:** Using **thiazide diuretics** (e.g., hydrochlorothiazide) with **loop diuretics** (e.g., furosemide) can cause therapeutic duplication if both are used to manage conditions like heart failure or hypertension. Both types of diuretics increase urine output, potentially leading to severe dehydration, electrolyte imbalances, and renal impairment.

b. **Potassium-Sparing Diuretics and Other Potassium-Sparing Diuretics:** Combining **potassium-sparing diuretics** (e.g., spironolactone) with other potassium-sparing agents (e.g., triamterene) can result in therapeutic duplication. Both drugs increase potassium levels, increasing the risk of hyperkalemia.

5. Antidepressants

Definition: Therapeutic duplication occurs when multiple antidepressants with similar mechanisms of action are used, potentially leading to excessive serotonin levels or other adverse effects.

Examples:

a. **SSRIs and SNRIs:** Using **Selective Serotonin Reuptake Inhibitors (SSRIs)** (e.g., sertraline) with **Serotonin-Norepinephrine Reuptake Inhibitors (SNRIs)** (e.g., venlafaxine) can lead to therapeutic duplication. Both classes of antidepressants affect serotonin levels, increasing the risk of serotonin syndrome, characterized by symptoms such as agitation, confusion, and increased heart rate.

b. **MAOIs and Other Antidepressants:** Combining **Monoamine Oxidase Inhibitors (MAOIs)** (e.g., phenelzine) with other antidepressants (e.g., tricyclic antidepressants) can result in therapeutic duplication and increase the risk of severe side effects like hypertensive crises.

Managing Therapeutic Duplication:

1. **Review Medication Regimens:** Regularly review patients' medication lists to identify and avoid therapeutic duplication.
2. **Assess Drug Necessity:** Ensure that each drug in a regimen has a distinct therapeutic purpose and that combined therapies are justified.

3. **Monitor for Adverse Effects:** Observe patients closely for signs of adverse effects related to therapeutic duplication.
4. **Educate Patients:** Inform patients about the importance of adhering to prescribed therapies and avoiding over-the-counter medications that may duplicate therapy.
5. **Consult Healthcare Providers:** Collaborate with healthcare professionals to optimize drug therapy and manage potential therapeutic duplication.

Multiple-Choice Questions (MCQs)

1. What is the definition of pharmaceutical incompatibilities?
   a) The beneficial interaction between two drugs
   b) Undesirable interactions between pharmaceutical substances
   c) The increase in drug efficacy when combined
   d) The mixing of drugs in the same container
2. Which of the following is an example of physical incompatibility?
   a) Oxidation
   b) Precipitation
   c) Neutralization
   d) Complex formation
3. What happens during phase separation in pharmaceutical incompatibilities?
   a) A solid forms from a solution
   b) Two liquids separate into distinct phases
   c) A color change occurs
   d) The drug decomposes
4. Which type of incompatibility involves a chemical reaction that leads to the breakdown of a drug?
   a) Physical incompatibility

b) Biological incompatibility

c) Chemical incompatibility

d) Therapeutic incompatibility

5. What is a common result of neutralization reactions in pharmaceutical incompatibilities?

a) Precipitation

b) Phasc separation

c) Reduced therapeutic effects

d) Increased drug efficacy

6. Which type of incompatibility occurs due to changes in the drug formulation or conditions like pH?

a) Chemical incompatibility

b) Physical incompatibility

c) Biological incompatibility

d) Pharmaceutical incompatibility

7. What is a key characteristic of biological incompatibilities?

a) Formation of insoluble complexes

b) Toxic effects or unexpected side effects

c) Cloudiness or turbidity

d) Phase separation

8. What should be done to manage physical pharmaceutical incompatibilities?

a) Use stabilizers and appropriate excipients

b) Combine drugs in the same container

c) Increase the pH of all solutions

d) Avoid consultation with professionals

9. Which of the following is an example of a degradation reaction?

a) Mixing epinephrine with sodium nitrite

b) Combining calcium chloride and sodium carbonate

c) Mixing insulin with glucose solutions

d) Exposure of penicillin to high pH solutions

10. Which type of incompatibility is associated with toxic effects due to drug interactions?

a) Physical incompatibility
b) Pharmaceutical incompatibility
c) Chemical incompatibility
d) Biological incompatibility

11. What is a potential outcome of synergistic effects in therapeutic incompatibilities?

a) Reduced therapeutic effect
b) Enhanced therapeutic effect
c) No change in drug efficacy
d) Complete neutralization

12. Combining two antihypertensive agents may lead to which of the following effects?

a) Increased blood pressure
b) Synergistic effect
c) Antagonistic effect
d) Physical separation

13. What type of therapeutic incompatibility occurs when one drug reduces the effect of another drug?

a) Synergistic effect
b) Additive effect
c) Antagonistic effect
d) Physical incompatibility

14. Which of the following represents an additive effect in therapeutic incompatibilities?

a) Combining acetaminophen and ibuprofen for pain relief
b) Using naloxone with morphine

c) Mixing warfarin with aspirin

d) Combining beta-blockers with beta-adrenergic agonists

15. What type of interaction occurs when grapefruit juice affects the metabolism of statins?

a) Physical incompatibility

b) Pharmacodynamic interaction

c) Pharmacokinetic interaction

d) Therapeutic duplication

16. What is the primary concern when therapeutic duplication occurs?

a) Reduced therapeutic effect

b) Increased risk of adverse effects

c) Enhanced drug efficacy

d) Improved patient outcomes

17. Which type of incompatibility involves the formation of insoluble complexes between drugs and metal ions?

a) Physical incompatibility

b) Chemical incompatibility

c) Biological incompatibility

d) Therapeutic incompatibility

18. Which of the following strategies is important for managing chemical pharmaceutical incompatibilities?

a) Increasing the temperature of all drug formulations

b) Avoiding the use of stabilizers

c) Conducting compatibility testing

d) Ignoring pH adjustments

19. How can therapeutic duplication be prevented?

a) Combining similar drugs to increase efficacy

b) Regularly reviewing and optimizing medication regimens

c) Avoiding the use of complementary therapies

d) Ignoring patient history

20. What is the result of combining insulin with glucose solutions in the context of pharmaceutical incompatibilities?

a) Phase separation

b) Neutralization reaction

c) Formation of a new compound

d) Increased solubility

Short Answer Type Questions (Subjective)

1. Define pharmaceutical incompatibilities and explain their significance in healthcare.
2. What are the different types of pharmaceutical incompatibilities?
3. Describe the process of phase separation in physical incompatibilities with an example.
4. Explain the concept of degradation reactions in chemical incompatibilities.
5. How do neutralization reactions affect the therapeutic efficacy of drugs?
6. What role does pH play in pharmaceutical incompatibilities?
7. Describe a situation where biological incompatibilities might occur.
8. How can physical pharmaceutical incompatibilities be managed effectively?
9. What are the potential outcomes of synergistic effects in therapeutic incompatibilities?
10. How can antagonistic effects lead to therapeutic failure?
11. Explain the concept of additive effects in therapeutic incompatibilities with an example.
12. What are pharmacokinetic interactions, and how do they affect drug therapy?
13. Discuss the risks associated with therapeutic duplication.
14. How does temperature affect chemical pharmaceutical incompatibilities?
15. Describe a scenario where complex formation leads to reduced drug efficacy.

16. What is the importance of compatibility testing in preventing pharmaceutical incompatibilities?
17. Explain how food-drug interactions can lead to pharmacokinetic incompatibilities.
18. How can healthcare professionals prevent and manage therapeutic incompatibilities?
19. Describe the impact of oxidation reactions on drug stability.
20. How does patient education play a role in managing pharmaceutical incompatibilities?

Long Answer Type Questions (Subjective)

1. Discuss the different types of pharmaceutical incompatibilities and provide detailed examples of each.
2. Explain how physical, chemical, and biological incompatibilities can affect drug stability, efficacy, and patient safety.
3. Analyze the role of pH and temperature in pharmaceutical incompatibilities and discuss strategies to manage them.
4. Describe the potential consequences of therapeutic incompatibilities, including synergistic, antagonistic, and additive effects, with relevant examples.
5. Discuss the importance of pharmacokinetic and pharmacodynamic interactions in drug therapy and how they contribute to therapeutic incompatibilities.
6. Explain the concept of therapeutic duplication and its implications for patient safety. Provide strategies to identify and prevent it.
7. Discuss the significance of compatibility testing and professional consultation in managing pharmaceutical incompatibilities in clinical practice.

8. Analyze the role of patient education in preventing and managing pharmaceutical incompatibilities, especially in complex drug regimens.
9. Explore the impact of food-drug interactions on pharmacokinetic incompatibilities, providing examples and strategies for management.

Answer Key for MCQs

1. (b) Undesirable interactions between pharmaceutical substances
2. (b) Precipitation
3. (b) Two liquids separate into distinct phases
4. (c) Chemical incompatibility
5. (c) Reduced therapeutic effects
6. (d) Pharmaceutical incompatibility
7. (b) Toxic effects or unexpected side effects
8. (a) Use stabilizers and appropriate excipients
9. (d) Exposure of penicillin to high pH solutions
10. (d) Biological incompatibility
11. (b) Enhanced therapeutic effect
12. (b) Synergistic effect
13. (c) Antagonistic effect
14. (a) Combining acetaminophen and ibuprofen for pain relief
15. (c) Pharmacokinetic interaction
16. (b) Increased risk of adverse effects
17. (b) Chemical incompatibility
18. (c) Conducting compatibility testing
19. (b) Regularly reviewing and optimizing medication regimens
20. (b) Neutralization reaction

CHAPTER – 13

SEMISOLID DOSAGE FORMS

INTRODUCTION:

Semisolid dosage forms are a category of pharmaceutical preparations that have a consistency between liquids and solids. They are used for topical, ophthalmic, and rectal administration. Here's an overview of their characteristics, types, and uses:

Characteristics of Semisolid Dosage Forms

1. **Consistency**: They are thicker than liquids but can be spread or applied easily. Their viscosity allows them to remain in place at the application site.
2. **Application**: Typically used for external applications on the skin, mucous membranes, or for localized treatment in the body.
3. **Absorption**: They may provide local or systemic effects depending on their formulation and the active ingredient.

Types of Semisolid Dosage Forms

1. **Ointments**
    a. **Definition**: Ointments are greasy, lipid-based semisolid preparations intended for external application to the skin or mucous membranes.
    b. **Base Types**: They can be hydrocarbon bases (e.g., petrolatum), absorption bases (e.g., hydrophilic petrolatum), or water-removable bases (e.g., creams).
    c. **Uses**: Often used for their emollient properties, to deliver active ingredients like anti-inflammatory drugs, or for protective purposes.

2. **Creams**
    a. **Definition**: Creams are emulsions of oil and water, providing a less greasy alternative to ointments.
    b. **Types**: They can be oil-in-water (O/W) or water-in-oil (W/O) emulsions.
    c. **Uses**: Suitable for conditions where a less greasy application is desired, such as for moisturizing or delivering medications like corticosteroids.
3. **Gels**
    a. **Definition**: Gels are semisolid systems where a gelling agent is used to stabilize a liquid phase. They are typically clear and non-greasy.
    b. **Types**: Can be aqueous gels or hydroalcoholic gels.
    c. **Uses**: Often used for their cooling and soothing properties, for delivering drugs like anti-acne agents or for personal care products.
4. **Pastes**
    a. **Definition**: Pastes are thicker than ointments and contain a higher percentage of solid particles.
    b. **Uses**: Provide a protective barrier and are often used in situations where a more occlusive effect is needed, such as in diaper rash treatments.
5. **Emulsions**
    a. **Definition**: Semisolid emulsions can be similar to creams but may have a thicker consistency.
    b. **Uses**: Used for both cosmetic and pharmaceutical applications, including moisturizers and therapeutic agents.

Formulation Considerations

1. **Stability**: The physical and chemical stability of the active ingredient must be ensured throughout the shelf life of the product.

2. **Compatibility**: The choice of base or vehicle must be compatible with the active ingredient and the intended application site.
3. **Release Rate**: The formulation should control the release rate of the drug, allowing for effective therapy with minimal side effects.

Applications

1. **Dermatological Treatments**: Used for skin conditions like eczema, psoriasis, and fungal infections.
2. **Ophthalmic Applications**: Gels and ointments for eye infections or dryness.
3. **Rectal Administration**: Used in suppositories or topical treatments for conditions like hemorrhoids.

DEFINITIONS OF SEMISOLID DOSAGE FORMS

1. **Ointments**

a. **Definition**: Ointments are viscous, greasy, and lipid-based semisolid preparations designed for external application to the skin or mucous membranes. They are typically composed of a base or vehicle, which can be either anhydrous (without water) or containing a small amount of water.

b. **Characteristics**: They are occlusive, providing a barrier that can enhance the absorption of active ingredients and moisturize the skin. Ointments can be used for both local and systemic drug delivery.

2. Creams

a. **Definition**: Creams are semisolid emulsions of oil and water, with a consistency that is less greasy than ointments. They are typically composed of a combination of water, oils, and emulsifiers.

b. **Characteristics**: Creams are spreadable and are designed to be absorbed into the skin more easily than ointments. They can be formulated as oil-in-water (O/W) or water-in-oil (W/O) emulsions, depending on the desired properties.

3. Gels

a. **Definition**: Gels are semisolid systems consisting of a liquid phase that is stabilized by a gelling agent. They are typically clear and have a jelly-like consistency.

b. **Characteristics**: Gels are non-greasy and often provide a cooling effect upon application. They are used for their ease of application and quick absorption, and can be formulated as aqueous gels or hydroalcoholic gels.

4. Pastes

a. **Definition**: Pastes are thicker than ointments and contain a high percentage of solid particles dispersed in a base. They have a more substantial and less spreadable consistency.

b. **Characteristics**: Pastes form a protective layer on the skin and are used when a more occlusive and prolonged effect is desired. They are often used for their emollient and barrier properties.

5. Emulsions

a. **Definition**: Emulsions are semisolid preparations that consist of a mixture of two immiscible liquids (e.g., oil and water) stabilized by emulsifiers. They can vary in consistency but are generally thicker than creams.

b. **Characteristics**: Emulsions can be formulated to be either water-in-oil (W/O) or oil-in-water (O/W), depending on the intended use and desired properties. They are used for both cosmetic and therapeutic purposes.

6. Suppositories (Rectal Semisolids)

a. **Definition**: Suppositories are semisolid dosage forms designed for insertion into body cavities (rectal, vaginal) where they dissolve or melt to release the active ingredient.

b. **Characteristics**: They are formulated to be solid at room temperature but melt or dissolve at body temperature. They are used for localized or systemic effects, depending on the medication and the site of administration.

CLASSIFICATION OF SEMISOLID DOSAGE FORMS

Semisolid dosage forms can be classified based on their consistency, composition, and intended application. Here's a detailed classification:

1. Based on Consistency

a. **Ointments**

i. **Greasy Ointments**: Composed of hydrocarbons or petrolatum (e.g., Vaseline). These are highly occlusive and protect the skin from moisture loss.

ii. **Absorption Ointments**: Contain emulsifiers that allow them to absorb water or other fluids (e.g., hydrophilic petrolatum). They can be used to deliver medications through the skin.

iii. **Water-Removable Ointments**: Similar to creams, they contain a water-soluble base that is less greasy and easier to wash off.

b. **Creams**

i. **Oil-in-Water (O/W) Creams**: Oil droplets dispersed in a water phase. They are less greasy and more easily absorbed by the skin.

ii. **Water-in-Oil (W/O) Creams**: Water droplets dispersed in an oil phase. They are more emollient and form a protective barrier on the skin.

c. **Gels**

i. **Aqueous Gels**: Contain water as the main component and a gelling agent (e.g., carbomers). They are typically clear and non-greasy.

ii. **Hydroalcoholic Gels**: Contain alcohol and water, often used for their quick-drying properties and antibacterial effects.

d. **Pastes**

   i. **Thick Pastes**: Contain a high percentage of solids dispersed in a base. They are less spreadable but provide a protective barrier (e.g., zinc oxide paste).

e. **Emulsions**

   i. **Cream-like Emulsions**: Intermediate in consistency between creams and gels, often used in pharmaceutical and cosmetic applications.

   ii. **Thick Emulsions**: Have a more substantial consistency and can be used for prolonged contact with the skin or mucous membranes.

f. **Suppositories**

   i. **Rectal Suppositories**: Designed for insertion into the rectum, often used for localized or systemic effects.

   ii. **Vaginal Suppositories**: Intended for insertion into the vagina, used for local treatment or hormonal delivery.

2. Based on Composition

a. **Hydrocarbon Bases**

   i. **Definition**: Ointments with bases like petrolatum or mineral oils. They are occlusive and protective.

   ii. **Uses**: Often used for their emollient and protective properties.

b. **Absorption Bases**

   i. **Definition**: Bases that can absorb water or other fluids, often used to enhance skin penetration.

   ii. **Uses**: Used for drugs requiring increased permeability through the skin.

c. **Water-Removable Bases**

   i. **Definition**: Bases that are easily removable with water, often used in creams and lotions.

   ii. **Uses**: Preferred for less greasy applications and easier removal.

d. **Gelling Agents**

  i. **Definition**: Substances like carbomers or alginates used to form gels.

  ii. **Uses**: Provide thickening and stabilizing properties for gels and pastes.

e. **Active Ingredient Combinations**

  i. **Definition**: Semisolid forms can be combined with various active ingredients, including anti-inflammatory agents, antibiotics, or corticosteroids.

  ii. **Uses**: Tailored formulations to address specific therapeutic needs.

3. Based on Intended Application

a. **Dermatological Applications**

  i. **Definition**: Used for conditions affecting the skin (e.g., eczema, psoriasis).

  ii. **Types**: Ointments, creams, and gels are commonly used.

b. **Ophthalmic Applications**

  i. **Definition**: Formulations designed for the eye area.

  ii. **Types**: Eye creams, gels, and ointments, often with specific safety and stability requirements.

c. **Rectal Applications**

  i. **Definition**: Formulations for rectal insertion.

  ii. **Types**: Suppositories and rectal creams or gels.

d. **Vaginal Applications**

  i. **Definition**: Formulations for vaginal insertion.

  ii. **Types**: Vaginal suppositories, gels, and creams.

MECHANISMS AND FACTORS INFLUENCING DERMAL PENETRATION OF DRUGS

The mechanisms and factors influencing dermal penetration of drugs from semisolid dosage forms are crucial for effective topical drug delivery.

Here's a detailed look at how drugs penetrate the skin and the factors that affect this process:

Mechanisms of Dermal Penetration

1. **Diffusion Through the Skin Layers**
    a. **Stratum Corneum**: The outermost layer of the skin is the primary barrier to drug penetration. Drugs must diffuse through this layer before reaching deeper skin layers.
    b. **Epidermis**: Once past the stratum corneum, drugs diffuse through the epidermis, which has a higher water content and is less dense than the stratum corneum.
    c. **Dermis**: The dermis, with its rich blood supply, allows for systemic absorption if the drug reaches this layer.
2. **Permeation Pathways**
    a. **Intercellular Route**: Drugs diffuse through the lipid matrix between corneocytes in the stratum corneum. This is the most common route for lipophilic (fat-loving) drugs.
    b. **Transcellular Route**: Drugs pass through the cells themselves. This route is less common and typically involves small molecules.
    c. **Follicular Route**: Drugs can enter the skin through hair follicles and sebaceous glands. This pathway can enhance penetration for certain drugs, particularly if they are lipophilic.
3. **Active Transport**
    a. **Carrier-Mediated Transport**: Some drugs use specific transport proteins in the skin to facilitate their movement across the skin barrier.
    b. **Electroporation**: Electrical fields can temporarily increase skin permeability, allowing for enhanced drug penetration.

Factors Influencing Dermal Penetration

1. **Drug Properties**

a. **Molecular Size and Weight**: Smaller molecules generally penetrate the skin more easily. Larger molecules may have reduced penetration.
b. **Lipophilicity**: Lipophilic drugs are more likely to diffuse through the lipid-rich stratum corneum. However, highly lipophilic drugs may also have difficulty in penetrating the aqueous layers of the epidermis.
c. **Solubility**: Drugs need to be soluble in the vehicle used in the semisolid dosage form to be effectively delivered. Both lipophilic and hydrophilic drugs must be compatible with the formulation base.

2. **Formulation Characteristics**
   a. **Base Composition**: The type of base (e.g., ointment, cream, gel) affects drug release and penetration. Ointments, for instance, tend to be more occlusive, enhancing drug absorption, while creams and gels may offer better skin compatibility.
   b. **Particle Size**: In formulations containing particulate matter (e.g., pastes), smaller particles can enhance penetration by increasing the surface area available for absorption.
3. **Skin Conditions**
   a. **Hydration**: Well-hydrated skin is more permeable than dry skin. Hydration can be influenced by the formulation's ability to provide moisture.
   b. **Skin Integrity**: Damaged or inflamed skin can have altered permeability, potentially enhancing drug absorption but also increasing the risk of systemic side effects.
4. **Application Factors**

a. **Occlusion**: Using an occlusive dressing (e.g., a bandage) can enhance penetration by preventing the loss of moisture and increasing the skin temperature, which can improve drug diffusion.

b. **Duration of Contact**: Longer contact times generally allow for greater drug penetration.

5. **Skin Site and Age**

a. **Site of Application**: Different areas of the body have varying degrees of permeability. For instance, areas with thinner skin or more hair follicles (e.g., scalp) may exhibit different penetration characteristics.

b. **Age**: The skin's barrier function and permeability can change with age. Infants and elderly individuals may have different absorption profiles compared to young adults.

6. **Physiological Factors**

a. **Blood Flow**: Increased blood flow to the skin (e.g., from exercise or heat) can enhance systemic absorption of topically applied drugs.

b. **Skin Temperature**: Elevated skin temperature can increase drug permeability by enhancing drug solubility and diffusion rates.

PREPARATION OF OINTMENTS

The preparation of ointments involves a series of steps to ensure the proper formulation, consistency, and effectiveness of the product. Here's a detailed look at the process:

1. Selection of Ingredients

a. **Active Ingredients**: The pharmaceutical agents intended for therapeutic action.

b. **Base**: The vehicle in which the active ingredient is dispersed. Bases can be hydrocarbon bases (e.g., petrolatum), absorption bases (e.g., hydrophilic petrolatum), or water-removable bases (e.g., creams).

c. **Additives**: May include preservatives, emulsifiers, stabilizers, or agents to enhance skin penetration.

2. Preparation of the Base

a. **Hydrocarbon Bases**: Often prepared by melting and mixing hydrocarbons (e.g., petrolatum) at elevated temperatures. This base is generally used for its occlusive properties.

b. **Absorption Bases**: Prepared by melting and mixing with emulsifiers that allow for the incorporation of water or aqueous solutions. These bases are used to allow for some degree of water absorption.

c. **Water-Removable Bases**: Prepared by blending emulsifying agents with water and other components to form a stable emulsion. These bases are less greasy and easier to wash off.

3. Incorporation of Active Ingredients

a. **Powdered Active Ingredients**: Should be finely powdered to ensure even distribution and to avoid grittiness. They can be incorporated using geometric dilution (mixing the powder with a small portion of the base and gradually adding more).

b. **Liquid Active Ingredients**: These are added directly to the base or mixed with a compatible solvent before incorporation.

4. Mixing and Homogenization

a. **Mixing**: The active ingredients are combined with the base using methods such as spatulation (using a spatula to blend ingredients on an ointment slab), trituration (grinding ingredients together), or by using a mechanical mixer.

b. **Homogenization**: Ensures that the ointment has a uniform texture and consistency. This can be achieved using a mortar and pestle, an ointment mill, or a homogenizer. Homogenization helps to eliminate lumps and achieve a smooth, consistent product.

5. Quality Control

a. **Consistency**: The final product should have the desired consistency and spreadability. This is assessed through various tests, including rheological testing.

b. **Uniformity**: The distribution of the active ingredient should be homogeneous. This can be checked through sampling and analyzing the ointment for active ingredient concentration.

c. **Microbial Testing**: To ensure the absence of harmful microorganisms, especially if the formulation does not include preservatives.

6. Packaging

a. **Containers**: Ointments are typically packaged in tubes, jars, or pots that protect the product from contamination and degradation.

b. **Labeling**: Proper labeling includes information on the active ingredients, usage instructions, expiration date, and storage conditions.

7. Stability Testing

a. **Storage Conditions**: The ointment is tested under various storage conditions (e.g., temperature, humidity) to ensure stability and efficacy throughout its shelf life.

b. **Shelf Life**: Determining the shelf life involves assessing the physical, chemical, and microbiological stability over time.

Additional Considerations

a. **Compatibility**: Ensure that all ingredients are compatible with each other and with the chosen base. Incompatible substances may affect the stability or efficacy of the ointment.

b. **Sterilization**: For certain applications, especially in ophthalmic or wound care, sterilization might be necessary to prevent contamination.

PREPARATION OF PASTES

The preparation of pastes involves creating a semisolid dosage form that contains a high proportion of solid particles dispersed in a base. Pastes are generally used for their thick consistency and protective properties. Here's a detailed look at the process of preparing pastes:

1. Selection of Ingredients

a. **Active Ingredients**: The therapeutic agents intended for topical application. These can be powders, powders that need to be finely ground, or other solid substances.

b. **Base**: The medium that holds the active ingredients. Common bases for pastes include:

i. **Hydrocarbon Bases**: Composed mainly of hydrocarbons like petrolatum, providing occlusiveness.

ii. **Absorption Bases**: Bases that can absorb water or aqueous solutions, such as hydrophilic petrolatum.

iii. **Water-Removable Bases**: Bases that are less greasy and easier to remove, often used in creams or gels.

c. **Additives**: These may include stabilizers, emulsifiers, thickeners, or preservatives, depending on the formulation needs.

2. Preparation of the Base

a. **Hydrocarbon Bases**: Typically prepared by melting the hydrocarbons at a controlled temperature. This base is used for its occlusive and protective properties.

b. **Absorption Bases**: Prepared by melting the base and mixing it with emulsifiers that can absorb water or aqueous solutions.

c. **Water-Removable Bases**: Prepared by blending emulsifying agents with water and other components to form a stable emulsion. These bases are generally less greasy.

3. Incorporation of Active Ingredients

a. **Powdered Active Ingredients**: These need to be finely powdered to ensure they mix well with the base and to avoid grittiness in the final product. The powders are usually incorporated using geometric dilution (mixing a small portion of the base with the powder and gradually adding more) or other mixing techniques.

b. **Liquid Active Ingredients**: If the active ingredients are liquids, they are usually mixed directly with the base or with a suitable solvent before incorporation.

4. Mixing and Homogenization

a. **Mixing**: The process of blending active ingredients with the base to achieve a uniform distribution. Techniques include:
   i. **Spatulation**: Using a spatula to mix ingredients on an ointment slab.
   ii. **Trituration**: Grinding powders together with the base using a mortar and pestle.
   iii. **Mechanical Mixing**: Using mixers or mills to blend the ingredients thoroughly.

b. **Homogenization**: Ensures that the paste has a consistent texture and that the active ingredients are evenly distributed. This may involve using a mortar and pestle, an ointment mill, or a high-shear mixer.

5. Quality Control

a. **Consistency**: Checking the final product to ensure it has the desired thickness and spreadability. This is usually assessed by rheological testing.

b. **Uniformity**: Ensuring that the active ingredients are evenly distributed throughout the paste. This can be tested by sampling different parts of the paste and analyzing them for active ingredient concentration.

c. **Microbial Testing**: Ensuring the paste is free from harmful microorganisms, especially if it does not contain preservatives.

6. Packaging

a. **Containers**: Pastes are typically packaged in containers that protect the product from contamination and degradation, such as tubes, jars, or pots.

b. **Labeling**: Proper labeling includes information about the active ingredients, usage instructions, expiration date, and storage conditions.

7. Stability Testing

a. **Storage Conditions**: Testing the paste under various conditions (temperature, humidity) to ensure it remains stable throughout its shelf life.

b. **Shelf Life**: Evaluating the paste's physical, chemical, and microbiological stability over time to determine its shelf life.

Additional Considerations

a. **Compatibility**: Ensuring all ingredients are compatible with each other and with the base. Incompatible substances can affect the paste's stability or efficacy.

b. **Viscosity**: The viscosity of the paste should be appropriate for its intended use. This may be adjusted by varying the concentration of solid particles or the choice of base.

PREPARATION OF CREAMS

The preparation of creams involves creating a semisolid dosage form that consists of a stable emulsion of oil and water. Creams are used for their ease of application, absorption, and moisturizing properties. Here's a detailed overview of the process:

1. Selection of Ingredients

a. **Active Ingredients**: Therapeutic agents that provide the intended medicinal effects. These can be in the form of powders, liquids, or other forms.

b. **Base Components**: The components of the cream base, including emulsifiers, stabilizers, and the oil and water phases.

   i. **Oils**: Provide the oil phase in the emulsion, contributing to the cream's texture and moisturizing properties.

ii. **Water**: Provides the aqueous phase, which helps in the spreadability and absorption of the cream.

iii. **Emulsifiers**: Agents that stabilize the emulsion by reducing the surface tension between the oil and water phases.

2. Preparation of the Base

a. **Oil Phase Preparation**:

i. **Heating**: The oil phase components, including oils, emulsifiers, and sometimes waxes, are heated to melt and mix thoroughly.

ii. **Homogenization**: Ensuring the oil phase components are well-dispersed and free from lumps.

b. **Water Phase Preparation**:

i. **Heating**: The water phase components, including water, any aqueous-soluble emulsifiers, and other ingredients, are heated to a temperature that helps in the mixing with the oil phase.

ii. **Mixing**: Ensuring that any solutes in the water phase are fully dissolved.

3. Combining Oil and Water Phases

a. **Emulsification**:

i. **Addition**: The oil phase is slowly added to the water phase while continuously stirring to form an emulsion.

ii. **Mixing**: Using high-shear mixers or homogenizers to ensure the oil and water phases are thoroughly mixed and the emulsion is stable.

iii. **Cooling**: As the emulsion cools, it should be stirred gently to maintain consistency and prevent separation.

4. Incorporation of Active Ingredients

a. **Powdered Active Ingredients**: If the active ingredients are powders, they should be finely ground and incorporated into the base. This is often done using geometric dilution, where the powder is mixed with a small portion of the cream base and then gradually combined with the rest of the base.

b. **Liquid Active Ingredients**: These are usually added directly to the cream base, either during or after the emulsification process, depending on their stability and compatibility.

5. Mixing and Homogenization

a. **Mixing**: Ensures that the active ingredients are uniformly distributed throughout the cream. Techniques include spatulation, mechanical mixing, or using homogenizers.

b. **Homogenization**: Achieved using high-shear mixers or homogenizers to ensure the cream has a smooth texture and the active ingredients are evenly distributed.

6. Quality Control

a. **Consistency**: The cream should have the desired texture and spreadability. This is assessed through rheological testing.

b. **Uniformity**: Checking that the active ingredients are evenly distributed throughout the cream.

c. **Microbial Testing**: Ensuring that the cream is free from harmful microorganisms, especially if it does not contain preservatives.

7. Packaging

a. **Containers**: Creams are typically packaged in tubes, jars, or pumps that protect the product from contamination and degradation.

b. **Labeling**: Includes information about the active ingredients, usage instructions, expiration date, and storage conditions.

8. Stability Testing

a. **Storage Conditions**: Testing the cream under various conditions (temperature, humidity) to ensure it remains stable throughout its shelf life.

b. **Shelf Life**: Evaluating the cream's physical, chemical, and microbiological stability over time to determine its shelf life.

Additional Considerations

a. **Compatibility**: Ensuring that all ingredients are compatible with each other and with the base to prevent issues such as separation or degradation.
b. **pH Level**: The pH of the cream should be suitable for its intended use, especially for dermatological applications.
c. **Viscosity**: Adjusting the viscosity of the cream to meet the desired texture and application properties.

PREPARATION OF GELS

The preparation of gels involves creating a semisolid dosage form that typically consists of a gelling agent dispersed in a liquid medium. Gels are valued for their transparency, ease of application, and ability to deliver active ingredients to the skin. Here's a detailed overview of the gel preparation process:

1. Selection of Ingredients

a. **Active Ingredients**: Therapeutic agents intended for topical application, which may be in the form of powders, liquids, or other types of solutes.
b. **Gelling Agents**: Substances that form a gel network when dispersed in a liquid. Common gelling agents include:
    i. **Polymers**: Such as carbomers (e.g., Carbopol), alginates, and hydroxyethyl cellulose.
    ii. **Clays**: Such as bentonite and kaolin.
c. **Solvents**: The liquid medium in which the gelling agent and active ingredients are dispersed, which can be water or aqueous solutions.
d. **Additives**: May include preservatives, stabilizers, pH adjusters, and other agents to improve the gel's properties.

2. Preparation of the Gel Base

a. **Solvent Preparation**:

i. **Heating**: The solvent, typically water, is heated if necessary to help dissolve the gelling agents and other solutes.

ii. **Mixing**: Ensure that the solvent is thoroughly mixed and any solutes are fully dissolved.

b. **Gelling Agent Preparation**:

i. **Hydration**: Gelling agents like carbomers need to be hydrated in the solvent. This often involves slowly adding the gelling agent to the solvent while stirring to avoid clumping.

ii. **Swelling**: Allowing the gelling agent to swell and fully disperse in the solvent. This may require a certain amount of time, depending on the gelling agent used.

3. Incorporation of Active Ingredients

a. **Powdered Active Ingredients**: Should be finely ground to ensure uniform distribution and prevent grittiness. They are typically added to the gel base in small amounts, using geometric dilution to gradually mix them with the gel base.

b. **Liquid Active Ingredients**: These are usually added directly to the gel base. If they are heat-sensitive, they should be incorporated after the gel base has cooled.

4. Mixing and Homogenization

a. **Mixing**: Ensures that the active ingredients are evenly distributed throughout the gel. Techniques include:

i. **Spatulation**: Using a spatula to mix ingredients manually.

ii. **Mechanical Mixing**: Using mixers or homogenizers to achieve a smooth, uniform gel.

b. **Homogenization**: Achieved using high-shear mixers or homogenizers to ensure that the gel has a consistent texture and that the active ingredients are well dispersed.

5. pH Adjustment

a. **pH Control**: Many gelling agents require a specific pH range to form a stable gel. Adjusting the pH of the gel may involve adding acidic or alkaline substances to reach the desired pH.

6. Quality Control

a. **Consistency**: The gel should have the appropriate viscosity and texture. This is assessed using rheological testing.

b. **Uniformity**: Ensuring that the active ingredients are evenly distributed throughout the gel.

c. **Microbial Testing**: Ensuring the gel is free from harmful microorganisms, especially if it does not contain preservatives.

7. Packaging

a. **Containers**: Gels are typically packaged in containers that protect the product from contamination and degradation, such as tubes, jars, or pumps.

b. **Labeling**: Includes information about the active ingredients, usage instructions, expiration date, and storage conditions.

8. Stability Testing

a. **Storage Conditions**: Testing the gel under various conditions (temperature, humidity) to ensure it remains stable throughout its shelf life.

b. **Shelf Life**: Evaluating the gel's physical, chemical, and microbiological stability over time to determine its shelf life.

Additional Considerations

a. **Compatibility**: Ensuring that all ingredients are compatible with each other and with the gel base to prevent issues such as separation or degradation.
b. **Viscosity**: Adjusting the viscosity of the gel to meet the desired application properties. This can be modified by varying the concentration of gelling agents or using different types of gelling agents.
c. **Clarity**: For clear gels, ensure that the formulation is free from particulates and has a smooth, transparent appearance.

EXCIPIENTS USED IN SEMI-SOLID DOSAGE FORMS

Excipients in semisolid dosage forms play crucial roles in the formulation, stability, and performance of the final product. They serve as vehicles for the active ingredients and help achieve the desired consistency, texture, and release characteristics. Here's a detailed look at the various types of excipients used in semisolid dosage forms:

1. Bases

a. **Hydrocarbon Bases**: These consist primarily of hydrocarbons like petrolatum or mineral oil. They are occlusive, providing a barrier to moisture loss and enhancing drug absorption.
   i. **Examples**: Petrolatum, mineral oil, paraffin.
b. **Absorption Bases**: These bases can absorb water or aqueous solutions, which can modify their properties. They are often used for their ability to incorporate active ingredients and provide better skin compatibility.
   i. **Examples**: Hydrophilic petrolatum, cetyl alcohol, lanolin.
c. **Water-Removable Bases**: Also known as water-washable or water-soluble bases, these are less greasy and easier to remove. They are suitable for a range of applications, especially where a non-occlusive base is preferred.
   i. **Examples**: Creams (containing emulsifying agents like stearyl alcohol), gels (containing carbomers).

2. Gelling Agents

Gelling agents are used to thicken and stabilize semisolid formulations by forming a gel network. They help achieve the desired viscosity and consistency.

a. **Carbomers**: Synthetic polymers that form gels when neutralized. They provide high viscosity and are used in clear gels.
    i. **Examples**: Carbopol 940, Carbopol 980.
b. **Hydroxyethyl Cellulose (HEC)**: A cellulose derivative used to thicken and stabilize aqueous solutions.
    i. **Examples**: Natrosol 250 HX, Klucel HF.
c. **Agar**: A natural gelling agent derived from seaweed, used in some gel formulations.
    i. **Examples**: Agar powder.
d. **Alginate**: Derived from brown seaweed, it forms gels in the presence of calcium ions and is used in gels and pastes.
    i. **Examples**: Sodium alginate.

3. Emulsifiers

Emulsifiers stabilize the mixture of oil and water phases in emulsions, preventing separation and ensuring a uniform texture.

a. **Surfactants**: Reduce the surface tension between oil and water phases to stabilize emulsions.
    i. **Examples**: Polysorbates (e.g., Tween 80), cetyl alcohol, stearyl alcohol.
b. **Lecithin**: A natural emulsifier derived from soy or eggs, used in various creams and lotions.

4. Thickeners

Thickeners are used to increase the viscosity of semisolid formulations, making them more stable and easier to apply.

a. **Xanthan Gum**: A natural polysaccharide that thickens and stabilizes gels and emulsions.

   i. **Examples**: Keltrol, Ticaloid.

b. **Sodium CMC (Carboxymethyl Cellulose)**: A cellulose derivative that provides viscosity and stability.

   i. **Examples**: CMC sodium.

5. Stabilizers

Stabilizers enhance the stability of the formulation, preventing degradation of active ingredients and ensuring uniformity.

a. **Antioxidants**: Prevent oxidation of active ingredients.

   i. **Examples**: Ascorbic acid, butylated hydroxyanisole (BHA).

b. **Preservatives**: Prevent microbial growth and extend shelf life.

   i. **Examples**: Benzyl alcohol, parabens (e.g., methylparaben, propylparaben).

6. Moisturizers and Humectants

These ingredients help retain moisture in the skin and improve the formulation's moisturizing properties.

a. **Glycerin**: A common humectant that attracts moisture to the skin.

   i. **Examples**: Glycerin, propylene glycol.

b. **Hyaluronic Acid**: A powerful moisturizer that attracts and retains water in the skin.

7. Solvents

Solvents are used to dissolve active ingredients or other excipients to achieve the desired consistency.

a. **Water**: The most common solvent used in aqueous-based formulations.

   i. **Examples**: Purified water, distilled water.

b. **Alcohols**: Used in some formulations to dissolve active ingredients or as part of the base.

   i. **Examples**: Ethanol, isopropanol.

8. Colorants and Fragrances

Colorants and fragrances are added to improve the appearance and sensory attributes of semisolid dosage forms.

a. **Colorants**: Used to give the product a specific color.
    i. **Examples**: FD&C dyes, natural colorants.
b. **Fragrances**: Added to provide a pleasant scent.
    i. **Examples**: Essential oils, synthetic fragrances.

EVALUATION OF SEMI-SOLID DOSAGES FORMS

The evaluation of semisolid dosage forms is crucial to ensure their quality, efficacy, and safety. This involves a range of tests to assess their physical, chemical, and microbiological properties. Here's a detailed overview of the evaluation process for semisolid dosage forms:

1. Physical Evaluation

a. **Appearance**: Assess the visual aspects of the product, including color, clarity, and homogeneity. The product should be free from visible particles or separation.
b. **Consistency**: Evaluate the texture and spreadability. This can be tested using:
    i. **Viscosity Testing**: Using a viscometer or rheometer to measure the thickness and flow properties of the semisolid. The consistency should match the specifications for the product.
    ii. **Spreadability**: The ease with which the product spreads on the skin. This is usually evaluated using a spreadability test where a known amount of the product is spread over a defined area and its spreadability is measured.
c. **Odor and Color**: Check for any unwanted odors or discoloration. The product should have the intended fragrance and color, if applicable.

2. Chemical Evaluation

a. **pH**: Measure the pH of the semisolid to ensure it is within the desired range for stability and compatibility with the skin or intended application. This is typically done using a pH meter.

b. **Drug Content**: Assess the concentration of the active ingredient(s) in the formulation. This can be done using techniques such as high-performance liquid chromatography (HPLC) or spectrophotometry.

c. **Stability**: Evaluate the chemical stability of the active ingredients over time and under various storage conditions. This involves:

   i. **Accelerated Stability Testing**: Storing the product at elevated temperatures and humidity levels to predict its shelf life.

   ii. **Long-term Stability Testing**: Storing the product under recommended conditions to assess its stability over the intended shelf life.

3. Microbiological Evaluation

a. **Microbial Limits Testing**: Determine the presence of harmful microorganisms to ensure the product is safe for use. Tests include:

   i. **Total Viable Count**: Measuring the number of viable microorganisms in the product.

   ii. **Pathogen Testing**: Testing for specific harmful microorganisms such as E. coli, Salmonella, or Pseudomonas aeruginosa.

b. **Preservative Efficacy Testing**: Evaluate the effectiveness of preservatives in preventing microbial growth. This test assesses whether the preservatives maintain their antimicrobial activity over the product's shelf life.

4. Rheological Evaluation

a. **Flow Properties**: Assess how the product flows under different conditions. This includes:

   i. **Shear Rate Testing**: Measuring how the viscosity of the semisolid changes with different shear rates.

ii. **Thixotropy**: Testing if the product exhibits a time-dependent decrease in viscosity with continuous shear and a recovery upon resting.

b. **Elasticity and Plasticity**: Evaluate how the product behaves under stress, which affects its spreadability and stability.

5. Sensory Evaluation

a. **Skin Feel**: Assess how the product feels upon application to the skin, including its absorption, greasiness, and residue.

b. **Consumer Testing**: Conduct surveys or tests with potential users to gauge their preferences and satisfaction with the product's sensory attributes.

6. Application Performance

a. **Spreadability**: Test how easily the product spreads on the skin or other intended surfaces.

b. **Absorption**: Measure how well the product absorbs into the skin or other surfaces, which impacts its efficacy and user experience.

c. **Washability**: Evaluate how easily the product can be removed from the skin or application site.

7. Packaging and Stability

a. **Packaging Compatibility**: Ensure that the packaging materials do not interact adversely with the product and provide adequate protection.

b. **Leakage and Integrity**: Test for any leakage or compromise in the packaging during storage and handling.

Multiple Choice Questions (MCQs)

1. What is the primary characteristic of semisolid dosage forms?

A) They are entirely solid

B) They are completely liquid

C) They have a consistency between liquids and solids

D) They are gaseous

2. Which of the following is NOT a type of semisolid dosage form?

A) Ointments

B) Tablets

C) Creams

D) Gels

3. What is the base of an ointment typically composed of?

A) Hydrocarbons like petrolatum

B) Pure water

C) Powdered solids

D) Alcohol

4. Which semisolid dosage form is typically used for its emollient and protective properties?

A) Gels

B) Pastes

C) Ointments

D) Suppositories

5. Creams are classified based on their emulsion type. Which of the following is an example of an emulsion type for creams?

A) Oil-in-water (O/W)

B) Water-in-air (W/A)

C) Oil-in-gel (O/G)

D) Water-in-silicone (W/S)

6. What is the main characteristic of gels as a semisolid dosage form?

A) They are greasy and occlusive

B) They are thick and contain a high percentage of solid particles

C) They are non-greasy and provide a cooling effect

D) They are solid at room temperature

7. Which semisolid dosage form is characterized by containing a higher percentage of solid particles than ointments?

    A) Gels

    B) Pastes

    C) Creams

    D) Emulsions

8. What type of base is used in water-removable ointments?

    A) Hydrocarbon base

    B) Absorption base

    C) Water-soluble base

    D) Oil-based base

9. What is the role of emulsifiers in semisolid dosage forms?

    A) To act as the active ingredient

    B) To stabilize the mixture of oil and water phases

    C) To increase the viscosity

    D) To provide color and fragrance

10. Which of the following factors does NOT influence dermal penetration of drugs?

    A) Molecular size of the drug

    B) Lipophilicity of the drug

    C) Color of the dosage form

    D) Skin integrity

11. What is the purpose of homogenization during the preparation of ointments?

    A) To dissolve active ingredients

    B) To achieve a uniform texture and consistency

    C) To package the product

    D) To add fragrance

12. Which type of gel base is commonly used for its clear and non-greasy properties?

A) Hydrocarbon gel

B) Aqueous gel

C) Silicone gel

D) Mineral oil gel

13. What is the purpose of viscosity testing in the evaluation of semisolid dosage forms?

A) To measure the drug content

B) To assess the thickness and flow properties

C) To test the microbial limits

D) To check the color stability

14. Which excipient is commonly used as a gelling agent in gels?

A) Carbomer

B) Stearyl alcohol

C) Lanolin

D) Glycerin

15. What is the primary function of preservatives in semisolid dosage forms?

A) To stabilize the color

B) To prevent microbial growth

C) To increase viscosity

D) To enhance fragrance

16. What is spreadability testing used for in the evaluation of semisolid dosage forms?

A) To assess the ease of spreading on the skin

B) To determine the microbial content

C) To measure the pH

D) To evaluate the fragrance

17. Which of the following is a common stabilizer used in semisolid dosage forms?

A) Ascorbic acid

B) Xanthan gum

C) Ethanol

D) Benzyl alcohol

18. What is a primary use of suppositories as a semisolid dosage form?

A) Topical application to the skin

B) Oral administration

C) Insertion into body cavities

D) Intravenous injection

19. What is the significance of stability testing in semisolid dosage forms?

A) To assess the color of the product

B) To determine the product's physical, chemical, and microbiological stability over time

C) To test the ease of packaging

D) To measure the spreadability

20. What is the role of thickeners in semisolid dosage forms?

A) To reduce the viscosity

B) To increase the viscosity

C) To act as a preservative

D) To dissolve active ingredients

Short Answer Type Questions (Subjective)

1. What are semisolid dosage forms and where are they typically used?
2. Define ointments and describe their typical characteristics.
3. Explain the difference between oil-in-water and water-in-oil creams.
4. Describe the role of gelling agents in the formulation of gels.
5. What factors influence the dermal penetration of drugs in semisolid dosage forms?
6. How are pastes different from ointments in terms of composition and use?
7. What are the main steps involved in the preparation of ointments?

8. How does the choice of base affect the properties of semisolid dosage forms?
9. What is the significance of rheological evaluation in semisolid dosage forms?
10. Describe the importance of preservatives in semisolid dosage forms.
11. How is pH measured in semisolid dosage forms and why is it important?
12. What is the purpose of stability testing in the evaluation of semisolid dosage forms?
13. Explain the process of homogenization and its role in preparing semisolid dosage forms.
14. What are the advantages of using gels over other semisolid dosage forms?
15. How do emulsifiers work in semisolid dosage forms?
16. What are the main considerations for packaging semisolid dosage forms?
17. Describe the role of excipients in the formulation of semisolid dosage forms.
18. What is spreadability testing and why is it important for semisolid dosage forms?
19. Explain the use of thickeners in the formulation of semisolid dosage forms.
20. What is the role of sensory evaluation in the development of semisolid dosage forms?

Long Answer Type Questions (Subjective)

1. Discuss the different types of semisolid dosage forms, including their composition, characteristics, and typical uses.
2. Explain the mechanisms of dermal penetration of drugs from semisolid dosage forms and the factors that influence this process.
3. Describe the preparation of ointments, including the selection of ingredients, incorporation of active ingredients, and quality control measures.
4. Explain the preparation process of creams and how emulsification plays a role in their formulation.

5. Discuss the evaluation methods used for semisolid dosage forms, including physical, chemical, microbiological, and sensory evaluations.
6. Describe the role of excipients in semisolid dosage forms and how they contribute to the product's stability and efficacy.
7. Explain the significance of stability testing in semisolid dosage forms and how it is conducted.
8. Compare and contrast gels and creams as semisolid dosage forms in terms of their formulation, uses, and advantages.
9. Discuss the importance of rheological properties in semisolid dosage forms and how they are evaluated.
10. Explain the preparation of pastes and the considerations for ensuring their effectiveness and stability.

Answer Key for MCQs

1. C) They have a consistency between liquids and solids
2. B) Tablets
3. A) Hydrocarbons like petrolatum
4. C) Ointments
5. A) Oil-in-water (O/W)
6. C) They are non-greasy and provide a cooling effect
7. B) Pastes
8. C) Water-soluble base
9. B) To stabilize the mixture of oil and water phases
10. C) Color of the dosage form
11. B) To achieve a uniform texture and consistency
12. B) Aqueous gel
13. B) To assess the thickness and flow properties
14. A) Carbomer
15. B) To prevent microbial growth

16.A) To assess the ease of spreading on the skin

17.A) Ascorbic acid

18.C) Insertion into body cavities

19.B) To determine the product's physical, chemical, and microbiological stability over time

20.B) To increase the viscosity